An Essential Guide

THE HISTORICAL JESUS

More *Essential Guides*

The Apostolic Fathers by Clayton N. Jefford

The Bible in English Translation by Steven M. Sheeley and Robert N. Nash, Jr.

Christian Ethics by Robin W. Lovin

Church History by Justo L. González

Feminism and Christianity by Lynn Japinga

Mission by Carlos F. Cardoza-Orlandi

Pastoral Care by John Patton

Preaching by Ronald J. Allen

Rabbinic Literature by Jacob Neusner

The Roman Empire and the New Testament by Warren Carter

Worship in Ancient Israel by Walter Brueggemann

An Essential Guide

THE HISTORICAL JESUS

JAMES H. CHARLESWORTH

Abingdon Press
Nashville

THE HISTORICAL JESUS
AN ESSENTIAL GUIDE

Copyright © 2008 by Abingdon Press

Library of Congress Cataloging-in-Publication Data

Charlesworth, James H.
   The historical Jesus : an essential guide / James H. Charlesworth.
      p. cm.
   ISBN 978-0-687-02167-3 (pbk. : alk. paper)
   1. Jesus Christ—Historicity.   I. Title.

BT303.2.C43 2008
232.9'08—dc22

2007044076

Unless noted otherwise, all scripture translations are those of the author.

08 09 10 11 12 13 14 15 16 17—10 9 8 7 6 5 4 3 2 1
MANUFACTURED IN THE UNITED STATES OF AMERICA

To

Harold W. Attridge,

John J. Collins,

James D. G. Dunn,

Ulrich Luz,

John P. Meier,

and

Gerd Theissen

Contents

Preface

This book is an essential guide to the life and thought of Jesus who was from Nazareth and died outside the western walls of Jerusalem sometime in the first century C.E. The book is for all who are eager to know something reliable about that incredible person from Nazareth.

I will keep in focus all the documents that may inform us about Jesus' context, life, and thought. Hence, I shall allow light to shine upon Jesus and his time from the Dead Sea Scrolls, the books left out of the Old and New Testaments, the Nag Hammadi Codices, the Jewish magical papyri, the Roman historians (Tacitus and Suetonius), as well as the Jewish historians of the first century: Philo of Alexandria and Josephus of Israel (and Rome).

Some claim that the ancients were subjective tellers of history and that only modern scholars can be trusted as objective historians, but Herodotus, Thucydides, and especially Polybius (book 12) developed a coherent and non-subjective historiography that influenced Josephus, the Jewish historian who describes life, thought, and reality during the time of Jesus and the Second Temple, and most likely Luke, who sought to impress his readers that he was a trustworthy historian, citing the need to write "an orderly account," having "followed all things closely for a considerable time," and consulting "eyewitnesses" (Luke 1:1-4).

The attentive reader may ask if anyone, ancient or modern scholar, can really be objective in writing history. Since the historian selects and orders data, some subjectivity is necessarily involved. As with all experienced historians who know that their work will be judged harshly if it is idiosyncratic and subjective, I shall seek to protect the exploration of Jesus' terrain from conclusions that are subjective or appealing only to theologians. I shall try to avoid any favoritism so that the reader may find this book reliable and helpful.

I have chosen to focus on Jesus' life and thought. His actions, as well as his recorded thoughts, help disclose his intentions and goals. Since the New Testament includes not only his teachings but also his private thoughts, and since it is fundamentally important to include all relevant data, I have eschewed the popular noun *teaching* and chosen the more inclusive noun *thought*.

Scholarly books are often boring and leave wide terrain for popular books, such as *The Da Vinci Code*, to seduce the naïve because they claim to pull back the curtain and expose an impostor as in *The Wizard of Oz*, and so provide a book that is captivatingly entertaining. I have avoided technical terms and endeavored to keep all readers interested. That seems warranted when telling "the greatest story ever told." Or is it only a story? That is yet to be seen.

To assist this task, and to allow a smooth flow of thought in this book, I have chosen to focus on twenty-seven questions, among others that will pop up during the venture, which will be explored consecutively; these twenty-seven questions are listed in the introduction. This book will include the major questions, even those that might seem blasphemous to the pious. I will not seek to provide clear or dogmatic answers to all the questions that will be raised, but I do expect that data will be provided and methods clarified so that readers may obtain answers or balance the most likely answers.

Our explorations will ask questions such as: Who was Jesus? What was his purpose? What was his fundamental message? What reliable historical information do we have concerning him? Did he attempt to establish a new religion that would be different from the Judaism he knew? Why was he crucified? And why did the Palestinian Jesus Movement not end with his death, as reflected in the dashed hopes of Cleopas: "We had hoped that he is (or was) the one about to redeem Israel" (Luke 24:21)?

Parts of this book were written in Princeton, others in Jerusalem (not far from Golgotha), Galilee (near Bethsaida), and Rome (not far from the Roman Forum). All translations are my own, unless otherwise noted. No footnotes are supplied, but the inquisitive reader will find abbreviations of major works at the front of the book.

I am indebted to the following for financial support: the Cousins Foundation, the Foundation on Christian Origins, Princeton Theological Seminary, the McCarthy Foundation, and the Pontificia Università Gregoriana in Rome. Finally, I am indebted to my editor at Abingdon Press for selecting me to write this book in their helpful *Essential Guides* series.

JHC
Rome, Jerusalem, Galilee, and Princeton
Spring 2007

Abbreviations

Abba	Jeremias, J. *Abba*. Göttingen: Vandenhoeck & Ruprecht, 1966.
AF	Charlesworth, J. H., and W. P. Weaver, eds. *What Has Archaeology to Do with Faith?* Philadelphia: Trinity Press International, 1992.
ANRW	*Aufstieg und Niedergang der Römischen Welt.*
Ant	Josephus. *Antiquities.*
Archaeology	Charlesworth, J. H., ed., *Jesus and Archaeology.* Grand Rapids: Eerdmans, 2006.
Beloved Disciple	Charlesworth, J. H. *The Beloved Disciple: Whose Witness Validates the Gospel of John?* Valley Forge, Pa.: Trinity Press International, 1995.
Birth	Brown, R. E. *The Birth of the Messiah.* Updated ed. New York: Doubleday, 1993.
Canon	Metzger, B. M. *The Canon of the New Testament.* Oxford: Clarendon Press, 1987, 1992.
Death	Brown, R. E. *The Death of the Messiah.* 2 vols. New York: Doubleday, 1994, 1998.
ET	English translation
Gospel	Benoit, P. *Jesus and the Gospel.* London: Darton, Longman and Todd, 1973.
Hillel and Jesus	Charlesworth, J. H., and L. Johns, eds. *Hillel and Jesus.* Minneapolis: Fortress, 1997.
JesusTalmud	Schäfer, P. *Jesus in the Talmud.* Princeton and Oxford: Princeton University Press, 2007.
Jesus the Christ	Dahl, N. A. *Jesus the Christ.* Ed. Donald A. Juel. Minneapolis: Fortress, 1991.
Jesus2000	Charlesworth, J. H., and W. P. Weaver, eds. *Jesus Two Thousand Years Later.* Harrisburg, Pa.: Trinity Press International, 2000.
JJew	Charlesworth, J. H., ed. *Jesus' Jewishness.* New York: Crossroad and the American Interfaith Institute, 1991.
JJ73	Vermes, G. *Jesus the Jew.* London: Collins, 1973.
JWithinJ	Charlesworth, J. H. *Jesus Within Judaism: New Light from Exciting Archaeological Discoveries.* New York: Doubleday, 1988.
MessExegesis	Juel, D. *Messianic Exegesis.* Philadelphia: Fortress, 1988.
Messiah	Charlesworth, J. H., ed. *The Messiah.* Minneapolis: Fortress, 1992.
MillProphet	Allison, D. C. *Jesus of Nazareth: Millenarian Prophet.* Minneapolis: Fortress, 1998.
Mishnah	Neusner, J. *The Mishnah.* New Haven and London: Yale University Press, 1988.

MJ	Meier, J. P. *A Marginal Jew*. 3 vols. New York: Doubleday, 1991, 1994, 2001.
Nativity	Vermes, G. *The Nativity: History and Legend*. London: Penguin, 2006.
OTP	Charlesworth, J. H., ed. *The Old Testament Pseudepigrapha*. 2 vols. Garden City, N.Y.: 1983, 1985.
ParablesD	Dodd, C. H. *The Parables of the Kingdom*. 2d ed. London: Nisbet, 1935.
Peasant	Crossan, J. D. *The Historical Jesus: The Life of a Mediterranean Jewish Peasant*. New York: HarperSanFrancisco, 1991.
Plausible	Theissen, G., and D. Winter. *Quest for the Plausible Jesus: The Question of Criteria*. Trans. M. E. Boring. Louisville: Westminster John Knox, 2002.
PSB 86	Charlesworth, J. H. "From Barren Mazes to Gentle Rappings: The Emergence of Jesus Research." *Princeton Seminary Bulletin* 7 (1986): 221-30.
PTSDSS	Charlesworth, J. H., ed. *The Dead Sea Scrolls*. PTS Dead Sea Scrolls Project. 12 vols. Tübingen: J. C. B. Mohr; Louisville: Westminster John Knox, 1994–.
Quest	Schweitzer, A. *The Quest of the Historical Jesus*. Trans. W. Montgomery. New York: Macmillan, 1961.
Rabbi	Chilton, B. *Rabbi Jesus: An Intimate Biography*. New York: Doubleday, 2000.
Resurrection	Charlesworth, J. H., et al. *Resurrection: The Origin and Future of a Biblical Doctrine*. New York and London: T. & T. Clark, 2006.
ResurrSOG	Wright, N. T. *The Resurrection of the Son of God*. Minneapolis: Fortress, 2003.
Setting	Davies, W. D. *The Setting of the Sermon on the Mount*. Cambridge: Cambridge University Press, 1964.
So-Called	Kähler, M. *The So-Called Historical Jesus and the Historic, Biblical Christ*. Philadelphia: Fortress, 1964 [1892].
Word	Bultmann, R. *Jesus and the Word*. Trans. L. P. Smith and E. H. Lantero. London: Charles Scribner's Sons, 1934.

Introduction

1) Why is Jesus Research necessary?
2) How is Jesus Research possible?

The *Historical Jesus: An Essential Guide* presents a historian's view of Jesus of Nazareth—provided we recognize that it is impossible to separate too cleanly history from theology in such a search. In the twenties of the first century C.E., this man walked out of the hills of Nazareth and into world culture. What can be known about this man, and how did his culture and time help shape his life and thought?

The authors of the New Testament Gospels indicate that Jesus was devoted to Torah; that is, God's will that is preserved in Jewish Scripture. Jesus did, however, disagree with many regulations added to Torah and the interpretations of Scripture offered by some influential Jews in Jerusalem.

Jesus was driven by one desire: to obey God at all times and in all ways. For him, not one word of Torah may be ignored or compromised. To what extent does this man, Jesus of Nazareth, stand out as one of the most Jewish Jews of the first century? Readers will be able to answer that question as they ponder the issues raised in the following chapters.

What is new and challenging about "the story of Jesus Christ"? Jesus' story was told by writers that we call the Evangelists in the first century C.E., less than one hundred years after his death. Two thousand years later, in some significant ways, we may more accurately retell the story of Jesus. How is that possible?

More accurate historical knowledge. If Matthew and John, Jesus' disciples, wrote the Gospels bearing those names, then they knew Jesus and spent time with him. These two Gospels thus would contain eyewitness accounts of those who had been with Jesus, hearing his teachings and sharing life with him until he was crucified. This assumption drove Bruce Barton's *The Man Nobody Knows: A Discovery of the Real Jesus* (1925). Barton (1886–1967) aimed to demonstrate that Jesus was a man's man, the consummate executive, and "the founder of modern business" (preface). For Barton, the Evangelists remembered the events of Jesus' life as "scenes that burned themselves indelibly into their memories" (p. 60). This business executive desired to "read what the men who knew Jesus personally said about him" (preface).

Unfortunately, intensive examination of this widely held assumption and the attempts to prove that the authors of the canonical Gospels, at least Matthew and John, were not only Evangelists but also apostles (that is, in Jesus' inner circle) have ended with sadness and failure. Scientific and reflective research leads sometimes to surprising results, and these will not always be pleasing and may be heartbreaking (see chap. 2). For more than two hundred years most New Testament experts have concluded that the Evangelists did not know the historical Jesus; moreover, they wrote decades after his death.

The Evangelists were not eyewitnesses of Jesus' life and thought. For example, Luke makes it clear that he had to find eyewitnesses of Jesus (Luke 1:1-4). If Matthew depends on Mark as a source, as most scholars think, and if Mark is either someone unknown or Peter's scribe who never met Jesus, then Matthew cannot be the "Matthew" of the Twelve. The Evangelists worked on traditions they received. Most of these came to them in oral form and had taken shape over three decades (from the 30s through the 50s, at least).

Many scholars conclude that the Evangelists composed their Gospels shortly before or long after 70 C.E. This year was a significant divide in Jewish history. In September of 70 C.E., Titus (the future emperor) and the Roman legions conquered and destroyed Jerusalem and burned the Temple, bringing an end to the history of ancient Israel and Second Temple Judaism. However, Jesus lived when the Temple defined Judaism and the cosmos for most Palestinian Jews, even though there were many creative definitions of *Judaism*. Mark, Matthew, Luke, and the author of the *Gospel of Thomas* forgot, or never knew, the vibrant, exciting, and diverse Jewish culture that shaped and framed Jesus' brilliantly poetic insights. As may become evident in later chapters, John may be intermittently better informed of Jesus' time than the first three Evangelists. The Gospel of John, therefore, must not be jettisoned from consideration in seeking to find the historical Jesus.

Thanks to the recovery of a Jewish library containing scrolls once held by Jesus' contemporaries—the Dead Sea Scrolls—we can read about the hopes of some of his fellow Jews and discern how they interpreted God's word, Scripture. Studying these and other Jewish documents from Jesus' time allows us to learn more about the terms and concepts presupposed by Jesus and his audience. It seems obvious now, given the date of the Gospels and the struggle of the Evangelists to establish a claim that was unpopular to many Jews and Gentiles, that the Evangelists missed much of the dynamism in the pre-70 world of Jesus and the Jewish context of his life and thought. These now are clearer to us because of the terms, concepts, and dreams preserved in the Dead Sea Scrolls; that is, these documents that represent many aspects of Second Temple Judaism predate 70 C.E. and are not edited by later Jews or Christians.

If some of Jesus' concepts were intermittently confusing to his Jewish followers, it may be partly because many terms and concepts presupposed by Jesus had been used and thus clarified in learned circles. Terms such as *God's Rule* (the Kingdom of God), *the Son of Man,* and *the Messiah* are found in pre-70 Jewish writings that have been recovered over the past three centuries. Since Jesus' closest followers were fishermen or workers, it seems unlikely they had access to such documents or were conversant with such concepts and terms. However, because he was inquisitive, and occupied himself by discussing Torah with Pharisees and others, and was obsessed with knowing God and the traditions of Israel, Jesus probably knew such learned traditions and even perhaps some of the early Jewish documents that have been rediscovered in the past two centuries. While many of Jesus' terms might have been unfamiliar to his disciples, he might have clarified their meaning in private conversations (as in Mark 4:34). Also, one must not overlook that Jesus' followers are not portrayed asking him about the meaning of the terms he used.

Jesus, however, was also creative and developed some revolutionary concepts.

His concept of suffering was extremely challenging to those Jews who expected a triumphant Messiah. His inclusion of the outcasts and the marginalized was unprecedented and especially offensive to many priests in Jerusalem.

Jesus was a genius. While he spoke the language of his generation and was deeply influenced by early Jewish theology, he did not merely repeat or redefine earlier teachings or traditions. We shall explore these new perceptions and concepts in the following chapters.

More objective methods. The authors of our canonical gospels were Evangelists. That means that they were primarily focused on proclaiming Jesus. For them he was the Son of God, the Good Shepherd, and, especially, the long-awaited Messiah. They did not have the inclination to explore historical issues or ponder the complexities of Jesus' life. They belonged to an ostracized and insignificant "sect" within the Roman Empire, and they were struggling to survive. They knew it was necessary to focus solely on Jesus and to proclaim Jesus' relation to God and his place within God's final plan of salvation.

We may, and should, ask questions the Evangelists could not ponder. We should be more self-critical, especially in light of the perennial penchant to create a Jesus who is admirable, even worthy of worship, because he is like us. We have access to new scientific methods for asking historical and sociological questions. We should not be blind to the fuller landscape of Second Temple Judaism and Jesus' place within it.

To peer through history to Jesus' time, as with a telescope, now seems possible, thanks to monumental archaeological discoveries and refined historical sensitivities and methodologies. For example, we have many items last touched by Jesus' contemporaries, before they were discovered in archaeological trenches. These *realia* (real objects) include gold, silver, and bronze coins (Jewish as well as Greek and Roman), spears, arrowheads, pots, spoons, glass drinking vessels, hatchets, manuscripts, bronze tweezers with attached toothpicks, and nails designed for crucifixion. We can also walk on paved streets, climb up stone steps, enter rooms and houses, and sometimes crawl down into graves that have been or are being excavated. By perceiving how small a "lamp" was in Jesus' time, we can comprehend why the young women lost the light of their lamps and were left in the darkness (Matt. 25:1-12). Archaeology and sociology thus become important methods for re-creating and imagining Jesus' time and society.

Recent fascination with Jesus. The fascination with the historical Jesus is placarded by four recent popular events. Just before the turn of the millennium, some experts on the Dead Sea Scrolls claimed in some leading magazines and newspapers that "the Jesus Scroll" had been recovered. Some scholars were duped into thinking that this scroll was authentic, a Dead Sea Scroll, and that it referred to Jesus. Just after the turn of the millennium, a sensation was felt in many archaeological and literary circles. "The James Ossuary" had been recovered, and it was alleged to be the depository of the bones of "James, the son of Joseph, and the brother of Jesus." Mel Gibson's *The Passion of the Christ* focused on the brutal punishment and death Jesus suffered. *The Da Vinci Code* was published, telling a story in which the Vatican and church officials have hidden documents and gospel truths from believers, including Jesus' relation with Mary Magdalene.

"The Jesus Scroll" proved to be a modern fake, yet it aroused a sensation. The name "Jesus" is not in the text. It had been restored. "The James Ossuary" may well be an ancient ossuary (bone box), but many experts rightly conclude that the words "the brother of Jesus" have been added by someone, perhaps recently. *The Passion of the Christ,* though it was snubbed by Hollywood, grossed millions of dollars and set box office records, but it is more like the bloody *Braveheart* than Jesus' passion. *The Da Vinci Code* has set records, selling millions of copies in the United States and in many other countries, but it is only a novel that plays fast and loose with facts, playing with fears, concocting conspiracies, and titillating the imagination.

Clearly and cumulatively, these events reveal that many people throughout the world are eager to learn more about Jesus, the man. Millions are thirsty for reliable information. The attention given to Jesus in the past decade proves that Jesus still fascinates many.

Purpose. This book is a basic introduction to all the main issues involved in exploring what may be known about the man from Nazareth and why such knowledge is fundamental to Christian belief and thought. The work is shaped by interrogatives; that is, questions will be more central than putative factual answers.

What questions will be in central focus? Here they are: What can be known with some reliability about Jesus' life and thought? What methodologies help ensure refined historiography (the scientific study of history) and protect us from distorting the evidence? How can we peer into the past and catch a glimpse of Jesus?

The purpose of this book is to help readers to struggle with the issues involved in discerning what can be known, and with what assurance, about Jesus' life and essential message. Throughout the book, stress will be placed on the proper methodologies for discerning answers. This approach has been developed in the various Quests for the historical Jesus and especially in the current phase of the inquiry, called Jesus Research, which began in 1980. The task is to search behind the proclamations (kerygmata) of the Gospels to obtain a view of that mysterious and charismatic figure known as "Jesus, son of Joseph" (John 6:42).

History and Christian faith. How much reliable history can be discovered behind the proclamations concerning the one announced to be the Messiah? That question seems central, especially for Christians, since Christian faith is based on historical facts.

Once many experts and the average Christian were duped by Existentialism. This term refers to the philosophical system that asked us: What is the relevance of that over there for the meaning of my existence here? We were told that if anything is relevant or important, it is so because of its significance for our becoming better beings. We were once taught that facts regarding the historical Jesus were not relevant for faith since we are saved solely by faith, and that we first confronted Jesus in the preached Word.

That teaching distorts reality and miscasts Christian faith. We humans are fundamentally historical creatures. We learn about each other by asking questions focused on the past (e.g., Where did you grow up, where did you go to school, and where do you live?). Christians may hear about Jesus for the first time in preaching, but they presuppose that this man was a historical person who did something important for their lives and salvation. Should we not explore such a presupposition?

Summary. The life and teachings of Jesus and the landscape of Jesus' time are no longer *terra incognita,* or unexplored territory, thanks to more sources and a better means of asking honest questions. The approach in this book seeks to encourage the reader to ask questions, to obtain personal answers to all the major questions regarding Jesus of Nazareth, and to ponder some unresolved issues.

In this book I bring forward for reflection a consensus among specialists in Jesus Research. They conclude that we can know a lot about Jesus, the itinerant prophet and miracle worker, and that we have access to his fundamental message and essential purpose. In light of archaeological insights and sociological reflections, as well as the study of manuscripts once held by Jews contemporaneous with him, Jesus' message makes stunningly clear sense. His message, his concerns, and his dreams were shaped by and reflect a unique world: the Jewish world of Palestine from 37 B.C.E. to 70 C.E. The first date, 37 B.C.E., is the year when Herod the Great wrested dictatorial powers from all Jewish leaders and aristocrats—slaughtering any who dared oppose him, "The King of the Jews." The second date, 70 C.E., signifies the destruction of Jerusalem, the burning of the Temple, the cessation of the cult and sacrifices, and the end of ancient Israel and Second Temple Judaism.

In pursuing Jesus Research we must avoid two extremes. We must escape the temptations of abject skepticism, which leaves us only with unreliable impressions of Jesus bequeathed by the second generation of his followers. We also must resist historical positivism, which re-creates history without the necessary subjunctives and qualifications. That is, we must avoid the errors of the minimalists or the maximalists: those who believe we can know almost nothing about the historical Jesus, or those who believe our sources present a clear view of him.

Twenty-seven questions. In the following pages, the reader will confront most of the major questions involved in Jesus Research. Among the many questions the inquisitive reader may have, the following will be in central focus:

1) Why is Jesus Research necessary?
2) How is Jesus Research possible?
3) When did the study of the historical Jesus begin, and what has been learned?
4) Is it important to distinguish between what Jesus said and what the Evangelists reported?
5) What are the best methods for discerning traditions that originate with Jesus?
6) Do reports about Jesus exist outside the New Testament?
7) Are the Gospels objective biographies?
8) Was Jesus not the first Christian?
9) Was Jesus an Essene, Pharisee, Zealot, or Sadducee?
10) When and where was Jesus born?
11) Is there historicity in the virgin birth, and did some judge Jesus to be a *mamzer*?
12) Did Jesus travel to a foreign land to obtain wisdom and the powers of healing, or did he live with Essenes to obtain these powers?

13) Is there any reliable history in the noncanonical gospels that helps us understand Jesus' youth?
14) Was John the Baptizer Jesus' teacher?
15) Was Jesus married to Mary Magdalene?
16) Did Jesus perform miracles?
17) How and in what significant ways is archaeology important for Jesus Research?
18) What are the most important archaeological discoveries for Jesus Research?
19) Was Jesus a peasant?
20) What was Jesus' fundamental message?
21) When did Jesus imagine God would inaugurate his Rule?
22) What term did Jesus use for God?
23) What led to Jesus' confrontation with some of the leading priests?
24) Who crucified Jesus and why?
25) Has Jesus' bone box (ossuary) been recovered?
26) If Jesus' bones have been discovered, is resurrection faith possible?
27) Did Jesus rise from the dead?

These focal questions define Jesus Research not only in this book but also within the academy and the church. There is also a growing interest in Jesus within synagogues and among Jews here and abroad, as evident in the popularity of David Flusser's *The Sage from Galilee: Rediscovering Jesus' Genius* (2007).

Many of the twenty-seven questions cannot be answered with certainty; that is, they should be answered with qualifications and uncertainties. Sometimes our sources do not provide answers or keys to unlocking a mysterious issue; hence, I do not consider it representative of the sources, helpful to the reader, or wise to offer an answer that is not carefully qualified.

What questions are peculiarly shrouded in the mists of history? Here are some: Jesus was probably intimate with Mary Magdalene; but we cannot define what *intimacy* means in this instance, and we possess no data that allows us to decide if he had been married to her. We may also catch only a glimpse of what Jesus thought about himself; that is true for two reasons: his followers—especially the Fourth Evangelist—often shaped the passages in which we might discern such self-understanding. Likewise, Jesus was more interested in speaking about God and God's Rule than about proclaiming who he was. We shall see that Jesus knew more precisely whose he was than who he was. We also may not be able to discern the motives of Judas and his complex relation to Jesus. The often impossible task of obtaining historical answers does not preclude us from asking and exploring such questions, however.

Faith and history. In exploring ways to answer these twenty-seven questions, we must perceive that it is often difficult to distinguish between history and faith. Jesus' history was preserved by those who believed in him, and his traditions were recorded by those who made unique claims about him. That is, the Evangelists and others, notably Paul, were primarily interested in Jesus because of their faith in him as the Messiah, the Son of God, and the Savior of the world. This truth has misled some scholars, mostly theologians, into the erroneous assumption that Paul and the Evangelists had no interest in history or in the Jesus of history. In the following pages we shall see why most of the leading experts in Jesus Research are now stressing that Paul and the Evangelists were keenly aware of the importance of Jesus' life and teaching, knew a lot about the historical person, and considered some of this knowledge fundamental for faith and belief.

Terms. With this perspective it is wise now to define the leading terms. By *the Jesus of the Gospels* is meant the Jesus proclaimed by the Evangelists. The term *the historical Jesus* denotes the life and teachings of Jesus that are reconstructed by specialists in Jesus Research. *The Jesus of history* is the real person of history who will always remain elusive and cannot be presented again on a reconstructed stage of history. The term *the Christ of faith* signifies the present and living Lord known by Christians in various church liturgies and in daily life. *Christian faith is based on the Jesus of history, but that person is elusive, except perhaps through spiritual experience; the closest approximation to this person is via* the historical Jesus, *who is tentatively disclosed by Jesus Research.*

1) *Why is Jesus Research necessary?* Readers should be provided data and perspectives that help them answer this question. First, a misperception needs to be clarified and then replaced.

Once Christians assumed they knew who wrote the Gospels. The Gospels of Matthew and John were composed by the apostles, Matthew and John, who had spent at least three years with Jesus. The Gospel of Luke was composed by Luke, the physician and companion of Paul. The Gospel of Mark was penned by Mark, Peter's scribe, who is most likely also John Mark of Jerusalem. It was once easy to imagine that the Gospels were factual biographies that were beyond reproach or criticism. Such "Gospels" were composed by eyewitnesses or based on harmonious eyewitness accounts of what Jesus actually did and said. It was assumed that the Gospels were unedited and presented an inviolate record of Jesus' life and teaching. Thus, there was no need for a Quest or Jesus Research.

Since the eighteenth century, scholars have learned and emphasized that the Gospels were not composed by Jesus' disciples. The Gospels are selected and edited traditions. They reflect the needs of communities aflame with Easter faith.

The necessity of Jesus Research thus becomes clear in a way that would seem shocking and too perplexing if confronted before we discerned that the Gospels are highly edited reports about Jesus; that is, that are either based on unreliable eyewitnesses or devoid of any firsthand witness. It is most likely that Matthew and Luke worked from a copy of Mark similar to the one in our New Testament, and that means they depended on a writer who had never met Jesus. They also felt free to change Jesus traditions, including altering words attributed to Jesus. Note this parallel comparison, which is presented in chronological order from left to right:

Mark 9:1	Matthew 16:28	Luke 9:27
And he said to them, "Truly, I say to you that there are some standing here who will not taste death	"Truly, I say to you that, there are some standing here who will not taste death	"But I tell you truly, there are some standing here who will not taste death

before they see that the Kingdom of God	before they see *the Son of Man*	before they see *the Kingdom of God."*
has come with power."	*coming in his kingdom."*	

Most readers will immediately perceive that first Matthew and then Luke were working from a copy of Mark similar to our own. They may not observe, however, that Jesus' prediction in Mark is embarrassing since "the Kingdom of God" did not arrive "with power" while those who knew Jesus were still alive. What is at stake is monumentally important. It concerns not only Jesus' knowledge and the truthfulness of his predictions concerning the coming Rule of God (which will be explored in chap. 8) but also the trustworthiness of the traditions in the Gospels.

Both Matthew and Luke read Scripture more attentively and thoughtfully than most ministers and priests today. The Evangelists knew that what Mark reported was embarrassing, and that they had to change what Mark had attributed to Jesus. They do so in different and independent ways. Matthew more severely edits the text, adding to Jesus' prediction the title "the Son of Man," which for Matthew clearly denotes Jesus—who has come—and is associated with "his kingdom" (cf. esp. 20:21). Luke omits that the Kingdom of God will come dynamically in the life-time of those standing by Jesus, and includes (or attributes to Jesus) later a saying that makes it clear that the Kingdom became present among, or within, Jesus' followers (cf. 17:21).

This one example clarifies why Jesus Research is necessary. If one reads the Gospels as if they are this morning's newspaper, then the truth in them will be distorted and the mysteries unperceived.

2) *How is Jesus Research possible?* The possibility of Jesus Research will appear more clearly in the following chapters. In chapter 2, we shall focus on how and with what methods one can discover Jesus' own traditions that are included among the traditions attributed to him.

CHAPTER 1

No Quest, the Old Quest, the New Quest, and Jesus Research (Third Quest)

3) When did the study of the historical Jesus begin, and what has been learned?

4) Is it important to distinguish between what Jesus said and what the Evangelists reported?

We have seen that Jesus Research is necessary, primarily because the Gospels were composed after Jesus' death and shaped by post-Easter theology and proclamation. This research does not assume that our Gospels are unreliable. It recognizes that we need to sift out Jesus' own actions and thoughts from acts and words attributed to him. No one devoted to discovering what Jesus said and did would be satisfied with what an Evangelist imagined or added. Fortunately, in the twenty-first century we can learn from scholars' past mistakes and insights. For the purpose of discerning the developments in the study of the historical Jesus, the past two thousand years may be meaningfully (if not neatly) separated into five phases (dates are approximate):

1. No Quest (worship of Jesus as the Christ): 26–1738
2. The Old Quest: 1738–1906
3. The Moratorium on the Old Quest: 1906–1953
4. The New Quest and Its Demise: 1953–ca. 1970
5. Jesus Research (Third Quest): 1980–the present

1. No Quest (worship of Jesus as the Christ): 26–1738. Interest in Jesus did not begin as scientific study; it commenced with worshiping him as the Christ, the Son of God, and God. Early Christians had no doubt that the Gospels were composed by Jesus' disciples or the followers of Peter or Paul.

The Evangelists attempted to reveal what had been promised in the Old Testament: God would send the Messiah into the world to save it. In their minds, that had been fully accomplished by Jesus Christ. Further, the differences among the four Gospels were not a problem because they could be harmonized. The productions of harmonies began about the middle of the second century C.E., and the most influential harmony of the Gospels was compiled by Tatian about 175 C.E. Although the original is lost, its significance and missionary power are evident today, since it is preserved in Old Latin, Syriac, Greek, Persian, Armenian, Arabic, Old German, as well as in other languages.

1

In this period, speculation and study were not focused on the historicity of the Gospels. In the earliest centuries of Christianity such historicity was assumed and affirmed. Instead, thought was focused on Christological issues, such as the relation between Jesus, God, and the Holy Spirit. The first council to discuss these issues was held in 325 C.E. at Nicea. It was attended by Christians who were Greeks and Romans; some were anti-Jewish.

2. *The Old Quest: 1738–1906.* In *The Quest of the Historical Jesus* (1910 [German: 1906]), Albert Schweitzer attributed the origin of the "Old Quest" to H. S. Reimarus (1694–1768), and this claim is repeated in many handbooks on the historical Jesus. It is misleading. The English Deists are the real precursors of critical Jesus study. The works of John Locke, Matthew Tindal, and Thomas Chubb shaped the world's culture because they sought a "reasonable Christianity." In the year 1738, Chubb published *The True Gospel of Jesus Christ Asserted.* Chubb "discovered" that Jesus' true message was the imminent coming of God's Rule (the Kingdom of God) and the true gospel was to be found in Jesus' preaching of good news to the poor.

David F. Strauss and other influential biblical scholars developed in Tübingen, a university city east of the Black Forest in Germany, a critical and scientific approach to the Bible. The Tübingen School initiated a new means of studying Christian origins, the Gospels, and the historical Jesus. The worship of Jesus was shifting to a quest for what can be known reliably about this man from Nazareth. In 1835, Strauss composed the first "life of Jesus"; it is his *Das Leben Jesu* (*The Life of Jesus*). Strauss was the first to comprehend the importance and complexity of myth and mythological language. Stories, like the Gospels, are possible only because of mythological language. Some myths evolve from poetry, others derive from philosophical truths, and still others develop from actual historical events. The only way to communicate the memorable and eternal is via mythical language. Strauss's insights into myth are fundamental; they would be more influential today if he had not couched his *Das Leben Jesu* within the threefold Hegelian dialectic of thesis, antithesis, and synthesis. As many philosophers have indicated, Hegelianism is too simplistic; human development has not developed in a unilateral, and optimistic, direction.

The Old Quest (1738–1906) was clearly motivated by theological concerns. Martin Kähler crafted one of the most influential books, *The So-Called Historical Jesus and the Historic, Biblical Christ* (1892; ET in 1964). There Kähler emphasized that the Gospels are post-Easter narratives. Unfortunately, he argued that our gaze should not be on the historical but only on the historic; that is, the historical Jesus should be replaced by the Christ of faith. What is important for the Christian, according to Kähler? It is the historic, biblical Christ. The denigration of historical biblical research and an emphasis on theology made sense in a world dominated and defined by the anti-Christian thoughts of Darwin and Freud, but Kähler's false dichotomy between the historical Jesus and the Christ of faith would have been abhorrent to the Evangelists and to the Reformers, especially Martin Luther, John Calvin, and John Wesley. Nevertheless, Kähler's dichotomy unfortunately cast a dark shadow on almost all the brilliant Christian theologians of the twentieth century, including the great "B's": Rudolf Bultmann, Karl Barth, Emil Brunner, and Dietrich Bonhoeffer, as well as Paul Tillich.

After the conquests, then explorations, of the Middle East by the French and the British at the end of the nineteenth century, much had been accomplished to foster the study of the historical Jesus, especially in philology and lexicography. Indeed, some of our major lexicons originated in the second half of the nineteenth century. But in biblical studies many were creating hidden mines and placing them in the erstwhile peaceful waters of biblical theology.

Three luminaries illustrate this point: Julius Wellhausen, Emil Schürer, and Adolf von Harnack. Each of these professors taught in Germany where almost all scientific and advanced biblical research was centered.

Wellhausen (1844–1918) stressed that four sources defined the compilation of the Pentateuch: literary strata J (the Yahwist), E (the Elohist), D (the Deuteronomic compiler), and P (the Priestly source). Yet along with virtually all biblical scholars, he was swept forward by the times, which were characterized by optimistic evolution, Christocentricity, triumphalism, and "man's invincibility" (recall the story of the "unsinkable" *Titanic*). No Christian scholar used terms like *Hebrew Bible* and *Tanakh* (now well-known terms in many seminaries and universities). They assumed that the Bible was the Christian canon, and that the canon was closed by the fourth century C.E. The important books prior to the New Testament were the inspired "Old Testament." Scholarship was controlled by European circles, and these were dominated by Christians.

Scholars were confident that they could arrange the books of the Christian Bible in precise chronological order, and they perceived an evolution of thought from prophecy to fulfillment. The Holy Spirit had been guiding the elect and faithful to deeper insights, and the prophets predicted the coming of Jesus Christ. Jesus "was no Jew," an influential German stressed, and his life was seen not as a part of Judaism but as a dimension of Greek and Roman culture (cf. *JJew*) and part of the history of the church. The "intertestamental" books were mined for gems that shined light on Jesus' uniqueness and messiahship.

Under the industriousness of such masterminds as Emil Schürer (1844–1910), the study of Judaism flourished, but it was subsumed under the mantle of Christocentricity and was conceived as the "background" of the New Testament. Note in particular the title of Schürer's encyclopedic and multivolume work: *The History of the Jewish People in the Age of Jesus Christ (175 B.C.–A.D. 135).* Rather than celebrating the genius and integrity of Second Temple Judaism, too often Schürer denigrated Jews contemporaneous with Jesus. For example, Schürer announced that during the time of Jesus, Jewish prayer was bound in the rigors of a fettered legalism.

At the end of the nineteenth century, Adolf von Harnack (1851–1930) was the recognized master of Christian origins and early Christian dogma. He focused on the mission and expansion of Christianity and situated Jesus within that history. Uninfluenced by Jewish apocalyptic and eschatological thought and virtually uninterested in Judaism, Harnack sought a Jesus who represented the best in German culture. He found it by positing it in the sources.

What did Harnack conclude? Stressing the essence of Christianity, Harnack claimed that Jesus was a revelatory genius who illustrated the fatherhood of God, the brotherhood of all men, and the binding ethic of love. "What a discovery!" "What a brilliant insight and so clear!" Those accolades accompanied the massive research project.

3

But something was amiss. With such a nonthreatening philosophy it is impossible to explain why Jesus was judged and condemned to death on a cross.

In retrospect, many nineteenth-century authors assumed they could write a biography of Jesus. These authors (some were not scholars) sometimes attempted to provide such a biography for those in the pews of the church so that Christians could have reliable historical knowledge about Jesus. Some authors concluded that Jesus was the perfect propagandist (Beverbrook); others claimed that he never existed (Bruno Bauer).

Ernest Renan, a distinguished French scholar of Near Eastern culture, composed a classic "biography" of Jesus. His *Vie de Jésus* (1863) has been heralded for changing the world's conceptions as much as Darwin's *Origin of Species* and Marx's *Das Kapital*. At times he read French Romanticism back into the life of the Galilean. For example, Renan suggested that Jesus wept in Gethsemane because he imagined the women he could have wooed in his life: "Perhaps he began to hesitate about his work.... Did he remember the clear fountains of Galilee where he was wont to refresh himself ... and the young maidens who, perhaps, would have consented to love him?" (p. 335).

Such so-called scientific research produced too many diverse and mutually exclusive conclusions. Slowly, scholars began to realize some errors in presuppositions and methodology. Had they myopically focused on an erroneous database: a putative closed canon? Had they employed an imprecise methodology?

At the beginning of the twentieth century, times were changing. The sinking of the *Titanic* exposed the error of Victorian optimism. The differences among the Gospels were becoming more evident, and the rediscovery of Jewish apocalyptic eschatology[1] signaled a need to perceive Jesus within his original Palestinian culture. Surely, a scholar would arise to point out that the liberal lives of Jesus were not the product of scientific and disinterested research.

3. *The Moratorium on the Old Quest: 1906–1953.* That person turned out to be Albert Schweitzer (1875–1965). In *The Quest of the Historical Jesus* (1906), Schweitzer convincingly demonstrated that those who had attempted a life of Jesus had only "discovered" an image of Jesus they wanted to see or assumed was correct. Schweitzer was the first since Reimarus (1694–1768) to perceive that Jesus' message was shaped by Jewish eschatology; that is, Jesus proclaimed the end of all time. Schweitzer argued, unconvincingly, that Jesus' message was defined by a thoroughgoing futuristic eschatology. Note the heart of Schweitzer's portrayal of Jesus:

> Jesus ... in the knowledge that He is the coming Son of Man lays hold of the wheel of the world to set it moving on that last revolution which is to bring all ordinary history to a close. It refuses to turn, and He throws Himself upon it. Then it does turn; and crushes Him. Instead of bringing in the eschatological conditions, He has destroyed them. The wheel rolls onward, and the mangled body of the one immeasurably great Man, who was strong enough to think of Himself as the spiritual ruler of mankind and to bend history to His purpose, is hanging upon it still. That is His victory and His reign. (*Quest*, pp. 370-71)

That is severe; yet it is laudatory and appreciative. Eventually, Schweitzer explained how he felt the call of Jesus: "He comes to us as One unknown, without a name, as of old, by the lake-side, He came to those men who knew Him not. He speaks to us the same word: 'Follow thou me!'" (*Quest*, p. 403).

Few scholars now devoted to Jesus Research and who conclude that Jesus' message was shaped by eschatology would agree with Schweitzer's thoroughgoing eschatology. The parables and the passages that stress the presence of God's Rule in Jesus' sayings and the Dead Sea Scrolls' view of time have combined to present a different concept of Jesus' eschatology (see chaps. 8 and 10).

Schweitzer's influence caused a moratorium on the Quest for Jesus in many circles for two main reasons. First, in Christian communities that hailed Jesus as divine, no preacher could proclaim belief in a man who seemed to be a deluded visionary. Second, no reputable biblical scholar could continue to be blind to the post-Easter theological interests and Christological claims that had shaped the portrayal of Jesus.

In the history of the study of the historical Jesus, the scholar who is most important and influential after Schweitzer is Rudolf Karl Bultmann (1884–1976). He sought ways to find history in the pre-gospel traditions. He was also a founder of Form Criticism, which sought to study the history of the literary forms in the Gospels. In *Jesus and the Word* (1934), Bultmann claimed that our only sources for obtaining reliable historical information of Jesus are the Gospels, but the Evangelists do not show any interest in the development of Jesus' personality or in history. Thus, any attempt at either is misperceived. Note Bultmann's words (which are often misrepresented): "I do indeed think that we can now know almost nothing concerning the life and personality of Jesus, since the early Christian sources show no interest in either, are moreover fragmentary and often legendary; and other sources about Jesus do not exist" (*Word*, p. 8).

In *The History of the Synoptic Tradition* (1963), Bultmann defended the Two Source Hypothesis. Matthew and Luke depended on Mark and a lost sayings source of Jesus (called Q) when they composed their Gospels. There are development and distance from Jesus' message in the twenties to the composition of the first Gospel, Mark, sometime around 70 C.E.

In his penetratingly brilliant, yet idiosyncratic, *The Theology of the New Testament* (1951), Bultmann emphasized that Jesus is the presupposition of New Testament theology, and that faith as a personal decision "cannot be dependent upon a historian's labor" (1:26). While this is certainly axiomatic as expressed, it implies that faith has no need of a Jesus of history, and the door is thrown wide open for the claim that Jesus never existed, historical knowledge of Jesus is irrelevant, or the Jesus of history has been replaced by the Christ of faith. None of these conclusions would have been endorsed by the Evangelists, Paul, or any New Testament author.

Bultmann sought a methodology that would enable him to remove the unattractive and dated mythological language in the Gospels. He sought to show how through "demythologization," we are no longer mired in antiquity in which the "ancients" had no difficulty of virgin births and God-men performing supernatural deeds, such as walking on the water. What is important is to perceive eternal truths.

What is an example of such truths, and how does it enable the good news in the

Gospels to be heard afresh? In the preaching of the Word we are confronted by the One who calls us to authentic existence; that is, the living and resurrected Christ calls us and frees us for salvation. It becomes apparent that Bultmann has read the philosophy of Existentialism back into the Gospels.

Most scholars who have assessed the period from 1906 to 1953 assume that Schweitzer's influence was universal and that he not only influenced all scholars but also convinced them. This is certainly true of the Bultmannian School; it is especially apparent in the life of Jesus published by H. Conzelmann (Bultmann's student). However, as W. P. Weaver discovered and explained in *The Historical Jesus in the Twentieth Century, 1900–1950*, Schweitzer's work was not universally well received.

In England, Schweitzer's influence was barely noticeable in many universities. Books were written on Jesus as if Schweitzer had never published his work or he was simply incorrect. Notable among the books on Jesus by English scholars are T. W. Manson's *The Teaching of Jesus* (1931) and C. H. Dodd's *The Parables of the Kingdom* (1935). Dodd showed that some of Jesus' teachings, especially the parables, evidenced a "realized eschatology" (a misleading term that Dodd later withdrew, though many scholars miss his later publication and retraction). Although Dodd's *The Founder of Christianity* did not appear until 1970, it represented Dodd's life work.

Even on the Continent, Schweitzer's influence was not determinative. Major books that focused on the historical Jesus appeared, notably M. Dibelius's *Jesus* (1939) and his *The Sermon on the Mount* (1940). In Tübingen A. Schlatter proceeded to work as if Schweitzer had never existed or was confused. His numerous books—especially his *Die Geschichte des Christus* (1923 [2nd ed.]; i.e., *The History of Christ*) and *Kennen Wir Jesus?* (1937; i.e., *Do We Know Jesus?*)—proceed on the assumption that one can know much about the historical Jesus and that such knowledge is essential for authentic faith.

J. Jeremias demonstrated that Jesus' chosen noun for "God" was *Abba* (1966) and popularized a study of Jesus' prayer life in *The Prayers of Jesus* (1967). He not only wrote a masterpiece on Jesus' parables (1963 [3rd ed.]), but also published a classic work, *The Sermon on the Mount* (1961). He shared thoughtful insights in *The Eucharistic Words of Jesus* (1966 [rev. ed.]), in which he proved that some of the traditions of the Last Supper, though developed in the Palestinian Jesus Movement (my term), derive authentically from Jesus' last supper with his disciples in Jerusalem. He also published one of the best studies of life in Jerusalem during the time of Jesus: *Jerusalem in the Time of Jesus: An Investigation into Economic and Social Conditions During the New Testament Period* (1967).

Despite these exceptions, the era from 1906 to 1953 is not characterized by a fascination with the historical Jesus. In contrast to the nineteenth century and the period after 1980, this virtual half century is characterized by a partial denigration of the historical Jesus. That era was shaped by Bultmann, Barth, Brunner, and Bonhoeffer, as well as Tillich. These theological giants were focused on Christian theology and built their theological edifices on the Christ of faith. None of them was interested in archaeology, historiography, or a search for the historical Jesus. They were not so much influenced by Schweitzer as by events in the West, especially the effects of "The Great War" (World War I), the Great Depression, and

World War II. These gifted minds were too shocked by contemporary events to launch out with a disinterested scientific search for a Jesus who lived millennia ago in a distant country. Not only Existentialism but living faith seemed to demand a Christ who was real and present. Certainly, no Christian wanted to follow a historical person who, in some ways, may be a little embarrassing.

4. *The New Quest and Its Demise: 1953–ca. 1970.* In 1953, Ernst Käsemann, a volcanic orator who shook the terrain of scholars in public, demonstrated before his teacher Rudolf Bultmann and his other students that the Gospels do contain reliable information regarding the historical Jesus, that we do know more about the historical Jesus than Bultmann and most of his followers assumed, and that such knowledge is relevant for authentic Christian faith. Käsemann's "The Problem of the Historical Jesus" appeared in 1964 in English in his *Essays on New Testament Themes.* Following Käsemann's dynamic lecture, scholars in Germany and the United States felt more confident to focus again on the historical Jesus. The period from 1953 until about 1970 has been designated the "New Quest of the Historical Jesus."

During this period major books on Jesus appeared by Bultmann's students, who had become distinguished professors. In his *Jesus* (1973), Conzelmann took Bultmann's critical method and thought to their logical conclusion. He claimed that much of what had been perceived as Jesus' self-consciousness was actually created by "the church" after Easter. Far more solid and reliable, if not as creatively brilliant, is Bornkamm's *Jesus of Nazareth* (1960). He wrote what would be the best attempt at a biography (while denying such was really possible) during the New Quest of the historical Jesus.

While it is widely claimed that the New Quest began in 1953, with Käsemann's stirring lecture, this perspective is as pan-Germanic as Schweitzer's claim that the Old Quest began with the German Reimarus and not with the Englishman Chubb. Lost in a focus on Käsemann's leadership are the publications of three sterling New Testament scholars: Pierre Benoit, Nils A. Dahl, and W. D. Davies. These scholars represent three different nations, and each had been arguing Käsemann's main points before 1953. Against the tide of the Bultmannian flood, they struggled to show that there is reliable history in the Gospels, and that such knowledge is essential for authentic Christian faith. Each man became a luminary in the New Testament field, not only in his own country but in the world community.

A French New Testament expert, Benoit taught in the École biblique de Jerusalem, was a heralded Greek philologist, an expert who showed how important archaeology is for Jesus Research, and one of the first editors of the Dead Sea Scrolls. Against the scholarly flow that found no reliable history in the Gospels, Benoit rightly claimed in 1946: "Perhaps an interest in history as such is not *the* dominant motive which governed the formation of the gospel tradition; but it is at least *one* of them and deserves to figure alongside the others, apologetic, polemic and so on" (*Gospel,* p. 33).

A Norwegian famous for his Christological studies, Dahl argued that the historical Jesus is not inaccessible. In 1952, Dahl argued: "We must expect of dogmatic work in Christology that it not avoid the problem of the historical Jesus but have a concern for a better solution than the historical life-of-Jesus theology and the dehistoricizing kerygmatic theology" (*Jesus the Christ,* p. 109). Dahl's insightful words may serve as a corrective to some recent claims that suggest historical Jesus research is not paradigmatically important for Christian faith (as in L. T. Johnson's *The Real Jesus*).

A British expert, W. D. Davies demonstrated that Paul must be studied within Judaism and that there are reliable historical traditions concerning Jesus. Though published in 1960, his work had evolved over more than eight years (see *Union Seminary Quarterly Review* 15 [1960]). Davies developed his thoughts in *The Setting of the Sermon on the Mount* (1964), which remains a classic. In this work he perceived that while the early followers of Jesus selected and edited Jesus' sayings, the Jesus traditions did *not* develop "over vast stretches of time" like "vague, folk tradition," but "the actual words of Jesus had a fair chance of survival" (pp. 417-18).

Why did the New Quest of the historical Jesus wane and eventually disappear? There are many reasons. First, it had been grounded on kerygmatic theology and the claim that the Gospels had evolved from kerygma, the preaching of the "early church." Scholars began to recognize that the Palestinian Jesus Movement (which the scholars in the New Quest called the "church") developed out of more than a focus on kerygma. There were many kerygmata (proclamations), and concerns beside proclamation shaped the earliest communities as they re-presented Jesus' life. The most important of these other activities in the Palestinian Jesus Movement are *didache* (teaching and study of scripture) and worship.

Second, the New Quest was shaped by Existentialism. Theologians eventually demonstrated that this philosophy is misleading or only partially accurate. A perception began to dawn that humans are not so much "beings" as *historical creatures* with an avid interest in historical questions and issues. Christians became interested in history and were not satisfied with only the existential meaning of a text (e.g., what does the text mean to me for salvation).

Third, the whole enterprise of the New Quest was essentially theological, and the jargon of academic theology was not interesting or comprehensible to most Christians. Scientific archaeology, interest in topography, and recognition of the history in the Gospels were being perceived by scholars; and no longer were all of them Christians.

The study of Jesus' time was becoming an obsession in the modern state of Israel, which had not existed before 1948. A new appreciation of the historical Jesus was being affirmed by many Jews, including Albert Einstein, Joseph Klausner, Samuel Sandmel, Geza Vermes, and David Flusser. Einstein is often not mentioned in the list of Jews who admired the historical Jesus. In *Einstein and Religion,* Max Jammer quotes an interview with Einstein in 1929; here are Einstein's words: "I am a Jew, but I am enthralled by the luminous figure of the Nazarene.... No one can read the Gospels without feeling the actual presence of Jesus. His personality pulsates in every word. No myth is filled with such life" (p. 22).

Finally, research on the Dead Sea Scrolls (recovered in 1947), the Old Testament Pseudepigrapha, and eventually New Testament archaeology significantly helped redefine *Christian origins*. Historians, archaeologists, and philologists (scholars interested in texts and language) began to play a more prominent role in New Testament research.

5. *Jesus Research (Third Quest): 1980–the present.* About 1980 a new trend

emerged. Leaving Existentialism behind—or not ever being influenced by it—many experts on the New Testament joined colleagues who were specialists in the study of Second Temple Judaism. It became apparent something new had begun. It is a scientific study of Jesus in his time in light of all relevant data. For the first time the study of texts was assisted by a systematic examination of archaeology and topography. Although the Old Quest, the partial moratorium on the Quest, and the New Quest were motivated by theological agendas and concerns, Jesus Research (or the Third Quest) began without such allegiances. Thus, this more scientific study of Jesus is led by a wide variety of experts. It is often not asked—or even obvious—if an author is a Roman Catholic priest, a dissident Roman Catholic layperson, a secular Christian, a liberal Christian, a conservative Christian, a Jew, an agnostic, or an atheist. Such labels are usually misleading if one is a research scholar, a skilled text expert, or an experienced archaeologist.

This development does not indicate that a putative Christ of faith is to be dichotomized from the Jesus of history. Scholars defined by Jesus Research (not to be confused with what some, like M. Borg, are doing in the Third Quest) are engaged in "disinterested" Jesus studies. Some of them also proceed to explore the continuities between the historical Jesus and the Christ affirmed and confessed by the Evangelists. The problem of separating the Jesus of history from the Christ of faith sprang up in the nineteenth century by focusing only on the New Testament and Christology, and misinterpreting the context of the texts involved. Too many theologians thought historiography was misperceived as detrimental to Christian faith. Now scholars include within focus additional necessary dimensions of Jesus Research, especially the topography of the Holy Land, archaeology, and texts on the so-called fringes of the canon. They ask, "What can be known about the life and thought of Jesus from Nazareth?"

Some leading Jesus Scholars are Jews. These experts obviously are not interested in revealing a Jesus who can be worshiped or in converting others to Christianity. They display a refreshing appreciation of Jesus from Nazareth and approach this Jew from within a mastery of Second Temple Judaism and early Rabbinics. Notable among them are two scholars.

One is the Jerusalem scholar, David Flusser. He was a charismatic showman with a genius for languages, history, and texts. A leading light in the first generation of exceptional professors at the Hebrew University, Jerusalem, Flusser was willing to call Jesus "Lord," and he had great admiration for the man, but refused to consider him God. His *Jesus* appeared in the sixties and was rewritten and expanded in 1998. One highlight of his book, which has appeared in many editions, is the focus on Jesus' concept of love, which he claimed was unique within Judaism and an example of pure genius (see chap. 11). He revised his masterpiece on Jesus, and it was completed by R. S. Notley; it now appears as *The Sage from Galilee: Rediscovering Jesus' Genius* (2007).

The second Jewish expert taught at Oxford University. Geza Vermes was once a Christian but is now again a Jew (yet these terms often mean something quite different within the academy). He has sought to demonstrate that Jesus should be seen in light of the Galilean miracle workers who were near contemporaries or contemporaneous with Jesus. Vermes has been dedicated to Jesus Research, and he is a prolific writer. His books on the historical Jesus include *Jesus the Jew: A*

Historian's Reading of the Gospels (1973, 1981, 2001), *Jesus and the World of Judaism* (1983, 1984), *The Changing Faces of Jesus* (2000), *The Authentic Gospel of Jesus* (2003), *Jesus in His Jewish Context* (2003), *The Passion* (2005), and *The Nativity* (2006).

Liberal as well as conservative Christians have devoted their skills and time to Jesus Research. Perhaps the most distinguished liberal is E. P. Sanders. Sanders's *Jesus and Judaism* (1985) has been widely influential. He emphasized that we can ascertain Jesus' fundamental message and that Jesus' teaching makes sense within pre-70 Judaism. What makes Sanders special is his focus on Jesus' deeds. Exploring what led to his crucifixion, Sanders found the answer in Jesus' turning over the tables of the money changers, and this act symbolized his prediction that the Temple would be destroyed. Such a charge against Jesus is evident in the meager reports of his so-called trial in the Gospels. Sanders's *The Historical Figure of Jesus* (1993) is a well-written, popular development of his method and conclusion. Sanders's major contributions are to demonstrate that anti-Semitism, even a lack of appreciation of Judaism, has marred Jesus Research, that Jesus should be understood within Judaism, and—perhaps most important—that we do know a lot about Jesus (contra Bultmann) and what we do know about him makes sense within Second Temple Judaism.

Many liberal and conservative thinkers have obviously been attracted to Jesus Research. M. J. Borg was "converted" to following Jesus as a result of his exploration of Jesus and his message. In 1984 with his *Conflict, Holiness, and Politics in the Teaching of Jesus,* Borg entered the field with an insightful and careful study of Jesus' concept of holiness. His *Meeting Jesus Again for the First Time: The Historical Jesus and the Heart of Contemporary Faith* (1994, 1995) reveals his position and clever use of English. Borg is convinced that Jesus' message was not shaped by Jewish eschatology. The main contribution of Borg's work is the passionate affirmation of the importance of the historical Jesus for our lives today. With Flusser, Borg would insist that Jesus' message contains answers to our daily problems.

A well-known and erudite conservative scholar is N. T. Wright. Wright's books include *Who Was Jesus?* (1992), *Jesus and the Victory of God* (1996), *The Challenge of Jesus: Rediscovering Who Jesus Was and Is* (1999), and *The Resurrection of the Son of God* (2003). He is an independent thinker and works with a careful, refined methodology. Wright asserts that Jesus was deeply influenced by Judaism, rejects Sanders's interpretation of Jesus' acts in the Temple, and is convinced that God raised Jesus from the dead.

Another influential and popular British scholar is J. D. G. Dunn. His latest book on Jesus is *Jesus Remembered* (2003). Along with Wright, Dunn concludes, rightly, that Jesus' thought was influenced by Jewish apocalyptic eschatology; that is, Jesus often imagined that the present world would soon end, perhaps was ending, and that a new world was dawning. Dunn's major contribution is the stress that oral traditions were alive between Jesus' time and the time of the Evangelists. He also rightly emphasizes that Jesus probably imagined that he was God's eschatological agent, was intimately linked to God through "sonship," and most likely hoped for a final acknowledgment of this role.

Two important and influential Jesus Scholars are Roman Catholic. Both are Americans where the majority of the interest in Jesus is now centered (though significant publications appear from Israel, Germany, and Britain). The two scholars are very different. J. P. Meier, a priest, is dedicated to a thorough and encyclopedic study of Jesus. Meier's *A Marginal Jew: Rethinking the Historical Jesus* now extends to three large volumes (1991–2001).

Much less confined by ecclesiastical restraints and somewhat iconoclastic is one of the best writers in the field of Jesus Research, the free-thinking J. D. Crossan. His *The Historical Jesus: The Life of a Mediterranean Jewish Peasant* (1991) has led many specialists to assume that Jesus was a peasant (but see the discussion in chap. 7).

Other influential scholars are not easy to categorize. These scholars include G. Theissen who introduced the importance of sociology into the study of Christian origins. His *The Shadow of the Galilean* (1987) is a captivating reconstruction of Jesus' time and some of his life. While imaginative, the book is based on a sensitive reading of Josephus's histories and other documents.[2] Theissen's book provides a narrative in which a reader catches a glimpse of life in Palestine when the Temple was still standing and when Jews struggled for meaning in a Land promised to them but overrun by Roman governors and Roman soldiers. Of Theissen's major contributions one is singularly important: it is now impossible to see the Jesus of history, but we can see him moving within the shadows preserved in the Gospels.

His *The Historical Jesus: A Comprehensive Guide* (1998), written with A. Merz, is a helpful guide to Jesus Research. Valuable insights into the proper methodology for pursuing Jesus Research are contained in his *The Quest for the Plausible Jesus* (2002), co-authored with D. Winter.

B. Chilton brings to Jesus Research his mastery of the Targumim (the translations of the Hebrew scriptures into Aramaic, Jesus' mother tongue). In *Rabbi Jesus: An Intimate Biography* (2000), Chilton speculates that Jesus may have been born in a Galilean village called Bethlehem. He argues that Jesus may have been a *mamzer* (one who could not prove that his father and mother were full Jews).

Three of the best books on Jesus Research are written by distinguished scholars who are women. Paula Fredriksen has published two major works: *From Jesus to Christ* (1988) and *Jesus of Nazareth, King of the Jews* (2000). In *The Misunderstood Jew*, Amy-Jill Levine insightfully illustrates how Christians have wrenched Jesus out of his Jewish environment and thereby contributed to anti-Judaism.

My work cannot be categorized easily into a liberal or a conservative camp. In "The Historical Jesus in Light of Writings Contemporaneous with Him" (*ANRW* 2.25.1 [1982]), I rejected the claim that *the Kingdom of God* was a creation of the early "church." I drew attention to the appearance of the words *the Kingdom of God* and related concepts in Second Temple Judaism. In 1986, in "From Barren Mazes to Gentile Rappings: The Emergence of Jesus Research" (*PSB* 7), I announced that a new phase in the study of the historical Jesus had commenced; I called it "Jesus Research." In *Jesus Within Judaism: New Light from Exciting Archaeological Discoveries* (1988), I endeavored to claim that Jesus must be studied within his religion, Judaism, and that monumental archaeological discoveries, including the Nag Hammadi Codices and the Dead Sea Scrolls, as well as excavations in sites frequented by Jesus, have changed the landscape of Jesus Research. It is evident that Jesus focused his ministry in the northwestern section of the Sea of Galilee, the area defined by Bethsaida, Chorazin, and Capernaum. It is now clear that

Pharisees and Essenes influenced Jesus, but he should not be labeled a Pharisee or an Essene. *The Gospel of Thomas* (found in a full Coptic form among the Nag Hammadi Codices) should be included in a search for Jesus' authentic words.

In *Jesus' Jewishness: Exploring the Place of Jesus in Early Judaism* (1991), with others, including many Jewish experts on Second Temple Judaism or the historical Jesus, I pointed out that Jesus was not only a Jew but one of the most Jewish Jews of the first century. In *Jesus and the Dead Sea Scrolls* (1992, 1995), along with Qumran experts, I helped to discern how and in what ways the unique teachings in the Scrolls enable us to better comprehend and appreciate Jesus' life, perspectives, and claims. In some sayings, Jesus appears pro-Essene; in many others, he seems anti-Essene. Yet Jesus should not be defined as an Essene or anti-Essene.

Jesus and Archaeology (2006) brings together major insights obtained by archaeologists. Discussions are directed to texts and to sites frequented by Jesus or important for Jesus Research. Jesus did teach in synagogues, and while almost always a "synagogue" was an ordinary place of gathering, some pre-70 edifices were constructed as synagogues. The Gospel of John surprisingly is not only a theological masterpiece; it also preserves some remarkable historical and architectural information. Some of Jesus' contemporaries most likely branded him a *mamzer*; that is, a man who could not prove to their satisfaction that his parents were demonstrably Jews and were married by Jewish law and custom. It is certain that, henceforth, those who engage in Jesus Research must be more focused upon, and informed by, archaeological discoveries and their assessments.

Conclusion

Today, it is no longer possible to report that Jesus Research is practiced by many who are disinterested in following Jesus. I am impressed, however, that many scholars in this field of research are able to work with scientific rigor and also affirm the essential need and importance of this scientific and historical research for Christian faith today. They demonstrate that Christian faith benefits from careful scientific and historical research.

The results of historical study may be intermittently disappointing. Yet through such painstaking study, a person looms large, perhaps not easy to understand or follow but at least not a projection or a creation of a believer's mind. For Christians, knowledge of Jesus is imperative if we are to comprehend what it means then and now to follow him.

Most scholars concur regarding Jesus' thought. It makes sense only within pre-70 Palestinian Judaism, and not later. For example, Jesus' teachings against Jewish purity laws make sense only between 20 B.C.E. and 70 C.E. That period saw the increased emphasis upon spirituality and holiness caused by the rebuilding and enlargement of the Temple. During that period, *mikvaot* (Jewish ritual baths) defined Jewish religious life in Judea and Lower Galilee; moreover, only then were stone vessels customarily being made, sold, and bought. *Mikvaot* (to ensure spiritual purification) and stone vessels (to protect their contents from contamination from impurity) were demanded by the excessive Jewish rules for purification being developed by priests in Jerusalem. In that setting, Jesus' words ring with special meaning: "Listen to me, all of you, and understand: there is nothing out-side a person that by going in can defile, but the things that come out are what defile" (Mark 7:14-15 NRSV).

Jews, Roman Catholics, and Protestants highly trained in Jesus Research emphasize a common conclusion. Jesus' major message was the proclamation of the present dawning of God's Rule, the Kingdom of God, and this message is deeply influenced by Jewish thoughts and concepts, especially Jewish apocalyptic eschatology.

Some consensus may be discerned as developing among Christian scholars devoted to Jesus Research (or the Third Quest). First, some knowledge of what Jesus did and intended to accomplish is necessary to comprehend the reason for his crucifixion, to perceive the meaning of his resurrection, and to be able to believe in him with an honest and enlightened commitment. Blind faith without any historical knowledge is not the faith in Jesus we find in the Evangelists and Paul. After all, Jesus warned that when the blind lead the blind, both will fall into a pit (Matt. 15:14).

Second, we need to avoid Kierkegaard's misleading counsel that the Christian is one who makes a leap of faith. Following this advice, some theologians want faith to be so risky that a Knight of Faith is required to battle the dragons of dis-belief. That actually turns the hero from Jesus to the Knight of Faith, and thus accomplishes precisely what the theologians sought to avoid. That is, such an emphasis shifts the focus from Jesus to a preoccupation with oneself; the result may be reminiscent of Narcissus's fate (he fell in love with his own image and, according to some myths, eventually committed suicide).

While Christian faith transcends scientific logic, it does need historical facts. Without some historical control, a putative Christian may jump into a theological black hole or be hoodwinked by Gnostics who thought Judas was the hero of the Gospels. Christian faith today should be continuous with the faith of the first dis-ciples, and they knew far more about the Jesus of history than any historian will ever be able to provide.

Third, Christians should not search for an objectivity that would guarantee faith. Authentic faith needs no guarantees. Historians and archaeologists cannot form faith, but their insights are necessary to inform faith. The Christian believes the paradigm of particularity: a particular person did something particularly sig-nificant in a particular place and time that is particularly foundational for faith.

The historian thus clarifies the scandal of Christianity and lays the foundation for a poetic vision. From the beginnings of Christian faith, it has been scandalous to believe that a man crucified publicly as a common criminal could be the Messiah, or the Son of God. It is equally absurd, in the minds of humanists, to believe that Jesus died and was resurrected. Poetic faith allows for the affirmation that something special happened in and through the life and death of Jesus, and that his life and thought are paradigmatically important because their meaning is experienced today anew. Such a poetic imagination sees more than a mangled body hanging on a tree outside Jerusalem's walls.

Fourth, there is continuity from the teaching of the Kingdom of God by Jesus to the preaching of the Christ by Jesus' earliest followers. They never categorized as paradigmatically distinct the historical Jesus and the Christ of faith. The followers of Jesus, and even Paul, claimed that the resurrected one was the Jesus who had been crucified. Thomas even wanted to place his hands and fingers in the wounds of the one who had the marks of crucifixion. Confronted by the risen Lord, Thomas knew it was not necessary to touch what he perceived.

Fifth, along with the best Jesus Scholars, we need to allow Jesus to be what he was and not portray him so he will appear attractive and easy to follow. That is the perennial problem. Schweitzer fell into it, even though he had imagined the pits full of those who sought to find the Jesus of history. That is, Schweitzer perceived that Jesus was different from the nineteenth-century liberals' portrayal of an attractive moralist. Yet in finding that eschatology defined Jesus' time and message—with his fondness for mysticism—he created a Jesus that was far more eschatological and mystical than the man who had lived.

From the Irishman George Tyrrell (1861–1909), an Anglican who became a Roman Catholic priest, we learn that we must not stare down the well of history looking for Jesus only to see our own faces. This well-known adage, often incorrectly attributed to Schweitzer who cited Tyrell, helps us comprehend that we must be far more critical of our methodological presuppositions and philosophical or theological preferences. We should be bold and courageous to be willing to discover a Galilean Jew who may at times be rather offensive and insensitive to Gentiles. Perhaps then a real flesh-and-blood human being might be perceived, and he may again make God present and challenge us to be willing daily to take up a cross in following him (as Luke reported).

Our opening questions were the following: When did the study of the historical Jesus begin, and what has been learned? Is it important to distinguish between what Jesus said and what the Evangelists reported? We have seen that the Old Quest commenced not with Reimarus in 1778 but earlier with Chubb in 1738. We should have learned not to seek a Jesus who is a mirror reflection of what we deem to be ideal and desirable. We should not equate or confuse what Jesus taught with what the disciples thought, and yet there is continuity from Jesus to Paul and the Evangelists. We should avoid the false dichotomy that separates the Christ of faith from the Jesus of history. We now turn to a methodology that successfully helps us discern Jesus' own traditions among the Jesus traditions collected and edited by the Evangelists (chap. 2).

Notes

[1] Jewish apocalyptic eschatology denotes the Jewish belief or idea that the end [*eschatos* in Greek] of all normal time was fast approaching and that God or his intermediaries had provided a revelation [*apocalypse* in Greek] of what was about to happen. This revelation is not systematically described. It often includes a disclosure of what secrets are in the heavens and what is mandatory for the faithful to do now on earth. It often mentions the last Judgment, the fulfillment of all God's promises, the cessation of evil, the defeat of Satan and the nations that had conquered the Jews, and the future peace and prosperity promised for God's faithful.

[2] Josephus lived in the first century C.E. and was an eyewitness of the revolt against Rome (66–70 or 66–74). He wrote the only extant history of the Jews during Jesus' time.

CHAPTER 2

Jesus Research and How to Obtain Reliable Information

5) What are the best methods for discerning traditions that originate with Jesus?

Two insights have now become apparent. First, the Evangelists sometimes significantly and deliberately edited Jesus' sayings. Second, we have learned that it is imperative to distinguish between the Evangelists' theology and Jesus' thought. This is an important task. By what method can we reliably recover Jesus' own thought and actions?

Methodology

We have also seen that an imprecise methodology has led to a vast array of lives of Jesus, many of them absurd or fantastic and some of the most insightful marred by Hegelianism (Strauss) or Existentialism (Bultmann). As we begin to examine the proper methods to discover traditions that originate with Jesus, we may now emphasize four fundamental perspectives.

First, *methodology distinguishes the learned from the uneducated*. The proper method distinguishes professional athletes from school boys, musicians from beginners, and scholars from authors. It is imperative to choose and employ the best methods and then to be self-critical, seeking to ensure that our search has not been detoured by marred circuitous questioning.

It should now be obvious how dangerous and fruitless it is for one to begin a study with the intention of finding a Galilean we can admire and wish to follow. Despite decades of labor-intensive work, we have accomplished nothing if we allow a wish to be the parent of a result. This warning applies to all research scholars, those wishing to find a Jesus to admire and those seeking to prove something unattractive about him (or even to foster the conclusion that Jesus never existed).

Second, *the method must be inductive and inquisitive*. If we commence with a commitment to ask questions for which we do not have answers, we must remain honest questioners who explore all possibilities with integrity. We need to ensure that we can ask honest questions and not manipulate an attractive answer. We need to remain attuned to our commitment to ask questions that penetrate deep into the data and provide trustworthy, even if sometimes disturbing, answers. We must allow, and will discover, that some of Jesus' actions and statements are shockingly embarrassing to Christians today. We render no honor to the man from

Nazareth if we seek only to know him by praising him. Is he not reputed to have said that many will call him "Lord" but that he does not know them?

Third, *focus should be on sources* and not on scholars' opinions. Most readers are not primarily interested in a discussion of what Jesus Scholars have concluded. They are drawn to the sources and eager to learn what might be knowable, and with what reliability, about Jesus from Nazareth.

Fourth, *all sources and data must be included.* This is certainly the most important fundamental perspective. Too often a gifted scholar inherits a question and quotes a proof text that answers it definitively. What may be forgotten is that the question may antedate 40 C.E. and that the answer discovered in the New Testament reflects proclamations shaped by a dependence on prophecy and may only be the answer of one person or group in antiquity.

For example, one of the main questions is obviously, Where was Jesus born? Like others in the Palestinian Jesus Movement, Matthew had heard that question. His answer is unequivocal: "Jesus was born in Bethlehem of Judea" (Matt. 2:1 NRSV). The novice will be pleased and end a search at this point; the gifted thinker will ask more questions, among them these: What does Matthew report or imply elsewhere? What do Mark, Luke, John, and Paul imply or claim? If Jesus is from Bethlehem, then why is he always called Jesus from Nazareth? The probing thinker will focus on Matthew, chapter 2, pondering whether the source of Matthew's answer is history: Had he spoken with one of the three wise men whom he alone reports were present at Jesus' birth? Or was Matthew (or the author of his source) answering historical questions by studying prophecy? The skeptic will imagine that Matthew is simply affirming the fulfillment of prophecy, since only a few verses later, he quotes Micah 5:1-3, which prophesies that from "Bethlehem" shall come "a ruler" who will govern Israel. This one example should clarify that honest questions demand a perusal of all relevant data within and without the canon of the New Testament.

With these four caveats consciously and constantly before us, we may begin to seek to discern, with more honesty and self-control, how to sift the sources in search of Jesus' life and thought. Perhaps some readers will discover what I learned over the past forty-five years: Jesus Research provides insights and answers that can be shocking, disturbing, enlightening, challenging, and revealing.

Is It Possible to Obtain Reliable Information Regarding Jesus of Nazareth?

We may now ask, How does one discern Jesus' own actions and thought from those attributed to him? How do we discover possible authentic Jesus traditions among the traditions collected, preserved, and edited by the Evangelists? These questions have vexed New Testament specialists since the time of Chubb (1738) and the recognition that the Evangelists were not eyewitnesses of Jesus' life and thought.

Myopia. The first task is to overcome too focused a vision, or myopia. In the past scholars too often answered a question by focusing on only one verse. For example, a fundamental question concerns Jesus' concept of the coming of God's

Kingdom. Discussion has been often skewed by looking only at Mark 9:1. One should include all related passages, especially Mark 13:32. Note how relevant each verse is for the other:

> Truly, I say to you, there are some standing here who will not taste death before they see that the Kingdom of God has come with power. (9:1)

> Concerning that day or hour no one knows, not the angels in heaven, nor the Son, only the Father. (13:32)

Include all Gospels and extracanonical sources. Frequently, Jesus Scholars have allowed one gospel, or one collection of gospels that portray Jesus from the same viewpoint (notably the Synoptics), to dictate conclusions. Along with many scholars, I think that the Gospel of John must not be marginalized, that the *Gospel of Thomas* intermittently preserves some reliable, less edited, sayings of Jesus, that Josephus did refer to Jesus, and that all relevant sources, literary and nonliterary (e.g., archaeology), should be collected for examination if we are to obtain a clearer and more representative picture of the man from Nazareth (see chap. 3).

Second Temple Judaism. There is much more to include as we seek to comprehend Jesus' life and thought within his own culture (also see chap. 4). Only a historian familiar with the varieties of Judaism in the first century C.E. can answer some of the questions we are now raising (see esp. chap. 4). I think that Bultmann, who had studied the literature of Second Temple Judaism, perceived this insight when in his magisterial *The Theology of the New Testament* (1951), he warned about the necessity of a historian: "Only the historian can answer this question ..." (1:26).

When one does not know the rich varieties of early Jewish life and thought that antedate 70 C.E., one can easily claim that Jesus created the literary forms of the parables and beatitudes and such concepts as the Son of Man and the Rule of God (the Kingdom of God). By ignoring Judaism or seeing it only as the background of the Gospels, one arrives at a unique religion called Christianity. But this modern construct provides ammunition for those who want a triumphant supersessionistic Christianity (that is, a new religion divorced from Judaism and superseding it). This idea was rightly abhorred by Pope John Paul II and has been rejected by most church leaders; it certainly was a position that Paul argued against in Romans 11.

Jesus was a devout Jew (as most scholars now stress and we shall see). The varieties of Jewish thought are the presuppositions of Jesus' mind and those of his first followers. This insight should appear obvious as the reader reflects on two facts. First, not once are the disciples portrayed asking Jesus to define his terms, like *the Kingdom of God*. Second, never are the disciples depicted asking him to define or explain such concepts as the Messiah or the Son of Man.

Methodology and Jesus' uniqueness. Terms and concepts once seen as creations by Jesus or his first followers are now clearly evident in pre-70 Jewish thought. "Son of Man" appears in *1 Enoch* 37–71, and despite the assumption of too many New Testament professors, this text is not only obviously Jewish but also clearly pre-70 C.E. These conclusions are now evident in the proceedings of the Enoch

17

Symposium. The concept of the Rule of God or God's Kingdom appears in many Jewish documents that antedate Jesus (cf. the *Angelic Liturgy*). Despite the advice of some influential New Testament experts, the term, phrase, and concept the Kingdom of God or Rule of God did not originate for the first time within the post-Easter community of Jesus' followers.

Seeking Jesus' uniqueness is a very tricky task. At the beginning of this task, it is imperative to comprehend that uniqueness does not lie in what is missing from a thinker's context. Uniqueness resides in what words have been chosen and which words are stressed. A cluster of words or concepts indicates the creativity of thinkers who are always constrained by the images, symbols, concepts, terms, and words used by those in their own time and culture. Hence, Jesus' unique words were shaped by contemporary Jewish thought and especially by the interpretation of scripture by his fellow Jews. To communicate to others in his culture, Jesus had to use their words, concepts, hopes, and fears. Jesus' words, in turn, shaped the minds of those who composed the Gospels.

Where does the burden of proof lie? In searching for the authentic Jesus, most scholars commence by assuming that a Jesus tradition is inauthentic until proven authentic and that the burden of proof lies with any expert who would argue for authenticity. This assumption is not objective or unbiased; it interjects into scientific research a bias against authenticity.

Since our sources assume a Jesus tradition is authentic, we also should assume a tradition is authentic until evidence appears that undermines its authenticity. Only this position is faithful to the intention of our Evangelists. Within a few decades of Jesus' death his followers handed on many reliable traditions. Along with many experts, I stress that some of those who had been with Jesus remained alive to preserve the authenticity of many traditions. Most, but not all, of these traditions were shaped by oral teaching and preaching. These took shape within a decade of Jesus' life.

In summation, a method that interjects initial and continuing doubt is discordant with the sources that present the data as reliable. Ultimately, as with other scientific endeavors, the burden of proof lies with the one making an argument. It thus becomes imperative to develop a sound, sensitive, and scientific method for discerning Jesus' traditions among the traditions attributed to him. Additional preliminary comments are necessary before presenting the five most important methods.

Composition of tracts within a generation of Jesus. Hillel (c. 60 B.C.E. to 20 C.E.) was a Jewish genius and theologian who lived before and during Jesus' life (c. 7/6 B.C.E. to 30 C.E.). His thought is so similar to Jesus' words that some scholars conclude, incorrectly, that Jesus was a disciple of Hillel.

Hillel traditions are almost always compiled and added to texts that are more than two centuries after he lived (cf. *Hillel and Jesus*). The Jesus traditions, in contrast, originated in and took a written form in tracts within a decade or two of his death. This seems evident when we study the pre-Marcan and pre-Johannine traditions; for example, the parables collected *en masse* in Mark 4 and the numbering of "signs" beginning in John 2:11. Learned Jews, a few clearly from Bethsaida, Capernaum, or Jerusalem, claimed in the first century and even before 70 C.E. that Jesus had said and done what is recorded in Mark and the earliest sections of

Matthew, Luke, and John. And the communities of the Evangelists included those who contended that a witness to Jesus was trustworthy (cf. John 1:14b; 19:35; 21:24; cf. Luke 1:1-4). Our sources for Jesus reflect controls against falsifying traditions about his life and original message.

The fundamental question may remain: How much reliable historical information has been supplied or guaranteed by the oral witnesses? And if we do find evidence of an eyewitness, how reliable is that witness?

In the past few years an emphasis upon the reliability of the oral tradition has begun to shape Jesus Research. R. Bauckham, an erudite and careful scholar, has recently claimed, in *Jesus and the Eyewitnesses* (2006), that the Gospels are based on eyewitnesses who knew Jesus personally. In his *Memory in Jewish, Pagan and Christian Societies of the Graeco-Roman World* (2004), D. Mendels shows that memory is a complex human perspective; it is the vehicle for transmitting reliable historical facts. We who have many means of refreshing our memories often lose the capacity to remember as did the early Jews who knew Jesus. Thus, while the Jesus tradition was once widely perceived as being shaped fundamentally by the Evangelists and social forces that postdate 70, a new, and promising, emphasis has been placed on the early nature, and reliability, of the traditions about Jesus. His original meaning is now widely seen as preserved in the Gospels, even though his exact words may be altered.

More and more experts in Jesus Research insist that Jesus' earliest followers were not incompetent or simple people. Although they were not trained like Rabbis, some of Jesus' followers were gifted and well trained, knew Hebrew and Greek, and were experienced in life and thought. All the disciples were not poor, ignorant peasants or rustic fishermen as earlier critics assumed. Archaeological research shows continuity between the culture in the Galilean villages and the cities, such as Sepphoris, Tiberias, Jotapata, and Gamla.

Polemical ambience. We need to pay heed to the social and historical context in which the Jesus traditions first took shape. They took definite shape within fifteen years of his life. Moreover, they did not evolve within a speculative or academic setting. They developed within Galilee and especially in Jerusalem among Jews who had known Jesus. They were refined within a polemical ambience in which it was foolhardy to fabricate traditions.

For example, the Passion Narrative appeared within a hostile context in Jerusalem and in the thirties. Then and there, many Jews knew that Jesus had been crucified as a criminal or insurrectionist, and some of them felt there were reasons why Jesus should have been put to death (breaking of Sabbath laws, disrespect for the high priest, blasphemy, presumption of being God's son). No reputable historian would deny that the early proclamation (kerygma and kerygmata) about Jesus took place within a very hostile setting. It appeared within Jerusalem, among Jews, and before eyewitnesses of his actions and teachings. The claims were public and could have been heard by influential priests, Roman authorities, merchants from Egypt and Persia, and others. The Roman centurion Cornelius was not far away and was most likely intermittently present. Pilate remained as governor until 36 C.E.

This hostile environment kept the Evangelists honest. This fact is apparent in their reports and the embarrassing aspects of the passion: James and John sought thrones, Judas betrayed Jesus, Peter denied him, and Jesus was publicly crucified. The Gospels evolved out of and within a polemical ambience; thus, fabrication and denial would undermine the success of any proclamation.

A perception of the polemical ambience in which the Jesus traditions took shape helps us comprehend the process of transmission. Yet we should avoid an assumption that there was a "college" of scholars in Jerusalem in the thirties and forties who were authenticating Jesus traditions. We should not fail to observe that eventually the Evangelists certainly did take incredible liberties in shaping the Jesus tradition; and that means we need to be ever cognizant of the best scientific method for separating what the Evangelists received and what they added.

Proclaiming the Proclaimer. We need to avoid all positivistic methods and conclusions; that is, the data allows us to obtain only relatively probable conclusions. We need to be aware that almost always the Jesus traditions appear to be shaped by other than historical concerns, and that raises the issue of inauthenticity. That is, it soon becomes readily apparent to the attentive researcher that traditions about Jesus often are shaped by the belief in his resurrection and the needs of the post-Easter Palestinian Jesus Movement. The transmitters of tradition and compilers of the Gospels were never interested first and foremost in giving us an uninterpreted life of Jesus. They proclaimed the one who had been the consummate Proclaimer.

We also have come to recognize that we do not have the ability to present a life of someone without interpretation. Most of us would admit that if such were possible, we would not be interested in it. It would be as dull and dead as many of the inscribed papyri and ostraca (broken pottery) that simply state a certain unknown man had crushed a certain commodity of wheat.

As is true for most of those who study the Gospels, the reader is most likely interested in learning something significant about Jesus. I doubt you would be interested in a simple report that Jesus crushed some wheat on a certain day in Nazareth. You would want reliable and meaningful information about Jesus' actions and message. What did Jesus do and say, and how do these help us comprehend what he intended to accomplish?

Five major methodologies. All canonical and extracanonical gospels are edited versions of Jesus traditions. Hence, criteria for discerning within the Gospels the deeds and sayings of the historical Jesus have developed. What are the most reliable methods for discerning Jesus' own traditions from the Jesus traditions recorded by the Evangelists? Five are major.

Which of these is most important? Some scholars have hailed one method as more important than all the others. This is unfortunate, since a method obtains its importance only in relation to a particular text. When another text is examined, another method often is more important. Methods are tools; they are defined as useful by the context. As a screwdriver is better than a hammer in dealing with a screw, and a lug wrench better than pliers when repairing a flat tire, so each method now to be examined is best with some texts and misleading with others.

1) *Embarrassment.* This method develops from the observation that some deeds and sayings of Jesus were an embarrassment to the Evangelists who have preserved our primary sources for determining the life and thought of Jesus. What was an embarrassment to the Evangelists would not have been invented by them. And it would not have originated with others who lived within the Palestinian

Jesus Movement. They were teaching (*didache*) and proclaiming (*kerygma*) the good news regarding Jesus the Christ.

In evaluating reputed deeds or sayings of Jesus with the criterion of embarrassment, we need constantly to remind ourselves of the original context for the transmission of Jesus' actions and words. The polemical ambience helped protect against the excesses in later compositions, like the story of a walking cross that exits the tomb (the *Gospel of Peter*).

The Gospels originated with the proclamation that the crucified Jew was the exalted Messiah. The proclamation was often directed to those who had rejected Jesus' teachings. Much of the early Jesus tradition was clearly first fashioned within a city still dominated by autocratic high priests, namely, Annas and Caiaphas, who, according to the author and sources of Acts, diligently sought to extinguish the flame lit among Jews by Jesus. Jesus was only the first of the martyrs in Jerusalem; he was soon followed by Stephen, James, probably John, and then his brother James, and all before the conflagration that consumed Jerusalem and the Temple in 70 C.E.

It is clear that numerous events and sayings were embarrassing to Jesus' followers. As we observe how the record was embarrassing to the Evangelists, we discern that a saying or action is most likely authentic to Jesus.

Our proof often is evident in Matthew's and Luke's editing of Mark. For example, Jesus' claim that God's Rule (the Kingdom of God) would dawn while some of his hearers were still alive was an embarrassment to Matthew and Luke; hence, they edited and altered Jesus' words (Mark 9:1 and par.). So, by this criterion, Mark's version is authentic.

Only Mark clearly reports that Jesus "was baptized by John" the Baptizer (Mark 1:9). Luke, for example, places John in prison before Jesus' baptism; Luke thus avoids the embarrassing claim that John was superior to Jesus, because the superior baptizes the inferior. The polemic against the followers of John the Baptizer also shapes the narrative elsewhere, especially in John 1–4. According to Acts 19, disciples of John the Baptizer were active in Ephesus. It appears, therefore, that the disciples of Jesus had difficulty debating with the disciples of John because of the embarrassing fact that John had baptized Jesus. The criterion of embarrassment clarifies that John baptized Jesus.

Other embarrassing deeds bothered and embarrassed the Evangelists. Again, recall the Passion Narrative. Very embarrassing are the requests of James and John, the betrayal of Judas, "one of the Twelve," who may have been the treasurer of Jesus' group, Peter's denial, and Jesus' death as a public execution that was seen from Jerusalem's walls and on the major road to Joppa and Caesarea Maritima. None of these embarrassing details originated in the post-Easter Jesus community; they are part of the pre-70 history of Jesus.

Not only actions but Jesus' reputed sayings are occasionally embarrassing and disturbing. Embarrassing sayings include "let the dead bury the dead" to a young man who needed time to bury his father (a Jewish law), and the rebuke of the Syrophoenician woman (Jesus seems to call this wise woman a "dog"). Jesus' cry of dereliction from the cross—"My God, my God, why have you forsaken me?"— was embarrassing to the Fourth Evangelist. He changed Jesus' last words to: "It is finished" (John 19:30).

These embarrassing deeds and words could not be proclaimed comfortably about the Proclaimer. They perplexed the Evangelists, as becomes obvious as one studies the chronology of editing in the transmission of Jesus traditions. If such deeds and words are embarrassing to Jesus' followers, then they were not created after Easter in the Palestinian Jesus Movement. Thus, they most probably derive from history and represent the life and thought of Jesus. In many passages the criterion of embarrassment is the most helpful tool for retrieving traditions that represent the historical Jesus.

In summary, the criterion of embarrassment denotes that if an act or saying is an embarrassment to Jesus' followers and to others within the Palestinian Jesus Movement, then it did not originate with his followers. This criterion dredges up many aspects of the Jesus story that some Christians would prefer to keep in the closet. It indicates that the Jesus Movement lauded a scandal, emphasizes that Jesus was misunderstood even by his closest disciples, that on his last night those accorded distinction within his group could not remain awake, and that Jesus' last cry was one of abandonment. Until we feel the absurdity of the kerygma within its pre-70 Jewish setting, we cannot appreciate its theological logic. The offensive nature of Jesus' actions and teachings may be disturbing to the reader; but they are priceless evidence of his existence and humanity. Quite distinct and much broader yet within a similar precision of methodology is the next criterion.

2) *Dissimilarity.* The method of dissimilarity has been developed to isolate Jesus' sayings that are dissimilar both to early Jewish thought and to the thoughts and claims of his followers. This method assumes that what cannot be attributed to Jesus from Judaism or from Jesus' followers is most likely authentic to him. For seventy years this has been the most popular method. In his *Jesus and the Word* (1934) and also in his *History of the Synoptic Tradition* (1963), R. Bultmann used a form of this criterion. In *Rediscovering the Teaching of Jesus* (1967), Norman Perrin called dissimilarity the "strongest" method for discerning Jesus' own traditions among the Jesus traditions (p. 38).

But this method can be misleading and is too restrictive; the net is too loose and torn to catch reliable data from the historical Jesus. Much authentic Jesus data is lost by focusing only on his dissimilarity to other Jews. It is clear today that Jesus was a Jew and he was deeply influenced by his own religion. Jesus' parables are some of his most unique creations; yet parables abound in early Judaism. He crafted beatitudes, but beatitudes are found among the Dead Sea Scrolls (see *Beatitudes* [4Q525]). Some critics imagine that the Lord's Prayer was fashioned by Jesus' followers who knew he referred to God as "Abba," Father; yet the Lord's Prayer is in many places identical with early Rabbinic prayers.

Likewise, much authentic information on Jesus is lost by focusing myopically only on his differences from his followers. Using the principle of dissimilarity without caution produces a Jesus who was not influential and who either had no followers or none of them were in any way influenced by him. The results can be absurd, since one of the clearest facts about Jesus is that he had followers and that they were influenced by him. To employ the method of dissimilarity without insight and without use of other methods ultimately produces a Jesus who was not a Jew and who had no followers.

The criterion of dissimilarity thus mixes two different criteria. On the one hand, as we saw with the criterion of embarrassment, what is dissimilar between Jesus and the community he called into existence helps us find a historical Jesus, since his followers are the ones who have given us the Gospels.

On the other hand, to seek what is dissimilar between Jesus and Judaism assumes that Jesus was not a Jew. What he shares with Judaism is usually authentic to him (despite the claims of Bultmann and Perrin), since we find virtually no evidence of a Jew uninterested in Jesus attributing Jewish ideas to him. Those who after World War II used the principle of dissimilarity from Judaism to discover Jesus' authentic teachings claimed to discover three main unique features of Jesus' teaching: the Lord's Prayer, the Kingdom of God, and the parables. These scholars probably neither attended synagogal services in which the opening of the Lord's Prayer is recited in Hebrew nor intended to enter the world of Judaism, in which parables abound (esp. in early Rabbinics and the *Apocryphon of Ezekiel*). Moreover, God's Rule appears in many Jewish prayers and diverse documents.

Furthermore, what is Jewish in Jesus soon became an embarrassment to those who were filling the Palestinian Jesus Movement: Gentiles. In fact, the criterion of dissimilarity to Judaism too often looks suspiciously anti-Jewish or anti-Semitic. Recent publications contain the argument that Jesus was far more "Jewish" than Philo, Paul, or Josephus (see the "Suggested Readings"). That is, Jesus seemed hostile to Gentiles, affirmed the revelatory power of the Torah (or Old Testament) without casting it within Greek and Roman models of thought. He also most likely followed the Jews' dietary laws (known as Kasrut); and there is no evidence that he rejected the importance of circumcision.

The criterion of dissimilarity is only appropriate regarding Jesus' sayings; and it is helpful only when the dissimilarity is between Jesus' sayings and the linguistic and theological world evidenced by each Evangelist. So refined this method will prove helpful and remains one of our strongest methods. It should be employed with perception and with knowledge of Early Judaism, the Palestinian Jesus Movement, and in light of other methods.

In working with Jesus' sayings, the two most important criteria for authenticity are the criterion of embarrassment to his followers and the criterion of dissimilarity to the Christology and theology of the members of the Palestinian Jesus Movement. That is, if a saying is embarrassing or dissimilar to his followers' way of thinking, then it most likely did not arise with them. Since it is attributed to Jesus by the Evangelists, it may well have originated with him.

3) *Multiple attestation.* A third major criterion for ascertaining Jesus' own words and deeds among the Jesus traditions is multiple attestation. That is, a saying or action attributed to Jesus preserved in two or more independent primary sources is more probably original to Jesus than if it were found in only one source. The independent strata, in roughly chronological order, are the following (developed in chap. 3):

Q   a putative source of Jesus' sayings used by Matthew and Luke
S   a possible Signs Source ostensibly used by John
Pl   Paul's references to Jesus and quotations or allusions to words of Jesus
Mk Mark
J^1 John [first edition]

M   traditions inherited only by Matthew
L   traditions inherited only by Luke
A   preservation of the Jesus traditions by the author of Acts
J²   the second edition of John (without 7:53–8:11)
T   *Gospel of Thomas*

These ten literary strata (or sources) have been judged by a wide-ranging group of New Testament specialists to be independent (or to represent independent sources). Hence, multiple attestation signifies that a tradition in two or more independent sources must not only antedate each of those sources but also indicate a tradition that most likely derives ultimately from Jesus. Thus, one finds from the study of Mark, John, and the *Gospel of Thomas* (which occasionally may contain some independently transmitted sayings of Jesus) that Jesus' teaching was shaped by Jewish apocalyptic thought and was parabolic (i.e., ideas were often expressed through stories).

Yet this method is also to be used with caution and reflection. Multiple attestation has its limits. It should be used only to include traditions that may ultimately originate with Jesus. It should not be used to reject as inauthentic a tradition that appears in only one source. Sometimes it is clear that an authentic saying of Jesus was misunderstood, misleading, or embarrassing, and was then omitted by others. The best example seems to be the seed growing secretly, which is found in Mark 4:26-29 but not in Matthew, Luke, or John (cf. *Gos. Thom.* 21). Most likely this parable derives from Jesus and was omitted by other evangelists because its meaning seemed unclear and it did not seem fitting to their own theologies. Under the fourth criterion (next), we will be able to discern why this parable in Mark 4 might be authentic.

To the criterion of multiple attestation can be appended the criterion of *double affirmation*. This method affirms as authentic to Jesus what was affirmed by opponents as well as proponents. Thus, this method allows us to discern that Jesus performed what his contemporaries called miracles. Why? Not only his proponents reported that he performed miraculous deeds. His opponents also affirmed this fact when they claimed he was able to do so because he was in league with Satan or Beelzebub (cf. Matt. 12; Luke 11).

Also, related to the criterion of multiple attestation is *multiple forms*. A Jesus tradition appearing in multiple literary forms most likely derives from Jesus ultimately. The concept of God's Rule or the Kingdom of God derives from Jesus since it appears in parables, stories, and dominical sayings. The same method discloses that Jesus had compassion for and included sinners, people with leprosy, women, and other outcasts of society (those lost in social interstices). The same method proves that Jesus rejected the restricted definition of Shabbat (the Sabbath) created by some of his contemporaries (see chap. 4).

4) *Coherence.* When these three methods present a reliable Jesus tradition, we can turn to the criterion of coherence. When a deed or saying of Jesus is virtually identical with what has already been shown to be most likely authentic to Jesus, the deed or saying under scrutiny may also with some reliability be attributed to Jesus. Thus, the passage about the woman caught in adultery (John 7:53–8:11), although only later added to the New Testament, especially to John, may be

authentic to Jesus. It is coherent with many of Jesus' original sayings, and is harmonious with the portrait of Jesus found elsewhere, especially his nonjudgmental nature and acceptance of those discarded by priestly leaders.

What about the Parable of the Good Samaritan, which is recorded only by Luke? On the one hand, Luke could have created it, since it reveals his universalism and concern for the outcast. On the other hand, it coheres with what has already been proved to be reliable traditions from Jesus, especially the parables. It reflects knowledge of the terrain in Judea between Jerusalem and Jericho, and it fits perfectly the emphasis on pollution and purity, which was a hallmark of pre-70 Palestinian Jews living not only in Judea but in Lower Galilee. Finally, it is coherent with Jesus' inclusion of the marginalized.

Having introduced the criterion of coherence, we may now consider a previous question: Why is the parable of the seed growing secretly probably authentic? We may now entertain the possibility that it derives from Jesus because of the criterion of coherence. That is, the saying is a parable, and parables are typical of Jesus and not those who followed him. The saying is also coherent to many sayings already discerned to be authentic to Jesus. The Parable of the Seed Growing Secretly is harmonious with what has otherwise been determined to be Jesus' main message: an apocalyptic and eschatological emphasis on God's impending action—and without human involvement.

5) *Palestinian Jewish setting.* In contrast to the methods used in the New Quest of the historical Jesus, especially the attempt to use the method of dissimilarity to find authentic Jesus traditions, we need to recognize a *"criterion of historical plausibility"* (see *Plausible*). This criterion suggests that a tradition of Jesus may be authentic if it reflects his specific culture and time and not the world defined by the loss of Land and Temple after the destruction of Jerusalem in 70 C.E. This criterion is best explained by using examples.

What are the best examples of this fifth method for discerning Jesus' own traditions? Four examples must now suffice. First, since the 1940s this method has been recognized when working on specific passages, notably the story of the woman caught in adultery (John 7:53–8:11). Many Johannine specialists concluded that although this passage is not originally a part of the Gospel of John, it may well derive ultimately from Jesus because the story is historically plausible. That is, it fits into Jesus' Jewish environment (the setting is a realistic depiction of the time when the Temple was the center of worship). It accurately preserves the tension over oral legislation between Jesus and some scribes and Pharisees (8:3-5). It reflects the concerns and debates regnant in Palestine at that time (it represents the need for two witnesses: Jesus does not witness against her and no one else does; and it preserves evidence that stoning is the punishment for adultery [8:5]). The story assumes the Temple has not yet been destroyed so that Jesus may teach people in it (8:1-2). Those who use this method assume, with good evidence, that the Evangelists wrote or completed their Gospels in Rome or southern Syria (Mark), Antioch (Matthew), Ephesus (John), or elsewhere (Luke). When a Palestinian Jewish setting is discerned in a passage (pericope), then it represents Jesus' time and place and not an Evangelist's time or place. Thus, the action or saying may derive ultimately from Jesus.

Second, fifty years ago we had little evidence of the obsession for ritual purity among religious Jews before 70 C.E. In the early 1950s, cisterns were found at Qumran and some had divisions down the center; it was not clear what such divisions indicated. Stone vessels were also found at Qumran. In the 1960s, with the excavation of Masada and the Upper City of Jerusalem something challenging appeared in the debris that antedates 70–73/74. Now we know that the stone vessels were necessary for purity rules, and these stone cups and jars have been found in Judea and Lower Galilee (see John 2). We also learned that some cisterns are *mikvaot*, which are Jewish baths required for ritual purification. The compiler of the *Temple Scroll* (the longest of the Dead Sea Scrolls) reports that a woman with a dead fetus in her makes herself impure and contaminates all houses she enters and everything collected and preserved in an earthen vessel (col. 50). That means the house must be purified (by some unknown means but surely performed by a priest). It also means that everything in the clay vessel must be destroyed along with the vessel. Impurity seeps through clay; hence, a religious Jew must store what is important in stone, glass, or bronze. Now, for the first time we comprehend John 2 and the six stone jars standing there in this wealthy house. They are, as the Evangelist had reported but no commentator has so far comprehended: "for the Jewish rites of purification" (John 2:6).

Archaeologists and specialists on the Mishnah and Talmudim have helped New Testament experts comprehend the importance of purification (not cleansing of hands) and stone vessels. The earliest documentary evidence of the need for purification and the mention of "vessels of bronze" seems to be Mark 7:1-23 (see esp. 7:4). According to John 9, a man born blind is healed by Jesus. After healing him, Jesus tells him to go purify himself in the Pool of Siloam. Now we know this pool is the largest *mikveh* ever found. *Mikvaot* and stone vessels characterize Jewish religious life before 70 and not after it. Thus, this Jewish ambience helps anchor and date some Jesus traditions as most likely authentic to Jesus.

Third, the authors of Romans, Mark, John, Matthew, Luke, and Hebrews affirm two historical facts: Jesus was crucified, and this act took place outside Jerusalem. Archaeological research proves that Golgotha was outside Jerusalem's walls in 30 but within it in 44 C.E. when a wall to the west was built, enclosing the area around it. This historical fact is supported by their attempt to explain Jesus' crucifixion. Jesus' followers claimed that Jesus died according to scripture (*kata tas graphas*). The latter was a *tour de force* within Judaism because no pre-70 Jewish texts or scripture indicates that the Messiah was destined to die. There was no suffering Messiah in early Jewish theology. That idea appeared first in history within the Palestinian Jesus Movement in Jerusalem. The failure to find a suffering and dying Messiah in pre-70 Judaism is a disappointment for some Christians who specialize in Second Temple Judaism, but it is still an unperceived boon for Jesus Research. Was Jesus the first to obtain this perspective, or were the first to proclaim him, after 30, the ones who introduced this concept into the world of ideas?

Fourth, Jesus (but not the Evangelists) affirmed the importance of the Temple, including worship and sacrifice there. For Jesus the *axis mundi* (center of the world) seemed to be the Temple, but for the Evangelists it was Jesus. Recall how Jesus celebrated the importance of the Temple. He hailed it as "my father's house." The author of Acts knows that Jesus' disciples continued to worship in the Temple and to teach there; for example, Peter and John ascend the stairs leading up to the Temple Mount at "the hour of prayer" (Acts 3:1). Peter continues to proclaim Jesus' messiahship and "the resurrection from the dead" exactly where Jesus is reported to have taught (John 10:22-30). It is in Solomon's Portico (or Stoa), which includes the row of pillars and high ceiling that ran north to south on the eastern edge of the Temple Mount (Acts 3:11–4:4).

Many of those in the Temple who heard Peter's claims about Jesus had seen him worshiping rather recently in the Temple. Some of them would have been among the crowd that shouted out to crucify him. Who else were also in the Temple watching attentively? Annas and Caiaphas were still alive and powerful, and the Sadducees had no time for any fool who would believe in a resurrection of anyone. It was against this resistance that the oral tradition and first written tracts about Jesus began to take definite shape; at least some of these oral and written traditions were not lost because the Evangelists and others preserved them. The Palestinian Jewish setting and polemical ambience help anchor and ensure many Jesus traditions.

Many readers of Bultmann and especially his followers like Conzelmann often obtain the impression that all those who lived in Palestine before 30 C.E. and had "bumped into" Jesus were whisked away in a chariot like the one that took Elijah. We need to perceive that those who hated or were indifferent to Jesus were alive while the Jesus traditions took shape; they help preserve some reliability in the transmission of the Jesus traditions.

Ten additional supporting methods. In addition to these five major methods for recovering traditions that are probably authentic to Jesus, ten other methods provide supporting insight and information.

First, for more than one hundred years experts have studied how the New Testament text has been "edited" by later copying scribes. These scribes provided variants that removed unattractive theological concepts, clarified the meaning, improved the grammar, or harmonized the text so that it was similar to parallel texts. Studying the editing of apocryphal texts, especially the *Testaments of the Twelve Patriarchs,* the *Fourth Book of Ezra,* the *Testament of Adam,* the *Hellenistic Synagogal Prayers,* and the *History of the Rechabites,* has helped us comprehend better the development of the Synoptic and Johannine traditions. Dozens of examples prove that *often a core tradition is habitually edited at the beginning and the end.* This insight helps us grasp the editing of Mark by Matthew and Luke, and perhaps, at times, Mark's editing of the traditions he received. Also, Paul, in reporting Jesus' last supper, edits the tradition he received and passed on by supplying a qualifying sentence at the end of the tradition: "For as often as you eat this bread and drink the cup, you proclaim the Lord's death until he comes" (1 Cor. 11:26 NRSV). Thus, Paul adds a saying of Jesus that derives not from tradition but from his editing. By using this method, we can discern before and after editing (sometimes needed to continue the flow of the narrative) *some Jesus traditions in a core may represent earlier tradition.*

Second, *an explanatory expansion* of a passage may indicate that the Evangelist most likely received a tradition that needs clarifying for his community and readers, who clearly postdate the tradition and need some explanation. An example of the usefulness of this method is found in Mark 7. After stating that the Pharisees and the scribes who had come from Jerusalem to spy on Jesus observed that Jesus'

27

disciples "ate with defiled hands," the Evangelist needs to explain Palestinian traditions to his readers. He adds to his received tradition this explanation demanded by readers who do not know Palestinian Jewish customs: "For the Pharisees, and all the Jews, do not eat unless they purify themselves; and there are many other traditions which they observe, the washing of cups and pots and vessels of bronze" (Mark 7:3-4). Enlightening, furthermore, is the observation that Greek scribes who copied Mark, ignorant of what he was explaining, changed "purify" to "baptize" (or "wash"). Other verses reveal the distance that has developed from Jesus' culture to later Greek and Roman culture (note esp. "with (the) fist" after "wash their hands" in many early manuscripts of Mark 7:3 [esp. MSS A and B]).

Third, the *exhortation to search* may indicate that a contiguous passage was not shaped by the needs of proclamation or teaching in the Palestinian Jesus Movement. For example, Matthew reports that Jesus said to Pharisees who demanded that he explain why he ate with many tax collectors and sinners: "Those who are well have no need of a physician, but those who are sick" (Matt. 9:12). The passage leaves the exegete pondering the precise appropriateness of Jesus' reply. Matthew knew this and so continued Jesus' speech: "Go and learn what this means, 'I desire mercy, and not sacrifice'" (9:13). The ambiguity of Matthew 9:12 may indicate that it probably did not arise in the post-Easter Palestinian Jesus Movement. It thus looks suspiciously like tradition authentic to Jesus and his Judaism. A passage that exhorts the reader to search for the meaning of Jesus' saying might lead us back to pre-30 history.

Fourth, a study of *how and in what ways the Jesus tradition is developing* helps us understand direction. Paul edits his Jesus traditions. Mark and John edit their sources. Matthew and Luke edit Mark. The development of thought sometimes becomes clear; by reversing the process, we are led to the earliest phases of the tradition. That is, the development of the Jesus traditions sometimes ultimately leads us back to Jesus' own traditions.

An analogy might clarify this point. When one throws a pebble into a placid pond, it radiates out ripples. By following these ripples backward, one comes to the center, and that is where the pebble entered the water. By tracing the Jesus traditions backward, we are certainly led back to their origins; many are originally centered in Jesus from Nazareth. This method makes sense only with ample study and lengthy demonstration, which the reader should obtain in the following chapters.

Fifth, as the Jesus tradition developed, Jesus was clearly portrayed in a more exalted position. Reversing high Christology to low Christology leads us back, sometimes in surprising ways, to the Jew named Jesus, son of Joseph. According to the Logos Hymn, prefixed to the Gospel of John at a later stage of development, perhaps about 95 C.E., it is implied that Jesus is the Logos—the Word—and that he is to be perceived as God (John 1:1-2). Earlier, perhaps in 85, Matthew emphasized that Jesus means Emmanuel (Matt. 1:23; cf. 28:20). Sometime around 70 C.E., Mark wished to stress that Jesus was revealed to be the Son of God (Mark 1:11; 9:7). Even earlier, perhaps in the forties, an unknown follower of Jesus stressed that Jesus "emptied himself, taking the form of a servant," so that after his obedience God exalted him, bestowing on him a new meaning to the name Jesus, so that everyone may confess "that Jesus Christ is Lord, to the glory of God the Father" (Phil.

2:7-11). By tracing the development of Christology, which is almost always from a lower to a higher adoration of Jesus, we are often led to Jesus' own words; hence, it is likely that Jesus said, "Something greater than Solomon is here" (Matt. 12:42; Luke 11:31). Also from this earliest of strata is Jesus' question, "Why do you call me good? No one is good except God alone" (Mark 10:18). This method of *retracing the development* to observe a low Christology often leads us to a person who is sometimes impressively humble: Jesus.

Sixth, studying a gospel and becoming familiar with the author's own theology and tendencies make one aware of traditions that are contrary to them. *What is against the theology of an Evangelist would most likely not have been added by him and probably reflects earlier traditions*; it is an aspect of tradition that, if attributed to Jesus, may well derive originally from him. For example, Jesus must have affirmed that the Torah (or Law) was eternally valid, as indicated in the Sermon on the Mount (Matt. 5:17-20). Why? The Evangelist who recorded those words seems to have assumed that "the prophets and the Law" were only until John the Baptizer (Matt. 11:13). In the early centuries of the church some translators of the New Testament perceived this problem and did not copy the words "and the Law" (Syriac and Coptic manuscripts).

Seventh, the Evangelists composed the Gospels in Greek. Some of their sources, oral and written, were clearly in Aramaic. Thus, *the discovery of transliterated Aramaic in the Gospels is most likely evidence of traditions that have been received.* Although the earliest preaching in Palestine was in Aramaic, there is no reason to doubt some Aramaic sayings transliterated in Greek and attributed to Jesus most likely derive from him. Thus, *talitha koumi* (Mark 5:41 [reading the correct transliteration in MS A] and other manuscript witnesses), *ephphatha* (Mark 7:34), *Abba* (Mark 14:36), *Siloam* (John 9:7), and *Elōi, Elōi, lema sabachthani* (Mark 15:34) most likely should be seen as Jesus' own voice (*ipsissima vox Jesu*). These transliterated words were as foreign to Greeks as they are to Americans and Europeans today.

An Evangelist often felt the need to translate them. Note these examples: "And grasping the child's hand he [Jesus] says to her, '*talitha koumi,*' which is to be translated, 'Little girl, I say to you, arise'" (Mark 5:41). Jesus approaches a man who is deaf and dumb in the Decapolis, "he put his fingers into his ears, and he spat and touched his tongue, and looking up to heaven, he sighed, and says to him, '*ephphatha,*' which denotes 'Be opened'" (Mark 7:33-34). South of the Temple Mount Jesus tells a man born blind, "Go, wash in the pool of Siloam (which is translated 'sent')" (John 9:7). In Gethsemane Jesus prayed, "Abba, Father [omitted in Codex Beza], all things are possible to you; remove this cup from me; yet not what I will, but what you will" (Mark 14:36). From the cross Jesus shouts, "'*Elōi, Elōi, lema sabachthani?*' which is to be translated, 'My God, my God, why have you forsaken me?'" (Mark 15:34). With some justification, some Jesus experts urge us to consider that these are not only Jesus' own words, but they are also Jesus' own untranslated mother tongue (which was clearly Aramaic). The conservative nature of the Jesus tradition is revealed, and the attention of the Evangelists to preserve accurately the tradition at this point balances the liberty we saw when studying the copying of Mark 9:1.

This insight leads to other passages that also (using the criterion of coherence) antedate the Evangelists and may derive from Jesus and his time. That is, evidence of Semitics (Hebrew and Aramaic forms) usually indicates tradition received by the Evangelists. Examples include the use of *bar* (which means "son" in Aramaic) in phrases like Simon bar Jonah; *Golgotha*; the use of the divine passive so as to avoid using the name God; and poetic paronomasia (i.e., clever use of words and wordplays, as in straining the gnat [*qalma*] and swallowing the camel [*gamla*]).

Eighth, a *historical prediction* in a logion (a Jesus saying) *that contradicts what happened most likely was not created by an Evangelist*. It probably derives from Jesus himself. There are two outstanding examples. In the Parable of the Wicked Tenant Farmers, Jesus reveals that he is one of the prophets sent to Israel, and as the "son" will be stoned outside Jerusalem (like the prophet Jeremiah and the near contemporary Galilean miracle worker, Honi). Jesus also lamented over Jerusalem, "O Jerusalem, Jerusalem, you who kill the prophets and stone those sent to you" (Matt. 23:37; Luke 13:34), and imagined, as a prophet sent to Jerusalem, he would be stoned. Jesus was not stoned. Contrary to what he may have expected, he was crucified. Thus, none of the Evangelists, or anyone after 30, could have created these sayings. They surely represent Jesus' own words and his own self-understanding.

Ninth, *evidence of a creative genius who knew Semitics may reveal Jesus' own mind.* The Evangelists report that Jesus was a creative and poetic genius, and they attribute Semitic concepts and phrases to him. It is unlikely that all or most of these are to be attributed to some unknown Semitic poet who was a follower of Jesus. Examples abound, such as Jesus' teaching and actions regarding purity, Jesus' perception and actions on Shabbat (the Sabbath), and especially the poetic and well-couched Semitic phrases (such as the echo of *qalma* in *gamla*).

Tenth, the Gospels intermittently reveal that Jesus was a devoutly religious Jew. The Gospels were directed to Gentiles, almost always, so it is unlikely this aspect of Jesus' life was added by the Evangelists. *Passages (pericopes) in which Jesus is portrayed as very Jewish may well derive from reliable Jesus traditions.* Random examples are the following: Jesus' contention that the first commandment is the most important of all the commandments and his teaching on the importance of the Temple. Jesus may have worn a *sisit*, the show-fringe of a devout Jew's religious undergarment that protrudes outside the waist in fringes. Recall that a woman suffering from a hemorrhage touched the fringe of Jesus' garments in the hope to be healed; that would be the proper place to touch the power embodied in this Jew (Matt. 9:20).

Before proceeding to apply these five major and ten supporting methodologies, some caveats are warranted. Fruitful results are possible if we avoid the errors of minimalism and maximalism. Most important, we may obtain only probable, not certain, aspects of Jesus' life and thought; we must not succumb to historical positivism (that is, claim to have discovered unassailable objective facts). Here are some additional caveats:

1. We shall search not for Jesus' unedited words (*ipsissima verba Jesu*) but for the purpose and intent of this Galilean Prophet.
2. The Evangelists change Jesus' words and meaning. Thus, if Matthew and Luke alter Mark 9:1, then maybe Mark changed Jesus' words also; and what about those who preceded him?
3. One attractive feature of the Evangelists and Paul is that they did not merely

point back to a Jew from Nazareth; they enthusiastically proclaimed and affirmed the presence of the living Lord who was none other than the one who had been crucified, dead, and buried.

4. The members of the Palestinian Jesus Movement cumulatively warn us that the Jesus of history and the Christ of faith cannot be separated.

5. Jesus' followers moved from *ipsissima verba Jesu* (Jesus' own words) to *ex ore Christi* (words out of the mouth of Christ); that is, Jesus' own unedited words are at times virtually indistinguishable from the words that come "from the mouth of Christ" (the words of the resurrected Jesus).

6. When we discover words that have been added through editing, we may also discern earlier traditions that required editing.

Is an objective biography of Jesus now possible? Jesus Scholars widely acknowledge that an objective biography of Jesus is impossible. How is any biography possible? If there is available a vast amount of sources, as with Winston Churchill, then there is the problem of leaving out most data and selecting what seems representative according to some third-level set of presuppositions. As with Jesus and all ancient luminaries, almost all actions and sayings have been lost. With Jesus, we are left with a selection of deeds and sayings that were chosen not to provide a biography but to proclaim a message.

All biographies fundamentally reflect the personal knowledge of the author (including denigration or appreciation, emotional involvement, focus, and perspective on the person as well as on the meaning of life and destiny [or fate]). Biographies never tell us only about the biographee; they tell us something also about the biographer.

As we search the sources for reliable traditions that may originate with Jesus, we should always remember that our first Evangelist, *Mark,* whoever he was, *never was with Jesus in Capernaum or Jerusalem.* That means he could not appeal to his own memory for clarifying when and where Jesus said or did something. The earliest Evangelist was forced to create an order for Jesus' life. Mark's task may be compared to the attempts of someone who had broken a woman's pearl necklace and was forced to put the pearls back in their original order. That is as impossible as it was for Mark to re-create accurately the order of Jesus traditions.

What is possible for us today? First, we must not let our wishes and desires dictate methods or conclusions. If we ask honest questions, then we must honestly seek to answer them. That means being true to the questions without regard to possible answers. Otherwise we deceive ourselves into thinking we are honest. If our method is not informed and honest, we become incapable of learning the most probable answers.

We have examined the fifth question in this book: What are the best methods for discerning traditions that originate with Jesus? We have learned that there are five major methods: embarrassment, dissimilarity to the theology and Christology of those who followed him (including the Evangelists), multiple attestation and double affirmation, coherence, and the Palestinian Jewish setting.

We have reemphasized that *all data* that is possibly relevant in helping us discern Jesus' life and thought must be included in our search and under our scrutiny. That includes the ten independent sources, as well as early Jewish data, notably the social setting, topography, numismatics (the study of coins), and all relevant archaeological discoveries and perspectives.

The reader will most likely be impressed by the honesty of the Evangelists. All New Testament authors boldly state that Jesus died in public disgrace. He was crucified publicly as a criminal and seemed to shout out to God that he felt abandoned. Peter's denial is reported, and (in contrast to Jesus' baptism) there is no evidence of any attempt to deny it or explain it away. Judas's betrayal is clear, and more than any other member of the Twelve, he is defined as "one of the Twelve." The Twelve evidence continuous obtuseness even when Jesus is portrayed explaining details to them and decoding a parable.

At this point in the book, readers have begun to perceive that the proclamation (kerygma and various kerygmata) took shape within the circles of those who had been eyewitnesses of Jesus' teaching. Some of those who heard Peter's speeches in Jerusalem had heard Jesus' teaching in Solomon's Portico, had observed Jesus' rage in the Temple. Most of those who heard the new claims about Jesus and his resurrection by God had also seen Jesus' public castigation and crucifixion. In exploring and seeking to understand the methods used to discover Jesus' own traditions among those attributed to him, readers have also already learned a lot about what this man did and said. The recovery of the man of history has already commenced and will become more apparent as we examine the sources outside the New Testament.

Epilogue

The preceding reflections attempt to stay close to the consensus achieved by the leading experts in Jesus Research. These also are attuned to two new major challenges to the dominant conclusion among New Testament experts that the Gospels are neither biographies nor based on eyewitnesses.

In *What Are the Gospels?* (2004), R. A. Burridge argues that the Gospels should be seen as biographies similar to the "lives" produced in the Greek and Roman world (an idea championed in 1987 by D. E. Aune, *The New Testament in Its Literary Environment*). While there are no biographies or gospels in Rabbinics (as W. S. Green and J. Neusner showed), I would add that *Joseph and Aseneth*, which was composed by a Jew soon after 100 C.E., is tantamount to a romantic life of Joseph; and in it Joseph is portrayed as "the Son of God" (also see next chapter). Yet I would stress that there is no real analogy to the genre of Gospel in antiquity.

The second challenge to the status quo is by R. Bauckham. In his *Jesus and the Eyewitnesses* (2006), he argues that behind Mark lies "the official tradition of the Twelve as an authoritative body of eyewitnesses" (p. 413), and that the unique features in the Gospel of John derive "from a particular circle of disciples of Jesus in which the Beloved Disciple moved" (p. 414). I also pointed out earlier, in *The Beloved Disciple* (1995), that the only Gospel that claims to be based on an eyewitness is the Gospel of John. In this Gospel, those who edited what is reputed to be an eyewitness report affirm that the witness is true.

Finally, it is more likely now that the Gospels derive from oral and written reports that come from eyewitnesses. It does not follow that the Evangelists were eyewitnesses or that eyewitnesses are always trustworthy and unbiased.

CHAPTER 3

Sources, Especially Josephus

6) Do reports about Jesus exist outside the New Testament?

7) Are the Gospels objective biographies?

Questions numbered six and seven lead into this chapter, which concerns the sources for Jesus and an evaluation of their trustworthiness. This issue could easily fill one or more books, but as with an essential guide, only an overview is now appropriate.

1) *Tacitus and Josephus.* Tacitus (c. 56–118 C.E.), a Roman historian, and Josephus (38–100 C.E.), a Jewish historian, are the only first- or second-century historians who significantly mention Jesus.

Unfortunately, the extant manuscripts of Tacitus's *Annals*, which reviews Roman history from 16 to 66 C.E., do not preserve the period 29–32 C.E. Obviously, then, any reference by Tacitus to Jesus in these passages is now lost. Most likely, Tacitus did refer to Jesus, since he makes a comment about Jesus while describing the fire of Rome in 64 C.E. Tacitus reports that Nero blamed the "Christians" for the fire because many in Rome blamed Nero for the conflagration; note Tacitus's account and the significant aside to Jesus:

> Therefore, to squelch the rumor, Nero created scapegoats and subjected to the most refined tortures those whom the common people called 'Christians,' [a group] hated for their abominable crimes. Their name comes from Christ, who, during the reign of Tiberius, had been executed by the procurator Pontius Pilate. Suppressed for the moment, the deadly superstition broke out again, not only in Judea, the land which originated this evil, but also in the city of Rome, where all sorts of horrendous and shameful practices from every part of the world converge and are fervently cultivated. (*Annals* 15.44; Meier, *MJ* 1:89-90)

Experts now concur that this passage is genuine and that it was written near the end of Tacitus's life (he died in 118 C.E.). What do we learn about the historical Jesus? We learn that Jesus (the name is conspicuously absent) is called "Christ," and he was executed by the Roman governor Pilate (26–36) during the reign of Tiberius (14–37) in Judea. Jesus is the origin of the "deadly superstition" advocated by "Christians."

How did Tacitus obtain this information? He incorrectly calls Pilate a "procurator" when he was a "prefect," as we know from a stone inscription found in Caesarea Maritima. The inscription names Pilate and clarifies he was a "prefectus."

Most likely, Tacitus was not working from official documents. He probably obtained information about Jesus from conversations with others, in Rome, elsewhere, and perhaps during the time he was governor of the western portion of Asia Minor about 112 C.E.

The Jewish historian Josephus lived in Palestine and was in charge of the Galilee during the first year of the Revolt of 66–70 (73/74 for Masada). He reliably describes the terrain and topography of Palestine, especially Gamla, which indeed looks like a "camel" and is east of the northern end of the Sea of Galilee. His report of Jewish beliefs and the reasons for the War or Revolt are couched so as to be appealing to Romans and to present Judaism as a sophisticated religion to be admired. In this context Josephus presents Jesus as a troublemaker, yet gifted. Josephus's report (the *Testimonium Flavianum*) was transmitted by a tenth-century Christian Arab, Agapius, and much earlier copied in Greek by Christian scribes who added to his account; note the use of italics, which signifies their additions (parentheses circumscribe words that are essential in English or clarify a cryptic point):

> About this time there lived Jesus, a wise man, *if indeed one ought to call him a man.* For he was one who wrought surprising feats and was a teacher of such people as accept the truth gladly. He won over many Jews and many of the Greeks. *He was the Messiah.* When Pilate, upon hearing him accused by men of the highest standing amongst us, had condemned him to be crucified, those who had in the first place come to love him did not give up their affection for him. *On the third day he appeared to them restored to life, for the prophets of God had prophesied these and countless other marvellous things about him.* And the tribe of the Christians, so called after him, has still to this day not disappeared.

Two aspects of Josephus's reference to Jesus are notable (also see *JWithin]*). First, there is no reason to doubt why a scribe who was a Christian would feel the need to elevate the reference and evaluation of Jesus. Perhaps these additions were first placed in the margins and subsequent scribes imagined the notes were parts of the text that should not be left out.

Second, no Christian would have written this testimony to Jesus as it is preserved. No Christian would have categorized Jesus' miracles as "surprising works," or reported that Jesus was condemned because he was "accused by the first-rate men among us." That statement implies that Jesus was rightly condemned to crucifixion. Also the final sentence implies that this "tribe" will not endure.

The reader should read the testimony two more times: once without the italicized words, observing how the statement flows with grammatical accuracy and with historical clarity, and another time stressing only the Christian additions. The intent of the Jew Josephus and then of Christian scribes should become more obvious.

Why is Josephus's reference to another Palestinian Jew significant? What is important is that Josephus, near the end of the first century C.E., referred to Jesus and included a reference to him in passages about the brewing revolt in Palestine. Later in the same work he refers back to this passage when he mentions another person condemned. Josephus identifies him as "James, the brother of Jesus who was called the Christ" (*Ant* 20.200). While Josephus made a rather minimal reference to Jesus, he probably did so to answer the questions of Romans about the "new sect" that had appeared in Rome, and that Tacitus implied was a pernicious superstition.

In Rome and elsewhere in the Roman world, Josephus's portrait of Jesus would have contradicted the good news of the Evangelists. Josephus admitted that Jesus was a wise man who seemed to have performed "surprising" and wonderful works. He was a teacher who taught people who enjoyed something "unusual." He was followed by many Jews and Gentiles. Jesus, however, was also a rebellious person and one who disturbed the peace in Palestine. He was most likely wisely condemned by the leading Jews and the Roman governor, Pilate.

Josephus's account is more trustworthily transmitted by Agapius. This Christian Arab quoted Josephus, but noticeably absent in his excerpt are three passages. First and second, Agapius's version does not have the first two Christian passages (in italics earlier): *"if indeed one ought to call him a man"* and *"He was the Christ."* Third, he claims that Jesus' followers "reported [sic] that he had appeared to them three days after his crucifixion, and that he was alive." The Greek and the Arabic versions of Josephus's testimony shine a light into the dark regions of ancient Palestine and help emphasize the importance of discerning the truth regarding this man from Nazareth. The references to Jesus by a Roman historian and a Jewish historian disprove the absurd contention that Jesus never lived, a claim made by authors, often not scholars, during the past two hundred years, such as Bruno Bauer, P. L. Couchoud, G. Gurev, R. Augstein, and G. A. Wells.

2) *The Nag Hammadi Codices, Gnosticism, and the* Gospel of Thomas. Sensational claims have been made about the Coptic manuscripts found in Egypt in the mid-1940s. Some scholars have asserted that the Nag Hammadi Codices revolutionize our understanding of Jesus. The vast majority of scholars have replied that these are manuscripts of documents that considerably postdate Jesus and the first century. Surely, the Codices are extremely important for a study of the development of thought, Jewish, Christian, and various forms of Gnosticism; but they do not preserve a biography of Jesus and scarcely add to what is learned in the clearly earlier intracanonical Gospels, Matthew, Mark, Luke, and John.

One exception has rightly caught the attention of scholars of first- and second-century Christianity: the *Gospel of Thomas*. This gospel has been dated variously, from the middle of the first century C.E. to the early third century C.E. Most experts conclude that a date around 125 C.E. is about the time the *Gospel of Thomas* took its present form, though the Greek clearly preserves an earlier version (many of the parallels with the Gospel of John were added when the text was translated from Greek to Coptic).

The question thus concerns the sources of the *Gospel of Thomas*. The document is a collection of Jesus' sayings. Some are parallel to those in the intracanonical Gospels and some are independent. The document preserves traditions that are mixed; some scholars contend that its final form is "Gnostic" while others disagree. Some sayings of Jesus preserved in the *Gospel of Thomas* may help us understand either the transmission of Jesus' sayings or Jesus' own purpose. Thus, it is unwise either to highlight or to ignore this document. It will be included and accessed when we explore Jesus' sayings (see chap. 8).

3) *Jesus and the apocryphal works.* In the collections of the New Testament Apocrypha and Pseudepigrapha are many gospels composed from the second to

35

the fifth century C.E. Wild claims and counterclaims have filled journalists' reports and even scholarly publications. The gospels that have been judged by some to contain early Jesus traditions are the *Gospel of Peter,* the *Gospel of James,* and the *Gospel of Judas* (which has just been recovered, but it is a Gnostic text claiming to preserve a dialogue between Jesus and Judas). These texts clearly postdate the intracanonical Gospels and tell us virtually nothing about the historical Jesus.

Why are these apocryphal gospels important? They are very important for a comprehension of Jesus' life as understood by Christians in the second through fifth centuries. Characteristically, details not found in the Gospels are supplied, including the names of the wise men, Mary's birth and parents, Jesus' life during "the hidden years" when he was a youth, and the increasing blame placed on Jews for Jesus' crucifixion. As stated previously, one work in the apocryphal New Testament—found among the Nag Hammadi Codices—deserves special attention: the *Gospel of Thomas.*

The scholars who disparage all the apocryphal compositions miss the point that in the first three centuries no clear margin separated intracanonical from extracanonical texts. Indeed, some passages in the New Testament familiar and cherished by some Christians are now considered to be "apocryphal." The best two examples are the ending to Mark (that is, Mark 16:9-20) and the story of the woman caught in adultery in John 7:53–8:11. These verses were read formerly, certainly in my youth, as if they were as canonical as the Sermon on the Mount.

4) *The Talmud.* Due to the burnings of Talmud manuscripts by ecclesiastical authorities, the earliest manuscript evidence for the Talmudic Jesus is from the twelfth century. Despite the conclusion of some scholars (viz., the minimalist J. Meier) that the Talmudic traditions are too late to be helpful in reconstructing Jesus' life, P. Schäfer has demonstrated that the Talmud can be a source for Jesus Research, and that the Babylonian Talmud is in touch with early discussions of Jesus (*JesusTalmud*). Schäfer's challenge to include the Talmud in Jesus Research wisely confronts the tendency to ignore it.

Talmudic claims that Jesus practiced magic (b*Sanh* 107b) may be early and perhaps based on Mark. These traditions may well be authentic to Jesus' time. Most likely, early are Talmudic references to healing in the name of Jesus (e.g., t*Hul* 2:22-23; see Schäfer, *JesusTalmud,* pp. 138-39). Jesus' execution on the eve of Passover is probably historical (cf. b*San* 43a-b). Not all of these passages can be easily attributed to the traditions of the Gospels, since they are accompanied with other, often polemical asides, and Jesus was reputed to have been "hanged" (b*San* 43a-b). The references to Jesus' being stoned (b*San* 43a-b) are especially interesting, since Jesus may well have feared that he would be stoned, as had Jeremiah and the Galilean miracle worker called Honi (see chap. 6). No one would create such traditions after Jesus' crucifixion in 30 (see *JWithinJ,* pp. 139-45).

5) *The intracanonical Gospels.* The four Gospels, Matthew, Mark, Luke, and John, and the references to Jesus in other sections of what became the canonical "New Testament" are the primary sources for studying the historical Jesus because of their date (all date from the century in which Jesus lived) and their preservation of early, reliable traditions about Jesus.

In chapter 2, the reader learned about the ten independent strata in the New Testament that preserve Jesus traditions. In roughly chronological order, it is now the time to describe each source.

Q. Q (from the German *Quelle*, "source") is a putative source of Jesus' sayings used by Matthew and Luke but not by Mark. We know neither the date nor the author of this collection, and it may preserve up to three internal sources. Most likely the document, orally or written, took shape sometime before 50 C.E. somewhere in Palestine, but we do not have an extant copy.

S. S denotes a possible Signs Source ostensibly used by John. Why do experts think there is a Signs Source in John? The signs are numbered, and the numbering is not according to the signs, or miracles, presented in the Gospel of John. For example, in 2:11 we read, "This is the first of his signs which Jesus did in Cana in Galilee, and manifested his glory." Then after a reference to other miracles, especially the miraculous things that the Galileans had seen in Jerusalem (4:45), we read that Jesus' healing of an official's son in Capernaum "was the second sign that Jesus did when he had come from Judea to Galilee" (4:54). If there is a Signs Source embedded in the Gospel of John, it would have been composed, probably in or near Cana, before 50 C.E.

Pl. Many Pauline scholars contend that Paul had no interest in the historical Jesus; yet Paul is one of the earliest known witnesses to Jesus' life and teachings. Paul does not only allude to Jesus; he quotes him. In the early fifties, in his first known letter, Paul apparently alludes to a saying of Jesus not preserved in the Gospels:

> For this we declare to you by the Lord's word, that we who are alive, who are left until the coming of the Lord, shall not precede those who have fallen asleep. For the Lord himself will descend from heaven with a cry of command, with the archangel's call, and with the sound of the trumpet of God. The dead in Christ will rise first; then we who are alive, who are left, shall be caught up together with them in the clouds to meet the Lord in the air; and so we shall always be with the Lord. (1 Thess. 4:15-17)

As is well known, a crisis in Corinth enabled Paul, in the mid-fifties, to reveal he knew that Jesus had said something special during his last night with his disciples:

> For I received from the Lord what I also delivered to you, that the Lord Jesus on the night when he was betrayed took bread, and having given thanks, he broke it, and said, "This is my body which is for you. Do this in remembrance of me." In the same way also the cup, after supper, saying, "This cup is the new covenant in my blood. Do this, as often as you drink it, in remembrance of me." (1 Cor. 11:23-25)

This passage in Paul is singularly important. It proves that Paul knew about Jesus' life and also that he knows the story, since he states that Jesus' last supper was "on the night when he was betrayed." That signifies Paul knows at least some of the narrative about Jesus.

Mk. The Gospel of Mark is widely accepted as the earliest gospel. It was composed either just before or just after 70, since the Evangelist knows that Jerusalem will be (or has been) lost to the Roman armies that burned it in September of 70 (cf. Mark 13). Mark may have been completed in Rome, but it clearly reflects a Galilean theology. For example, Mark records that Jesus said, "But after I am raised up, I will go before you to Galilee" (Mark 14:28). Later a young man sitting in Jesus' empty tomb tells the women: "Go tell his disciples and Peter that he is going before you to Galilee; there you will see him, as he told you" (Mark 16:7). A study of the narrative of Mark indicates that this Evangelist is interested especially in Galilee. Further, Mark is the most apocalyptic of the Gospels, and the eschatological rush of the work is evident by the repetitive "and immediately"—Mark's favorite connective—as well as the abrupt ending "for they were afraid."

J^1. Almost all scholars who have focused their research on the Gospel of John have concluded that this gospel has been edited more than once. A first edition (J^1) can only be imagined; it would be what is left when additions were removed. Perhaps this first edition took shape in Jerusalem before 70 C.E.; but at this stage such comments are highly speculative. John is the only gospel that claims to be based on an eyewitness.

M. M is used to denote the passages in Matthew that are unique to this gospel. It thus denotes both editorial work and the evidence of traditions inherited only by Matthew. The latter are important for us now. The traditions unique to Matthew represent an unknown number of sources that date from the twenties (Jesus' time) to the eighties (Matthew's time). Matthew's gospel is very Jewish; the Evangelist stresses that Jesus is a "Rabbi," seeks to portray Jesus as being a new Moses (he goes up on a mountain and presents a new law), strives to prove that Jesus fulfilled all prophecies concerning the Messiah (the hermeneutic is like the Qumran *Pesharim*), and his reasoning is similar to the early Rabbinic traditions. Among Jesus' sayings found in M is the quotation attributed to the resurrected Jesus: "Go and make disciples of all nations" (Matt. 28:19).

L. L signifies passages unique to Luke; thus, L specifies both editorial additions and received traditions. The Jesus traditions unique to Luke would obviously antedate him, and some may derive from Jesus' own time. Luke is eager to convince the reader that he is a reliable historian, so he seeks eyewitnesses and strives to prepare an orderly account (Luke 1:1-4). His gospel emphasizes Jerusalem and is universalistic in scope; and his second volume, Acts, moves the good news from the Holy Land to Rome.

A. The author of Acts preserves Jesus traditions. These were edited by the author of Luke and Acts; they antedate this work, which took shape probably around 90 C.E. or later. If authentic to Jesus, a tradition would then antedate 30 C.E. Particularly interesting is the summary of Jesus' life in Acts 10:34-41.

J^2. J^2 signifies the second edition of John, which is basically the present version of the Gospel of John without the addition of 7:53–8:11, the passage about the woman taken in adultery. It is not present in our earliest copies of John. This gospel is also a very Jewish gospel. The Evangelist knows about the importance of stone for Jewish purification rites (2:6), portrays Jesus working in Judea (as well as Galilee), has Jesus state that "salvation is from the Jews" (4:22), and represents Johannine Jews striving with Synagogal Jews for the right to observe the festivals and to worship in the synagogue.

T. T represents the *Gospel of Thomas*, which was discussed when we reported on the Nag Hammadi Codices and the New Testament apocryphal gospels. It most likely antedates 125 C.E. and was composed in western Syria or perhaps Egypt.

These ten literary strata (or sources) preserve Jesus traditions and are independent witnesses to the Jesus of history. Thus, with Tacitus and Josephus, the historian has twelve possible sources to utilize in seeking to discern Jesus' authentic actions, intentions, and sayings. Clearly, the main sources are found in the four intracanonical Gospels. What can be known about these primary sources?

The Four Gospels: How Were They Composed and Why Were They Chosen?

A) *How were the intracanonical Gospels composed?* In the fourth century C.E., Alexander the Great, who was taught by Aristotle, united the Western world and established Greek culture as the ideal and the Greek language as the *lingua franca* (the language of commerce and diplomacy). Although Jesus' native speech was Aramaic, and most of his teachings were in Aramaic, the intracanonical Gospels were composed in Greek. Behind the Greek gospels one can often detect Aramaic sources, which are oral and perhaps (at times) written tracts.

Caveats. Some caveats are necessary. The focused research of New Testament experts since the eighteenth century has disclosed the following discoveries:

1) We do not know who composed Matthew, Mark, Luke, or John.
2) Tradition regarding the authors of the Gospels is late and appears for the first time about one hundred years after Jesus, in the second century C.E.
3) It is not certain that the titles given to the intracanonical Gospels belong to the text of the documents, as some experts contend (viz., Hengel), or were added later, most likely after 150 C.E. (as Koester concludes).
4) The author of Luke admits that he was not an eyewitness to Jesus' life; but he also adds that he has based his work on eyewitnesses' testimonies (Luke 1:1-4). Only the Gospel of John claims to be based on an eyewitness to Jesus' life and teachings (see *Beloved Disciple*).
5) We do not have one fragment of the New Testament from the first century. The earliest fragment of any intracanonical Gospel is P52 (Papyrus 52 preserved in the John Rylands Library in Manchester). The fragment contains words from the Gospel of John and dates from perhaps 115 to 125 C.E.
6) Three of the four intracanonical Gospels portray Jesus' life with the same perspective. These are the Synoptics: Mark, Matthew, and Luke. The latter two depend on Mark, according to almost all New Testament scholars. The Gospel of John presents a different perspective.

Non-literary sources. Usually, scholars select three sources from which to reconstruct Jesus' life and teachings: Mark, M, and L. We have focused on ten independent literary sources and two non-Christian sources. As rich as this database now seems, it is insufficient because it is purely literary. Those seeking to better understand Jesus in his context are not satisfied with only a literary portrait of him. Literature needs to be supplemented. Why?

Jesus' teachings are filled with images and descriptions he observed in the life and land around him. Ancient Palestine—the land of Israel—is truly a topographical wonder. It shaped Jesus' mind and perspective. The hills and mountains, like

Tabor and Hermon, lift one's eyes to the sky and heavens. The hills and valleys of Galilee are verdant, exploding in the late winter or early spring with brilliant colors that dazzle in the piercing Mediterranean sun. The ravines, or wadis, are dry most of the year; but in the late rainy season they fill rapidly with a torrent that moves with the force and speed of a rapid train. Before 60,000 B.C.E., a freshwater lake extended from the foot of the Hermon to the lower tip of the Dead Sea. In Jesus' time, it was one life-giving watercourse, proceeding southward from the Hermon, to the Huleh Lake, the Sea of Galilee, and the Jordan River. Then, at the lower part of our earth, all life ceases as the water turns deadly in the Dead Sea.

Walking from Galilee to the Holy City to observe Passover was arduous. Two steady companions were the heat of the sun and the choking desert dust and sand, as one walked from Capernaum to Jericho, and then up the winding paths of the treacherous Wadi Qelt to the hills of Judea, over the Mount of Olives to Jerusalem (see chap. 9).

Living in the Land helps one appreciate the claim that the land or topography is really the Fifth Gospel. Topography and the culture of daily life in ancient Palestine not only abound in Jesus' realistic stories; they provide silent sentinels pointing to meanings lost to a purely literary approach to the man who mystifies so many.

Jesus' parables are windows into his world and culture. In traditions attributed to Jesus, we hear frequently, among other things, about rocky ground, fertile ground, vineyards, wine presses, towers, stone fences, olive trees, sparrows, sheep, shepherds, fish, fishermen, a tempestuous sea, and valleys threatening death. And there is more, including nets, boats, swords, fringe garments, cloaks, coats, thatched roofs, and beds. Almost all of these now lie exposed or collected after two thousand years, thanks to painstaking archaeological excavations and research from Caesarea Philippi, in the north, to Eilat, in the south. Displayed for specialists to touch and examine are numerous *realia* (real objects once held by Jesus' contemporaries), including bronze objects, such as tweezers, toothpicks, swords, knives, spoons, weights, and ladles for serving wine mixed with water, and even two-thousand-year-old wooden objects, such as combs. The abundance of glass is exceptional, with virtually all colors of the rainbow represented: yellows, reds, purple, green, blue, brown, light blue, and translucent white. These glass receptacles were used for cosmetics, medicines, and fine spices or ointments. Ceramic objects abound from Jesus' time. These objects include lamps, cooking pots, mixing bowls or cups, drinking cups, and large clay vessels for storage.

Finally, coins abound, especially in Judea and the coastal plain. Lying on the surface, exposed by a winter's rain, excavated, or discovered as a hidden hoard while digging to plant a tree in a backyard, hundreds of people over the past fifty years have found thousands of gold and silver coins (usually Greek or Roman) and hundreds of thousands of bronze coins (Greek, Roman, and mostly Jewish). On the gold and silver coins are the faces of one of the emperors before or during Jesus' time, Julius Caesar, Augustus, or Tiberias. Looking at these faces, one is reminded of Jesus' answer to a well-known and pressing question. He asked his interrogator to see whose face is on the coin and to render to Caesar what is Caesar's and to God what is God's. As we hold such a coin, we have a source that assists us in understanding Jesus' words. As with those near him long ago, we may also ask: "Does anything really belong to Caesar?"

Suffice it to clarify now that such *realia* and nonliterary sources are fundamental for understanding the reason for and importance of some of Jesus' actions and sayings. For example, the discovery of stone vessels provides contexts for texts. We now take notice of words that once had no meaning or were passed over unnoticed: "And six stone jars were there for the Jewish rites of purification" (John 2:6).

Probing questions. A study of the four Gospels awakens in the reader some inconsistencies and perhaps contradictions. As we continue to seek to discern what Jesus actually did, said, and hoped to accomplish, it is challenging—even exciting for many—to ponder the following questions:

Was Jesus born in Bethlehem (Matt. 2; Luke 2) or Nazareth (Mark?; John?)?

Were wise men (Matt.) or shepherds (Luke) at Jesus' birth (or neither)?

Was Jesus baptized by John the Baptist (Mark) or not (Luke 3:19-21)?

Was Jesus' ministry one year (Mark; Matt.; Luke) or three (John)?

Was Jesus' teaching defined by the Rule of God (Mark; Matt.; Luke) that was offered in challenging parables or by "I am" proclamations (John)?

Did Jesus accept Peter's confession that he was the Messiah (Matt.) or not (Mark)?

Is the Lord's Prayer authentic to Jesus, and if so, which version is original, Matthew's or Luke's? If Jesus taught this prayer, then why is it absent in the two early and independent Gospels, Mark and John?

Did Jesus express a painful lament in Gethsemane (esp. Luke) or not (John)?

Did Jesus carry his own cross (John), or did Simon of Cyrene carry it for him (Mark; Matt.; Luke)?

Were Jesus' last words "My God, my God, why have you forsaken me?" (Mark) or "it is finished" (John)?

Were Jesus' first resurrection appearances in Jerusalem (Matt.; Luke; John) or Galilee (cf. Mark)?

Did Mary Magdalene (John) or Peter (Paul [1 Cor. 15]; cf. Matt. 28:9) see the resurrected Jesus first?

Such questions reflect not only an interest in discovering the historical Jesus behind the Evangelists' theology; they indicate an interest in how and why the Gospels evolved.

Shaping of the gospel tradition. Today scholars have basically agreed on how the Gospels took shape. At the beginning, of course, are Jesus' life and his teachings (ca. 7/6 B.C.E. to 30 C.E.). These were remembered by those who knew him (eyewitnesses) and were shaped by the teaching (*didache*) and proclamation (kerygma) in the Palestinian Jesus Movement ("church" being anachronistic).

Some early tracts of Jesus' traditions were probably written since such documents seem to explain the clustering of parables (Mark 4) and miracles (Mark 6:30-56) in the Gospel of Mark. A Signs Source may lie behind the Gospel of John. A lost document called Q, containing sayings of Jesus, probably was used by Matthew and Luke. Some experts (J. Dickson) think that the Epistle of James, which contains the most allusions to Jesus' thoughts in the New Testament corpus (except for the Gospels), derives from Jesus' brother (cf. P. H. Davids) and should be recognized as a source for Jesus. All these documents antedate the Gospels. They probably took shape between 30 and 60 C.E.

The first written gospel seems to be the Gospel of Mark, which was composed in the late sixties or early seventies. The Gospel of John evolved through numerous editions. The first one may conceivably antedate 70 C.E. Matthew was composed around 85. The "final" edition of John is dated about 95. The composition of Luke-Acts is usually dated around 80–90, though some experts now suggest perhaps between 90 and 110.

Key question. A key question is now central in the study of all gospels and in Jesus Research. Scholars are sharply divided as they seek to answer this question: How much tradition and how much addition shape the Jesus traditions in the gospels? The minimalists claim that the Evangelists have given us only their own unreliable editing of Jesus traditions. The maximalists contend that the Evangelists have preserved accurately the accounts of Jesus' birth, his life, and his words. Clearly, the intracanonical Gospels are edited accounts of what Jesus said and did, but editing is possible only because of some tradition to shape. Edition clarifies tradition. Does that mean that the Synoptics (Matt.; Mark; Luke) present somewhat accurately Jesus' fundamental message? The answer, as we shall see (chap. 8), is probably yes.

B) *Why were the names Matthew, Mark, Luke, and John chosen for the Gospels?* We have no clear and direct evidence of how and why four Gospels were chosen. There was no early church council that voted on what should be included and what should be excluded. Obviously, apostolic authorship or authority was important in deciding which gospels to include and which to exclude. The titles of such rejected gospels as the *Gospel of Thomas*, the *Gospel of Peter*, the *Gospel of Mary*, and the *Gospel of Judas* prove that mere titles did not secure acceptance into a selected canon.

In centers of learning in which Christianity was influential before the fourth century C.E., the social and theological needs of leaders and the average Christian were important criteria for choosing a gospel as "true." A standard or rule (= canon) was needed to define and shape faith, since dozens of gospels were circulating about 200 C.E.

Some of the criteria for deciding what is authoritative (or canonical) reflect a growing recognition by the masses that only four gospels are accepted (= canonical). Frequently, social custom and not theological insight was dominant. For example, Irenaeus, Bishop of Lyon, about 180 C.E. claimed that it was essential to have four gospels since there are four winds: "It is not possible that the Gospels can be either more or fewer in number than they are, since there are four directions of the world in which we are, and four principal winds ..." (*Adv. Haer.* 3.11.8). Irenaeus imagined that his readers accepted the custom of assuming there were only "four winds." In comprehending this claim, one should note that much earlier, Andronicus in Athens demonstrated that there are more than four winds, and that Irenaeus included in his canon as "Scripture" the *Shepherd of Hermas*. Irenaeus's criterion discloses that in his area four gospels had already been accepted as apostolic and authoritative. Apparently, he also could not appeal to any custom that the canon had been defined.

The limits of the canon were not defined in many areas until the Middle Ages. While the Festal Letter of 367 by Athanasius, Bishop of Alexandria, reflects a canon that is virtually identical to that used today in the West, it was not definitive in many cities in the fourth century. The Revelation of John was not accepted by the Greek Orthodox Church until about the tenth century. And this apocalypse is not "canonical" in the Syriac vulgate (the Peshiṭta), the canon of the Syrian Church. It is unrepresentative to assume that the canon was defined and closed by the fourth century C.E. B. M. Metzger and L. M. McDonald show that debates over the "canonical" status of some books continued much later, and even past the fourth century.

What were the major reasons for the development of the New Testament canon? Historians have no clear data to supply a definite answer; they must assess a wide variety of sources, and none of those were written specifically to answer questions related to the origins of our canon. A widespread acceptance of the sacredness of some texts, especially Paul's letters and the Gospels, preceded any theory of what belongs in a canon.

The following eight reflections represent recent research on why Christians chose certain documents and attributed to them unique authority and special sacredness. First, Marcion (died ca. 160) defined the "canon" as including only a version of Paul's letters and Luke; and Marcion removed from these any elements that he thought represented the capricious God of the Old Testament. He thus challenged the leaders of the church to devise a less corrupt version of the canon. Perhaps the threat from the Marcionites helped stimulate Tatian to compile the first influential harmony (the Diatessaron). Second, the Montanists revered as authoritative the apocalyptic and ecstatic oracles of Montanus, Prisca, and Maximilla, thus threatening, or removing, the authority of received and older apocalyptic compositions. Third, the Gnostics threatened developing orthodox Christianity with philosophical and mythological ideas that were not only against earlier traditions but separated individuals from the community (or church), stressing individual knowledge over tradition. Fourth, many Christians felt the need for a clear and definitive perspective on the meaning of Jesus' life and thought, so the Synoptics were first accorded widespread canonical status. Fifth, early Christian scholars stressed the necessity to stay close and in tune with the teaching of the first apostles (the criterion of apostolicity). Sixth, imperial edicts, like the ones in 303 and 304, which ordered copies of Christian Scriptures to be burned, demanded Christians to decide which books were sacred. Seventh, from the very beginning in the thirties in Jerusalem, Jesus was considered to be the source of what was sacred; as Metzger states, "the words of Jesus are taken as the supreme authority" (*Canon*, p. 73). Thus, the "good news" about Jesus' life and thought became a criterion for acceptance of a work into the canon. As the canon took definite shape, it became the basis for catholic (universal) confessions and creeds. Finally, and most important, many perceived the need for a rule of faith (*regula fidei*) or a canon of truth so that Christians and those attracted to Christianity would understand what should be believed so as to avoid hell and enter heaven.

Answering questions six and seven. Our sixth question is, Do reports about Jesus exist outside the New Testament? We have drawn attention to three sources that are fundamentally important for our search: the writings of Tacitus (a Roman), the histories of Josephus (a Jew), and the *Gospel of Thomas* (composed by a Christian but perhaps influenced eventually by early forms of Gnostic thought).

Our seventh question is, Are the Gospels objective biographies? They certainly are not objective biographies. The degree to which the Gospels are biographies, in the sense used in the first century, will slowly take shape in the reader's mind as the search and study of the historical Jesus continues in the following pages.

An appreciation of what an ancient biography might look like is indicated by Suetonius (ca. 69–140?); it is his *Lives of the Twelve Caesars* (120 C.E.). The concept of biography in the Greek and Roman world needs to be supplemented by a study of biographical compositions in the Jewish world. They are very widely conceived. First, Josephus's *Vita* is not only history but also a defense of his actions. The life of Joseph the patriarch seemed especially interesting to early Jews, appearing "biographically" in various ways in the *Testament of the Twelve Patriarchs*, in *Joseph and Aseneth*, and in the *History of Joseph*. The life or biography of Job appears in the *Targum of Job* (found at Qumran) and the *Testament of Job*. The reverence given to Enoch in the *Books of Enoch* is unique but should be included for reflection. For at least three centuries in Galilee, Enoch was deemed perfect morally and one who had not died, so that he was eventually elevated and finally saluted with these words: "You are that Son of Man."

In antiquity, many were hailed to be born of virgins or from divine intervention (esp. Alexander the Great and Augustus), and objectivity was shunned for celebration and the search for a model life. History and biographies were studied not for entertainment or curiosity; they were essential reading to comprehend, and achieve, the good or beneficial life. While educated Greeks and Romans wanted a good or true life, the Evangelists pointed to Jesus, who defined an obedient life. Whether or how they achieved that goal and—more importantly—how Jesus was obedient and to what or whom will be explored in the following chapters.

CHAPTER 4

The Judaism of Jesus

8) Was Jesus not the first Christian?

9) Was Jesus an Essene, Pharisee, Zealot, or Sadducee?

Eyewitness source. To comprehend the Judaism of Jesus, we should know many things. We need firsthand knowledge of Palestinian Judaism before and after 70 C.E. We require descriptions of the topography of cities and villages known to Jesus. We desire descriptions of buildings and architectural features seen by Jesus. And we need this information provided by a reliable eyewitness. Is that possible? Yes, for such information we are indebted to Josephus.

Josephus is the most informative historian of first-century Palestinian Judaism. His major works are the volumes called *The Jewish War* and *The Antiquities of the Jews*. He was born in Jerusalem around 38 and died sometime after 100 C.E. He lived in Palestine, was a witness of the First Jewish Revolt (66–73/74), and moved to Rome in 70, after the Roman soldiers burned the Temple and Jerusalem. For centuries, New Testament scholars have accepted Josephus's description of first-century Judaism as if it were definitively accurate. According to Josephus, the Judaism of Jesus' time was defined by four sects: Pharisees, Sadducees, Essenes, and Zealots.

Questioning the "four sect" paradigm. Numerous issues arise with this division of Palestinian Judaism. Among the most prominent questions are the following: Should one talk about *sects*, and how should this sociological term be defined? What about the Samaritans? What about the baptist groups, especially the group led by John the Baptizer? Josephus referred to Jesus, but where do he and his group belong in such a description of Second Temple Judaism (ca. 300 B.C.E. to 70 C.E.)? Did the Zealots exist during Jesus' time, or did they appear only at the beginning of the revolt in 66?

When Josephus's description of the Judaism of Jesus' time was taken literally, scholars debated whether Jesus was a Pharisee, Essene, or Zealot. Scholars did not try to align Jesus with the Sadducees. He and they were far too distant theologically and culturally; for example, unlike the Sadducees, Jesus believed in the resurrection and did not reject all the oral traditions. Unlike them, Jesus was influenced by apocalyptic eschatology and expected (sometimes experiencing) the full dawning of God's Rule. The Sadducees were culturally defined by the Temple, but Jesus, while revering the Temple as God's house, felt God's presence in the Galilean hills. Jesus' possible relationship to the other three groups or sects was sought within misconceptions. On the one hand, Jesus' closeness to the Pharisees and Essenes was frequently either overlooked or exaggerated. On the other hand, Jesus' uniqueness was claimed to be either exceptional or minimal.

Any search for Jesus' uniqueness obviously must be pursued in terms of a perception of Jewish thought and culture during his time. As a first-century Jew, Jesus spoke the dominant language of his people: Aramaic. He obviously employed concepts that his fellow Jews could comprehend and appreciate.

How do we enter Jesus' world so as to perceive such concepts? First, we need to perceive that *Second Temple Judaism was not shaped by four sects*. Josephus misrepresented the Judaism he had experienced in Palestine. Now, a careful reading of Josephus in light of archaeological discoveries reveals that Josephus's account of Judaism is frequently selected, slanted, and edited to win the respect of Roman citizens and to defend the credibility of Judaism.

Today, thanks to a study of the Jewish apocryphal books and the Dead Sea Scrolls, we can imagine that more than twenty sects, groups, and subgroups defined Jesus' Judaism. To be included within Second Temple Judaism are such groups as the following: baptist groups (including John the Baptizer and his disciples), Enoch groups, Samaritans, Qumranites, scribes and their schools, Hillel's group, Shammai's group, the numerous feuding priestly families (esp. the Boethusians), and Jewish soldiers who guarded the Temple. It is also fundamentally important in grasping pre-70 Palestinian Jewish life and types of Jewish groups to recognize the sociological chaos caused by bandits, revolutionary units, and messianic pretenders. When all these are comprehended, analyzed, and described, we need to be aware we have focused only on religious groups.

Jewish life and thought were also shaped by non-religious groups. A mere list of these other groups can only be glimpsed. They would include Roman soldiers, caravan owners and their clientele, craftsmen, builders of Herod's monumental edifices, slaves, workers, engineers, athletes, artists, philosophers from many countries, pilgrims, shepherds, goatherds, vendors of pigeons and other animals to sacrifice, those who provided the oil and wood for fires, musicians, and money-changers in the Temple. It is patently obvious that a study of Jesus within Judaism includes most of these groups. Many of them have cast shadows on the background assumed by the Evangelists.

Is there a major group that has not been mentioned? Yes; one of the most important groups is never mentioned in publications of Jewish groups in Second Temple Judaism. It is Jesus and his group. Jesus' group must not be left out of a description of Second Temple Judaism. *Jesus and the Palestinian Jesus Movement belong within Judaism.* Among the most important insights we obtain from this observation is that we should avoid the term *Christian* when describing first-century sociology and history.

Paradigm shifts. The twenty-first century began with a worldwide recognition of paradigm shifts. Unfortunately, too many students and scholars tend to use commentaries and scholarly monographs without noting the date of publication. One cannot use scholarly works published from the early nineteenth century to the present assuming naïvely that scholars are examining the same texts with similar methodology, sophistication, and perception. Both the database and the methodology for perceiving and studying Jesus within Judaism have increased and been improved.

Works published after 1970, or 1980, are often paradigmatically different from those issued in the preceding nineteen hundred years. Earlier works are seriously dated by old perceptions, improper methodology, and a paucity of sources. Works published before 1980, the approximate year for the emergence of Jesus Research, are not to be confused with more recent informed research. Such a synchronic malaise obscures not only the development of research but also the recreation of first-century Palestine.

The preceding comments may be summarized by comparing the old and new paradigms for reconstructing the life and times of Jesus of Nazareth.

Old paradigm. For centuries scholars assumed that Second Temple Judaism was orthodox, monolithic, cut off from other cultures, especially the Greeks and Romans, and was defined by four sects: Pharisees, Sadducees, Essenes, and Zealots.

New paradigm. Now scholars are more critical of inherited assumptions. It is certain that Josephus was wrong to divide Jewish thought into four sects. Most likely, the most important and influential Jewish groups were the following:

- the conservative Sadducees, who were tied to the Temple;
- the Pharisees (who were extremely diverse with Hillel usually disagreeing with Shammai [if we may label these Rabbis Pharisees]), who were politically influential;
- the Essenes, who were diverse and usually learned;
- and the pugnacious Zealots, who may have appeared only at the beginning of the First Revolt (66–73/74 C.E.).

One can also perceive more than twenty groups, subgroups, and sects. First, the Samaritans are also Jews with a Pentateuch almost identical to that preserved in the *Tanakh* (or Old Testament). Second, one must include the baptist groups, whom we know about from the *Sibylline Oracles,* the *Apocalypse of Adam,* and the New Testament (esp. John the Baptizer). Third, we should recognize the importance of the Enoch groups, who seem to be localized in Galilee and existed for three centuries, at least, and have left us the *Books of Enoch* or *1 Enoch.* Fourth, Jesus and the Palestinian Jesus Movement were not as insignificant as many scholars have assumed; after all, the history of martyrdom in the movement discloses that the Romans and Jewish leaders found it to be noticeably threatening.

Some scholars have tended to think about Jewish thought before 70 C.E. as being chaotic and without some unifying center or creed; but chaos broke out in 66 C.E. when "hotheads" within Judaism insisted on melting plowshares into swords. Likewise some scholars see disunity within Second Temple Judaism and talk about "Judaisms." Other scholars are still influenced by late Rabbinic thought and imagine a unified Judaism or *Covenantal Nomism.* Such a term is not found in pre-70 Jewish texts; moreover, the definitions of *covenant* and *law,* like the Temple cult, often caused not only unity but also disunity among pre-70 Jews.

Most likely, there was a powerful and influential ruling party within Jerusalem, but it was mixed. It was composed of Pharisees, Sadducees, and other types of Jews (notably, the Boethusians [a special order within the Temple cult] were intermittently powerful). In addition to these influential Jews, there were the oppressive Roman legions and a Roman governor.

The common recitation of the Shema ("Hear, O Israel, the LORD, our God, [is] one LORD" [Deut. 6:4]) and the living liturgical use of the Psalter, as well as the celebration of the Festivals, in my opinion, helped to check the centripetal forces that eventually produced the ill-conceived Revolt (66–74 C.E.). After all, the Jews revolted against the Roman Imperium without an army and in the midst of what might be labeled a civil war.

Other concepts also tended to unite Jews, both in Palestine and in the Diaspora; among them are race, election, Land, and belief in a God who intermittently has and will act in history on behalf of those who remain faithful to God's will, which is embodied in the Torah (Old Testament).

This picture of Second Temple Judaism derives from examining sources not studied perceptively by earlier scholars and from sources completely unknown to them. They trusted as reliable history the reports in the New Testament, Josephus, and Rabbinics (esp. the Mishnah). These collections of ancient Jewish texts are sources that must be used with caution and in recognition of their shared tendencies to distort historical and social realities. The previously unknown primary sources are hundreds of Jewish documents that antedate 70 C.E. They were once held and read by early Jews, and therefore not altered, as are many of the Old Testament Pseudepigrapha, by later Christian scribes.

These newly recovered documents are the Qumran Scrolls (the Dead Sea Scrolls), and the corpus is now exceptionally voluminous. If 66 books define the Christian Bible, more than 900 documents are now known to be preserved, usually in fragmentary form, within the Qumran library of scrolls. In light of these clearly Jewish works, we can examine with new sensitivity the 65 documents in the Old Testament Pseudepigrapha. The study of the Old Testament Apocrypha and the Septuagint, which is now perceived to preserve ancient text types as well as translation additions and revisions, helps place images together in the massive attempt to re-create a vast jigsaw puzzle in which we may glimpse the world of Jesus' Judaism.

Jesus

Over the past forty years, scholars have generally come to comprehend that Jesus must not be understood over against Judaism. They are now also recognizing it may be misleading to think about Jesus *and* Judaism. Most leading Jesus Scholars are attempting to comprehend Jesus *within Judaism*.

There is an exception that should at least be noted. The well-known Jesus Seminar in the United States has consistently portrayed Jesus without the prerequisite sensitivity to his context within Second Temple Judaism. The members of the Seminar have argued for a Cynic Jesus, a Mediterranean peasant, and a man whose thought was not eschatological. A critic might label such productions as remnants of anti-Judaism in the academy. I would prefer to contend that the members of the Jesus Seminar have failed to learn from the archaeological excavations of sites frequented by Jesus. They, more importantly, have not focused on Jewish texts, like the Pseudepigrapha and the Qumran Scrolls. Thus, they miss the most important point provided by the latest Jesus Research: Jesus and his followers were deeply Jewish.

Jesus' devout Jewishness. Jesus was a very devout Jew. The claim by early Jews and some modern scholars that Jesus broke the commandments and did not honor Shabbat (the Sabbath) is misinformed. Jesus knew that according to Genesis

2, God continued his creating work on Shabbat, and then rested. Note the biblical text: "And *on the seventh day God finished the work that he had done,* and he rested on the seventh day from all the work that he had done" (Gen. 2:2 NRSV; emphasis added). The Torah's concept of God working on Shabbat to complete the works of creation informs a comment by Jesus that has often been misunderstood by exegetes and commentators. After healing the man who had been ill for thirty-eight years and lay beside the Pool of Bethzatha (Bethesda), Jesus alludes to Genesis 2: "And this is why some of the Judean leaders persecuted Jesus, because he did this on the Sabbath. But Jesus answered them, *'My Father is working still, and I am working'* " (John 5:16-17).

Jesus' devotion to Torah and Judaism is evident also in his actions. During his last week alive, Jesus was in Jerusalem. Why? He had ascended to the Holy City to celebrate Passover, as required by Torah. During this week, Jesus taught in the Temple and, quoting the revered prophet Isaiah, called the Temple "a house of prayer" (Mark 11:17; Matt. 21:13; Luke 19:46). According to the author of Acts, Jesus' followers, James and John (Acts 3:1), and later Paul (cf. Acts 21:26; 22:17) continued to worship in the Temple, observing the sacrifices and the cultic liturgy. According to Hegesippus, James, "the brother of the Lord," remained in the Temple, worshiping (but perhaps not sacrificing) and praying until his martyrdom (Eusebius, *HE* 2.23.4-18).

Thus, *Jesus should not be imagined as the first Christian.* He was a very devout Jew who observed Torah (the Law recorded in the Bible). Perhaps, as previously mentioned, he was so devout that he wore the religious garment of a conservative Jew, the *sisit*, which pours outside the outer garment with fringes (Mark 6:56; Matt. 9:20; Luke 8:44).

History in the Gospels. Seeking history within the Gospels, in light of what has been learned archaeologically (*realia*, sites, and texts) about pre-70 Judaism, has been enlightening. We have seen that the reference to stone vessels for the Jewish rites of purification makes best sense within Second Temple Judaism. We have noted that the reference to the Pool of Siloam involves Jewish purity customs, since this pool is the largest *mikveh* (Jewish pool for ritual cleansing) discovered (see also chap. 7); and the recent discovery of this pool disproves the pleas that the Fourth Evangelist created a story to stress Jesus' being sent into the world, since no Pool of Siloam from Jesus' time existed.

Jesus' words sometimes obtain their original meaning only when they are understood in light of newly discovered Jewish traditions. His comments often presuppose the Jewish hermeneutic of pre-70 Judaism when Jews differed significantly in their interpretations of Torah. Jesus affirmed Torah (the entire Old Testament) as God's Will; it must be followed accurately and perceptively. Thus, Jesus disagreed with the interpretations of Shabbat by some influential Jews, probably based in Jerusalem; he perceived their legislations to be against God's will.

Again, only two examples must suffice to illustrate Jesus' Jewishness and his engagement with pre-70 Jewish hermeneutics. Jesus' comment about leaving an animal in a pit on Shabbat makes no sense to a religious person: "What person among you, if he has one sheep and it falls into a pit on the Sabbath, will not lay hold of it and lift it out?" (Matt. 12:11). Religious persons would be disturbed by the cries for help by any animal; they would not leave it to drown in a pit. Thus, the original sense seems baffling and demands asking, For whom were such words addressed?

Jesus' intended meaning is now restored since we have found the context of this text. The *Cairo Damascus Document* contains a rule that one must leave an animal to die in a pit on Shabbat: "Let no man deliver (the offspring of) an animal on the Sabbath day. And if it falls into a pit or a ditch, let him not raise it on the Sabbath" (CD MS A 11.3-14; my translation). Jesus' words and the *Cairo Damascus Document* mention animal, the expression "falls into a pit," and Sabbath; but they provide paradigmatically different legislations. It is obvious why Jesus probably knew this rule; it would be widely known since the cries of an animal on a quiet day of rest would be a public nuisance.

The second example also significantly helps us perceive how Jesus' message was often directed against new legislation. Jesus' aside that the hairs of one's head are numbered by God again seems meaningless, even absurd. Recall the passage: "Even all the hairs of your head are numbered" (Matt. 10:30; Luke 12:7). The passive verb is a divine passive; that is, God has numbered all the hairs on one's head. What does that mean?

The recently published fragments of the *Cairo Damascus Document* contain legislation that one who has a disease of the head or beard should go and consult a priest who will count the hairs of your head and discern the cause of the sickness (4QD[a-h] 13-21). Jesus' comment that God has numbered all the hairs of one's head makes sense only when one knows this legislation; and it would be public knowledge, since the person with this sickness was ordered to shave his head (4QCD[a-h] 17). These two examples provide proof of how sometimes Jesus' intended meaning, once unknown and confusing, obtains clarification and importance in light of literary and archaeological discoveries. At other times, familiar terms—such as the Son of Man, the Messiah, and God's Kingdom—now obtain fuller meaning; that is, familiar concepts frequently become clarified as we see them used in early Jewish documents unknown to a previous generation of scholars.

Scholars once portrayed Jesus only by focusing on the New Testament and a putative "emerging Christianity." And that religion was frequently presumed to be basically Greek, since the New Testament was composed in Greek. Then, Jesus was imagined to be partially Jewish and comprehend with Judaism as a distant background. Now, many experts perceive Jesus to have been a very devout Jew whose life and thought must be grasped *within Second Temple Judaism*.

Before turning to the advent of "Christianity," it is pertinent to confront ten misconceptions of Judaism as it existed during Jesus' time. Some of these misperceptions derive from a reading of the New Testament texts without their Jewish context, the perennial penchant of many Christians to preach the superiority of Christianity, and the desire to convert Jews.

Ten Modern Misconceptions about Judaism during Jesus' Time

1) *Unconscious of sin and no need for forgiveness.* Since at least the earliest Christian council at Nicea in the early fourth century C.E., many (if not most)

Christians assumed that Jews during the time of Jesus did not recognize their sins and did not feel a need for forgiveness. For example, when the *Prayer of Manasseh* was rediscovered, Christian scholars (notably Fabricius, Migne, and Nau) assumed the document must have been composed by a Christian, since no Jew would have called on God for forgiveness of sins (see *OTP* 2:625-37). According to these specialists, Jews thought they were free from sin because they had faithfully obeyed the Ten Commandments. Despite the efforts of scholars, Christian preachers sometimes employ this misconception to stress the superiority of Christianity over Judaism by arguing that Jews claimed to be able to earn their own good relation with God (righteousness) by doing righteous deeds (works of righteousness). Such a falsehood is often connected with interpretations and sermons based on a misreading of Jesus' Parable of the Pharisee, who exalted himself, and "the Publican" (a sinful tax collector): "Two men went up into the Temple to pray, one (was) a Pharisee and the other a tax collector. The Pharisee stood and prayed thus with himself, 'God, I thank you that I am not like other men.... I fast twice a week, I give tithes of all that I get'" (Luke 18:10-12). Obviously, it is possible to imagine anywhere, even in the Temple, a person who was self-righteous. What was typical in Jesus' day?

No Jewish text indicates that anyone can earn favor with God or win God's blessing. The book of Job and the Psalms, especially Psalm 119, should make that point clear. In fact, Jewish texts stress the indelible sin that all humans inherit. For example, a Jew in the late first century C.E. portrayed Ezra asking, "O Adam, what have you done? For though it was you who sinned, the fall was not yours alone, but ours also who are your descendants" (*4 Ezra* 7:48 [118]; *OTP* 1:541). The author imagines that Jews collectively confess: "We have miserably failed," "we have lived wickedly," and "we have walked in the most wicked ways." Far from suggesting that Jews are not sinners, these passages reveal that Jews admitted that they knew their sins, confessed them, and sought forgiveness from God, and not because they performed a work: "The Most High ... is gracious to those who turn in repentance to his law; and patient, because he shows patience toward those who have sinned, since they are his own works; and bountiful, because he would rather give than take away" (*4 Ezra* 7:62[132]-65[135]; *OTP* 1:541). In these words one finds the concepts of grace and forgiveness.

One of the most elevated penitential prayers was composed by a Jew, and not by a Christian as already intimated. The author lived shortly before Jesus' time. This anonymous author imagined that he was Manasseh, the wickedest king of Judah. Note these words that represent the mindset of many Jews during Jesus' time:

> And now behold I am bending the knees of my heart before you;
> And I am beseeching your kindness.
> *I have sinned, O Lord, I have sinned;*
> And I certainly know my sins.
> I beseech you;
> *Forgive me, O Lord, forgive me!* (*Prayer of Manasseh* 11-13; my translation)

The spiritual sophistication of this composition is so advanced that leading scholars in the past assumed, as previously implied, that the work had to have been composed by a Christian. The poetic genius of the author is apparent in his reflection that he has bent his knees so repeatedly and so devoutly that the "knees" of his heart are bent before the Lord. In light of recent work on Jewish apocryphal compositions and the Dead Sea Scrolls, there is no longer any doubt that the author of the *Prayer of Manasseh* was a Palestinian Jew who lived prior to Jesus.

No one should any longer imagine that the *Prayer of Manasseh* must be a Christian composition. Christians inherited from early Judaism the consciousness of sin and the need for God's forgiveness. Both Jesus and his earliest followers frequented the Temple for prayer and worship. They would often have heard the Levites chanting on the Temple steps. Perhaps they heard them chant the great penitential prayer in the Psalter, the hymnbook of the Second Temple. Recall the well-known words:

> Have mercy on me, O God,
> > according to your steadfast love;
> according to your abundant mercy
> > blot out my transgressions.
> Wash me thoroughly from my iniquity,
> > and cleanse me from my sin....
> Create in me a clean heart, O God,
> > and put a new and right spirit within me (Ps. 51:1-2, 10 NRSV)

All faithful Jews knew they had sinned. They knew only God could forgive, and they asked God for forgiveness. They felt subsequently that God had cleansed them of their iniquities.

It is also clear that the reigning high priest knew and confessed publicly his own sins (cf. Lev. 16:6, "Aaron is to offer his own bull of sin offering, to make expiation for himself and for his household," *Tanakh*). Before those in attendance in the Temple, the high priest admitted his own sins each year on the Day of Atonement (Yom Kippur). The night before this day he ate little and stayed awake all night (presumably to pray, meditate, and read Torah, and remain ritually pure). When day broke and the first sacrifice was ready, he immersed himself five times in a *mikveh*. With his hands on the bullock, he confessed:

> O Lord, I have committed iniquity, transgressed,
> > and sinned before you, I and my house.
> O Lord, forgive the iniquities, transgressions, and sins,
> > which I have done by committing iniquity, transgression,
> > and sin before you, I and my house. (*Yoma* 3:8F; *Mishnah* [order mine])

Although this document was written after 200 C.E., most experts rightly perceive that it preserves pre-70 customs. Thus, Jesus and other Jews knew that confession of sin and forgiveness were deeply rooted in ancient Israel. In fact, they were ritualized. The high priest and all in the high priesthood, according to the yearly liturgy, openly and publicly confessed their sins and sought God's forgiveness.

2) *Legalistic laws.* Many Christians have been told and others assume that Judaism during Jesus' time was corrupted by legalism. They believe that laws and

legislation had replaced God and goodness. Obviously, one may discover legalism in Second Temple Judaism if one looks for it. A good example may be found in passages in *Some Works of the Torah* (which was composed at Qumran about 150 B.C.E.). Note these words:

> And concerning [his pu]re ani[mal:] It is written that one should not let it be inter-bred of two kinds. And concerning [his] clothes: [it is written that it should not] be of mixed material and he should not sow his field and [his] vi[neyard of mixed kind]s, because they are holy and the sons of Aaron are the h[oliest of the holy]. (MMT, composite text, 76-79; *PTSDSS* 3:245)

It is misleading to think or claim that such legalism defined Judaism during Jesus' time. As many scholars have emphasized for decades, the Torah was not a legalistic document. Jews perceived it to embody God's will. Torah evoked joy and celebration. Jews celebrated liturgically the joy of the Torah (Simhat Torah) because God was real and close to humans faithful to God. In the Torah, Jews found God's graciously revealed divine will for humans and creation.

The Torah (that is, the whole Hebrew Bible) was not a stagnant closed book in Jesus' day. Numerous text types of the Hebrew Bible (the Old Testament) existed in Second Temple Judaism. These living sacred texts did not define one sect or group from another, with the exception of the Samaritans. The five books of Torah (Genesis, Exodus, Leviticus, Numbers, and Deuteronomy) were very similar for all Jews, including the Samaritans who altered the ancient texts so that Gerizim, not Jerusalem, was the sacred site for worship. Even among the Samaritans the alterations to the Pentateuch are minimal, exposing a common sacred text shared by all Jews. Jesus' love of the Psalms, Jeremiah, and especially Isaiah is well-known and obvious from the words attributed to him in the Gospels. His quotations from the scriptures are in line, almost always, with the received text, the Masoretic Text used by Jews and Christians today. Most likely this text tradition was shaped by priests in the Temple, thus revealing again Jesus' connection with the Temple and mainstream Judaism.

3) *Election superiority.* Far too many historians fall into the *all-fallacy* when they write or speak about Early Judaism; that is, either they use the word *all* when talking about Jews, who had astoundingly diverse views before 70 C.E., or they imply that, for example, Jews (meaning all Jews) considered themselves superior and the "elect of God."

Documenting that claim is easy, but many different views are found in early Jewish texts. On the one hand, claims to superiority are obvious in early Jewish texts. However, these are often one Jewish group, or sect, claiming superiority over another *Jewish* group or sect. For example, the Qumranites stated explicitly that they, and only they, were "the Sons of Light" who were guided by "the Holy Spirit" and that all others, especially the Jewish priests running the Temple cult, were "the Sons of Darkness" who were led by Belial or Satan (viz., the *Rule of the Community* 3-4). On the other hand, Jewish attitudes to non-Jews were complex and diverse. Some Jewish texts seem anti-Gentile (viz., *Jubilees*, the *Pesharim*, and some of the *Sibylline Oracles*). Others are not anti-Gentile (*Sirach* and esp. the *Wisdom of Solomon*), and some are inclusive of Gentiles (e.g., *The Testaments of the*

Twelve Patriarchs, Philo's tomes, Josephus's *War,* and the Jewish strata of the *Odes of Solomon*).

It can be misleading to look for pro-Gentile thought in early Jewish documents. One must remember the contexts of these texts. The authors were treated as inferiors and lived in a land conquered successively by Persians, Greeks, and Romans. Surely, at least at times according to the Gospels, Jesus was anti-Gentile. Recall Jesus' commission to the Twelve: "Into the way of the Gentiles do not go and into a town of the Samaritans do not enter. But go rather to the lost sheep of the house of Israel" (Matt. 10:5-6). The all-fallacy dumps all Jews into one category and overlooks the rich and creative varieties of Jews mirrored in early Jewish texts.

4) *Polluted Temple.* Some Christian theologians assume or conclude that the Temple was polluted during the time of Jesus. Surely, it is easy to find evidence of the corruption by high priests, especially Alexander Jannaeus (103–76 B.C.E.), Annas, and Caiphas. The Kathros family, a powerful priestly family whose weights for measuring commodities was found in Jerusalem's Upper City, was denounced in Rabbinics for its fraud and injustice (Tosefta, *Minḥot* 13.21; Babylonian Talmud, *Pesaḥim* 57.1). To conclude, however, that some high priests were corrupt does not prove or indicate that all priests were corrupt or that the Temple cult was polluted.

Confusion in understanding Jesus' relation to the Temple has been caused by not perceiving four distinct categories. First, Jerusalem was "the Holy City"; many Jews claimed or assumed it was the center of the world (*Jubilees*). Second, the Temple was the quintessential residence of God on earth. Herod the Great extended the Temple Mount to the south and west, but these extensions were often not judged to be part of the Holy Temple by some Jews. Third, "the Holy of Holies" was within the Temple. Only the high priest, and only on the Day of Atonement, could enter this inner sanctum. Fourth, for centuries before Jesus' time, priests organized the cult so it magnificently ordered sacrifice and liturgy, including the Levites' chanting, which was accompanied by dancing, trumpets, cymbals, drums, and lyres. Different texts (esp. 1QS, CD) indicate that some Jews deemed the cult to be polluted, thus disclosing the need felt by many Jews, including the Essenes and Jesus, for a purified Temple and cult. Jesus' attitude to alms and a purified cult is reflected in the famous story of the widow's mite (Mark 12:42; Luke 21:2). Thus, historically, at least in general content, the early reports that Jesus was offended by the abuses in the cult and attempted "to cleanse" the Temple probably are reliable. Jesus frequented the Temple, taught in Solomon's Portico, worshiped in the Temple, and considered it as God's chosen sacred space. He probably called the Temple "a house of prayer" (Mark 11:17; Matt. 21:13; Luke 19:46), and he may even have called the Temple "my Father's House" (John 2:16). Thus, Jesus revered the Temple, celebrated the Temple liturgy, admired many of the priests, but was offended by some excesses in the cult and some of the injustices and abuses of some influential priests.

5) *Corrupt liturgy.* Despite the efforts of some New Testament specialists, numerous influential authors have claimed that Jewish liturgy in the home and elsewhere had become corrupt during Jesus' time. At the end of the nineteenth century a monumental and multivolume work appeared: *A History of the Jewish People in the Age of Jesus Christ.* The author, Emil Schürer, concluded that Jewish prayer during the time of Jesus "was bound in the fetters of a rigid mechanism"

(Div 2, vol. 2.2, pp. 115-25). Schürer's volumes were accepted widely as authoritative and definitive. Even in the last two decades, professed Christians in the United States have claimed that God does not hear the prayers of Jews. Anti-Semitism—the greatest Christian heresy—is unfortunately surviving and in some areas reviving.

But the Davidic Psalms (the Psalter) was the hymnbook of the Second Temple (ca. 520 B.C.E. to 70 C.E.). In the last two hundred years we have learned about other hymnbooks and collections of prayers and psalms. These are now called the *Psalms of Solomon*, the *Thanksgiving Hymns*, the *Angelic Liturgy*, the *Pseudepigraphic Prayers*, and *More Psalms of David* (*Psalms 151–155*). It is now certain that fresh psalms, hymns, odes, and prayers were being composed during the centuries before the end of the Temple sacrifice and liturgy in 70 C.E. These poetic and psalmic compositions constitute the most numerous works among the Dead Sea Scrolls.

Jewish prayers also appear sporadically in the Jewish apocryphal works and narratives. Jews left indelible impressions that prayers were a conversation between the human and the Creator, that these were efficacious and cosmic. Even angels prayed and chanted to God (see esp. *Angelic Liturgy* [4Q400-407]). It was on this foundation that Jesus constructed his own prayer life, which was stressed by Luke, who portrays Jesus praying before major events in his life. Jewish liturgy also provides words and phrases in Jesus' special prayer: the Lord's Prayer. Clearly, Jewish prayers during the time of Jesus are among the great masterpieces in the world's storehouse of liturgy; they were unfettered, and the heart of the created could commune with the heart of the Creator.

6) *Resurrection denied.* Far too many people think that only Christians believe in the concept of resurrection. This belief is often misunderstood and seldom defined. Resurrection belief constitutes three elements: a person was alive, has died, and will rise again from the dead, usually to enjoy eternal life.

Even when resurrection belief is clarified, many Christians proceed to declare that Jews do (and in Jesus' time did) not believe in an afterlife. Such misperceptions can be built upon the claim that Sadducees did not believe in the resurrection of the dead, as the author of Acts 23:8 reported, and the widespread assumption that because Jews do not believe in Jesus' resurrection, they do not believe in the concept of resurrection. The Sadducees seem to be an exception and should not be confused with a rule. As far as we now know, the only group of Jews in Jesus' day who denied belief in the resurrection was the Sadducees.

The belief in resurrection appears frequently in Second Temple Judaism and was not a belief that defined only one group or sect. The earliest clear reference to belief in the resurrection is in *1 Enoch* 22–27, which may date from as early as 300 B.C.E. It appears again in Daniel 12:2, which was composed about 164 B.C.E. According to *2 Maccabees* 14, Razis is depicted tearing out his entrails, hurling them at his enemies, and calling on the Lord to give them back again to him (14:45). A scroll found in the Qumran Caves is now labeled *On Resurrection*. In it the Lord is one who, conceivably through the Messiah, "shall heal the slain ones, and bring back life (again) to dead ones." The early Jewish liturgy, recited in synagogues, called the *Eighteen Benedictions*, contains resurrection belief. Note these words: "Blessed are you, O Lord, who resurrects the dead."

The earliest evidence of resurrection belief may appear in Zoroastrianism; but the extant texts date from the Middle Ages, and one has to consider the possibility of influences from Christianity and Judaism. An exploration of Greek texts reveals that Asclepius was hailed as one who "raised up the dead" (Apollodorus, *Bibliotheca* 3, 10, 3, 5-4, 1; Theodoretus, *Graecarum Affectionum Curatio* 8, 19-23). These seem to be isolated and perhaps unreliable claims. What is clear is the appearance of resurrection beliefs in many early Jewish documents. There is now no doubt that the concept of a general resurrection was developed by Jews long before Jesus. Thus, it should now be abundantly clear that Jews did believe in the resurrection, that some of Jesus' followers held that belief before the crucifixion (see John 11:24), and that the Christian belief in Jesus' resurrection is founded on Jewish concepts and beliefs (see *Resurrection and ResurrSOG*).

7) *Kingdom of God: A Christian creation.* In *Jesus and the Language of the Kingdom* (1976), Norman Perrin, a very influential New Testament expert, contended that from "the point of view of linguistic usage the form 'Kingdom of God' is comparatively late; it may even be specifically Christian" (p. 81). Today, New Testament scholars spend more time than they did in the 1970s studying and appreciating early Jewish texts. It has thus become clear that the concept of God as King and God's Kingdom or Rule is found in many Jewish texts that date from the time of Jesus and centuries earlier. The following texts illustrate this point, and each of them comes from the period of Second Temple Judaism:

Blessed are you (God) upon the throne of your kingdom. (Dan. 3:54)

And then indeed he (God) will raise up the kingdom for ever. (*Sib. Or.* 3.767)

Blessed be God who lives forever and his kingdom. (Tobit 13:1)

For being servants of his kingdom you did not judge correctly. (Wis. Sol. 6:4)

She (Wisdom) showed him *the Kingdom of God*. (Wis. Sol. 10:10)

And *the Kingdom of the Lord* will not be among you. (*T. Ben.* 9:1)

And the kingdom shall be to the God of Israel. (1QM 6.6)

And you are a fe[arful] God in the glory of your kingdom. (1QM 12.7)

The Kingdom of our God is for ever over the nations in judgment. (*Pss. Sol.* 17:4)

The Lord himself is our king for ever and ever. (*Pss. Sol.* 17:46)

His (God's) Kingdom will appear throughout his whole creation. (*T. Mos.* 10:1)

Glorified and sanctified be God's great name.... May he establish his kingdom in your lifetime and during your days.... (Qaddish)

Some of these texts were composed in Hebrew, others in Aramaic, and still others in Greek; thus, one should avoid talking about Hebrew as the only language for this expression and concept.

It should now be obvious that the form *Kingdom of God* is neither late in the history of Second Temple Judaism nor a Christian creation. God, his kingdom, his kingship, and the term *the Kingdom of God* (or Rule of God) are neither unique to early "Christian" preaching (kerygma) nor created by Jesus.

The excerpts just highlighted illustrate what is meant by the insight that Jesus—his life and thought—must be understood within Judaism. For example, since the opening of the Lord's Prayer is similar to the Qaddish and God's kingdom is praised as about to appear, we are led to ponder the following questions: To what extent was Jesus influenced by the Qaddish? Was the Kingdom of God (or Rule of God) Jesus' central teaching? We shall examine such questions in chapter 8.

8) *No concept of salvation.* Some scholars have assumed that the concept of salvation and a "Savior" appears for the first time in early Christian belief. In fact, these concepts were present prior to Jesus' time. Asclepius, the Greek and Roman god of healing, for example, was hailed as "the Savior" not only in inscriptions but also in *Orphic Hymn* 67. The author of the Wisdom of Solomon, sometime perhaps in the second century B.C.E., claimed that the serpent mentioned in Numbers 21:4-9 was a "symbol of salvation" (16:6), but God was "the Savior of all" (16:7). Jesus and his followers inherited a rich vocabulary, including the terms *salvation* and *Savior.*

9) *A distant God.* A cursory reading of the Jewish apocalypses and apocalyptic literature has given many persons the impression that Jews imagined God had abandoned his earth, and that meaning and truth reside only in one of the heavens or in some future age. There is some truth in this impression, but one needs to observe that the seers selected as visionaries by the Jewish authors of the apocalyptic works, such as Enoch, Levi, and Abraham, go into the heavens or the future to obtain wisdom, moral insight, and a perception of the future so that they can come back and help those *on earth.* So did Jesus really change the emphasis in apocalyptic thought when he taught his disciples to pray, "Thy kingdom come, thy will be done *on earth* as it is in heaven"?

10) *A deteriorated religion.* Kant and Spinoza, and many other influential thinkers, misled many in Western culture to imagine that Judaism during the time of Jesus had become corrupt. Each of these influential savants inherited the tendency to denigrate Judaism so as to elevate Jesus and Christianity. Despite current teaching in numerous universities and seminaries, many people in the United States believe that Christianity has "superseded" (gone beyond, improved, and replaced) Judaism. This is the heresy of supersessionism. What is wrong with this thought?

First, supersessionism fails to perceive Jesus within his mother religion: Judaism. Second, it miscasts Jesus as "the first Christian" or a non-Jew. Third, it misses the teaching of Paul who had to speak against supersessionism among some of his converts. Note his words in his most important, mature, and brilliant writing: "I ask, therefore, has God rejected his people? By no means!" (Rom. 11:1).

Jewish biblical exegesis. The *Pesharim* are biblical commentaries composed at

Qumran (where many of the Dead Sea Scrolls were copied or composed). Almost all of them date from the first century B.C.E. They provide a paradigm for assisting scholars to discern the ways early Jews prior to the Palestinian Jesus Movement understood scripture. The Qumranites presupposed that the books we call the Hebrew Bible or the Old Testament preserved God's Word. They assumed scripture had not been composed for the past; it was recorded (sometimes without insight or comprehension) for the present and only for "the Yaḥad," the Community. Their own community was defined by the special revelation and knowledge given by God solely to the Righteous Teacher (1QpHab 7), God's chosen one who defined Qumran theology. The Qumranites claimed God's promises were trustworthy. Members of the Qumran Community could see in their own history how God had mysteriously proved his trustworthiness. Such interpretation was aided by the Holy Spirit from God and was comprehended and communicated in light of the conviction that the present is the latter days in which God's promises would be fulfilled. These promises were especially clear in the prophets, notably Isaiah and Habakkuk, even though God had not disclosed to the early prophets the meaning of the words they recorded. Hence, it was even possible to correct the records of these prophets; that is, scripture could be corrected in the Qumran scriptorium.

Exegesis of scripture at Qumran was pneumatic, eschatological, and an example of fulfillment hermeneutics. The Qumranites, thus, thought the spirit in the latter days was fulfilling God's promises that pertained almost always only to the Qumranites and their history.

This Jewish Community at Qumran, which antedates Jesus and his group by at least one hundred years, helps us comprehend the exegetical moves and hermeneutical norms of the earliest members of the Palestinian Jesus Movement. Both at Qumran and within Jesus' group biblical interpretation was fulfillment hermeneutics; that is, the history of each group was portrayed as the fulfillment of prophecy. Two noted differences appear as we compare the *Pesharim* with the Gospels and Paul's earliest letters. While messianic belief tends to permeate Qumran theologies (cf. 1QS, *On Resurrection* [4Q521], CD, and the copies of Dan.), messianism does not shape the *Pesharim*. Only in the Palestinian Jesus Movement can one faithfully talk about messianic exegesis (*MessExegesis*). The perspective that the Messiah has come and all promises are fulfilled in him distinguishes Jesus' group from all others. Second, for the Palestinian Jesus Movement scripture obtains its full meaning only when it is explained in light of what is remembered about Jesus' life and thought.

The origins of Christology. What was the source of messianic speculation within the Palestinian Jesus Movement? First, of course, the source was Scripture, especially the ancient prophecies found in the Hebrew Bible or Old Testament.

Second, a major source for the origins of Christology was the speculation about the Messiah found in contemporary Jewish texts (*Messiah*). Only two texts must suffice now for illustration.

First Enoch is a voluminous collection of five or more books composed by Jews during Second Temple Judaism. The authors lived perhaps in Galilee from about 300 B.C.E. to maybe 44 C.E. They attributed their inspiration to Enoch, the seventh after Adam, who was morally perfect, and so he did not die. In these writings the Messiah is equated with or parallel to the Son of Man. Virtually no more theological development was necessary for Jesus' followers as they sought appropriate Christological concepts. What was needed was an exploration of how to transfer to Jesus of Nazareth the terms for The-Coming-One developed within Second Temple Judaism and a search for how and in what ways prophecy proved that Jesus was the Messiah.

The *Psalms of Solomon* are eighteen psalms composed by a Jew living in Jerusalem less than forty years before Jesus' birth. He and his community stressed that only God is King and that the Messiah is "his Messiah." When the Messiah comes, he will purge Jerusalem of the plague that has infected her. The sickness is the Romans. The Messiah will drive out the Romans from Jerusalem and the Land. He will not rely on weapons or horses. His sword will be the word that comes from his mouth.

Third, and far more fundamentally important as a source of messianic understanding for Jesus' followers, was the living memory of what Jesus had done and claimed. Thus, for example, while an exegesis of Isaiah's suffering servant passages is not present in Jewish messianic thought prior to Jesus and his group, such an interpretation defined his group. The source of the reflection is primarily a focus on the man who descended from the hills of Nazareth. Likewise, while the Messiah was not one who was to perform healing miracles, such undisputed aspects of Jesus' ministry defined messianism for Jesus' followers. In summation, the source of thought for Jesus' earliest followers was a vast store of written and oral traditions, all deemed revelatory and infallible; but the fundamental source of Christological thought within the Palestinian Jesus Movement was the one who founded and defined the Movement: Jesus from Nazareth.

Summary. In this chapter I have tried to organize and clarify the widely recognized perceptions and articulations that represent a new consensus emerging among historians and archaeologists devoted to re-creating first-century Palestinian social and religious phenomena. In them, we have not encountered the term *Christian* or the concept *church*. These two nouns are clearly anachronistic within first-century Jewish phenomena.

How may we re-present ancient social organizations without confusing them with modern concepts? As an example, we ought to bring to the task of translating New Testament Greek what we learned from examining and translating papyri. That is, we usually translate *synagōgos* as "assembly" in papyri; hence, we should translate this term in the Apocalypse of John 2:9 as "the assembly of Satan" and not "the synagogue of Satan," thus removing an anti-Semitism in the New Testament. Also, perhaps we New Testament translators should render *he ekklēsia* as "the assembly" and not "the church" in Acts 19:32 (cf. 19:39 also).

It should now be clear that what was once called Earliest Christianity is now perceived to be a Jewish phenomenon. It was centered in Palestine (a term that antedates the first century and is Herodotus's term for the land of the Philistines). It originated during the life and times of Jesus of Nazareth. Unlike Qumran that disappeared under the flames ignited by Vespasian and his troops in 68 C.E., the group became a movement. Hence, for a term such as *church,* many experts now use the term *Palestinian Jesus Movement.* This technical term is clear, descriptive, and does not transpose to early phenomena what developed much later, some time in the fourth century C.E.

As we have seen, the term *Christianity*—which is often understood as an antithesis to Judaism—is thus revealed to be misleading in describing first-century religious phenomena. The disciples of Jesus were labeled by some at Antioch as "Christian" (Acts 11:26); but most likely, they would have been as pleased with that label as the early Methodists were with the surrogate "Bible Moths." Paul prefers to refer to the followers of Jesus as a Jewish "sect" known as the "Way" (Acts 9:2; 22:4; 24:14, 22; cf. 24:5), and that brings into focus a concept and term well known from the Qumran Scrolls. The Qumranites, under the influence of Isaiah 40:3, portrayed themselves as members of the Way. As we proceed to improve and refine our terms by which we portray first-century social groups, we might come closer by using terms and concepts they themselves coined, inherited, and used.

For example, in the 1960s I used the term *Johannine Christians* to describe those within the Johannine Circle (or School). Now, more than forty years later, I prefer to refer to a struggle within Judaism between Synagogal Jews and Johannine Jews. As is well known, the term *aposunagōgos* (only in John 9:22; 12:42; and 16:2), which denotes being cast out of the synagogue, discloses not only that some in the Johannine Circle were being thrown out of the synagogue but also that they wanted to attend synagogal services. These followers of Jesus were clearly Jews.

These brief reflections help clarify the new perspectives of Judaism, the Gospel of John, Jesus, and the advent of "Christianity." Not only are the new methodology and perspectives more attuned to Jesus and his Judaism, but each opens avenues of communication with Jews, who have been miscast, castigated, and even murdered because of poor biblical exegesis and hermeneutics.

Conclusion

Questions eight and nine. Our eighth question is, Was Jesus not the first Christian? That question may have seemed well couched; now it seems naïve. Clearly, Jesus was not the first "Christian." Jesus was a devout and rather conservative Jew who could be extremely liberal on social issues.

Our ninth question is, Was Jesus an Essene, Pharisee, Zealot, or Sadducee? This question also is now exposed as uninformed. Jesus was certainly no Zealot or Sadducee. He was close in many ways to the Essenes and especially some Pharisees; but he was neither an Essene nor a Pharisee. The reader now observes that other groups should have been initially included.[1]

In the following chapters we shall explore whether Jesus is closer to one of these Jewish groups than others. Did Jesus break with John the Baptizer and set in motion a new "sect" or movement within Judaism? If so, why, and what was Jesus attempting to accomplish? With a grasp of the new consensus regarding Second Temple Judaism, we may now focus on Jesus and his life and thought within Judaism.

We first must begin with basic questions: Where was Jesus born? When was he born? Is there any history in the apocryphal gospels that describe his birth and youth?

Note

[1] For example, Was Jesus a Samaritan? Apparently, some Samaritans joined the Palestinian Jesus Movement and may even be present in the community in which the Gospel of John was written. Perhaps some of Jesus' early followers thought he was a Samaritan; they probably are responsible for the Samaritan sections in the Gospel of John. What leads to this supposition?

According to John 4, Jesus discusses theology with a Samaritan woman. The disciples are depicted startled or amazed that Jesus is talking with a woman, but not a Samaritan. Leaving Samaria for Galilee, Jesus is welcomed by the Galileans because they had seen "all that he had done in Jerusalem at the feast" (4:45).

What had just happened in Samaria? It may be that the Samaritans rejected Jesus, and this interpretation may be demanded by the statement with which Jesus leaves Samaria: "After the two days he departed for Galilee. For Jesus himself testified that a prophet has no honor in his own country" (4:43-44). Jesus has just left Samaria, which seems to be mirrored by the words "in his own country." Jesus is accepted by Galileans, thus, Galilee cannot be his "own country," because he is being honored by them. He has left Samaria; is that because "a prophet has no honor in his own country"? One can imagine that an early tradition now edited into a Johannine narrative clarified that "country" denoted Samaria. If so, we have discovered and isolated Samaritan traditions about Jesus within the Gospel of John.

Unfortunately, the passage is so heavily edited that it is impossible to comprehend to what extent some of Jesus' followers, perhaps Samaritans, imagined Jesus was related to Samaritans. The original episode is lost in the haze of history that lies hidden behind the theology of the Gospel of John.

According to John 8:48, some Judean leaders told Jesus: "Are we not right in saying that you are a Samaritan and have a demon?" Jesus replied that he had no demon (8:48-49). Why did he not deny he was a Samaritan? Is it because of the narrative or rhetoric of the passage? Is it because of the more devastating charge of having a demon, which was often addressed to Jesus? Was it because the Evangelist edited the text so it did not offend Samaritans in his community? Attentive readers will ask, "Why did Jesus not deny he was a Samaritan?"

Another group that should have been included in the question is: was Jesus a member of a baptist group? An answer is provided by the Evangelist John. He reports that Jesus began his ministry in "the land of Judea ... beyond the Jordan" (John 3:22, 26), with John the Baptizer, and that he "was making and baptizing more disciples than John" (John 4:1). Thus, according to these traditions, Jesus may have begun his public ministry within a baptist group related to John the Baptizer (see chap. 6).

CHAPTER 5

Jesus' Birth and Youth

10) When and where was Jesus born?

*11) Is there historicity in the virgin birth,
and did some judge Jesus to be a* mamzer?

*12) Did Jesus travel to a foreign land to obtain wisdom
and the powers of healing, or did he live with
Essenes to obtain these powers?*

*13) Is there any reliable history in the noncanonical gospels
that helps us understand Jesus' youth?*

The Gospels are heavily edited versions of Jesus' life and thought. That means the Gospels are not primarily history; they are fundamentally proclamations that Jesus is the Christ or God's Son.

There is wide disagreement among New Testament experts concerning the possibility that one of the Gospels derives directly or indirectly from an eyewitness and perhaps an apostle. Luke admits he needs to check with those who were eyewitnesses (Luke 1:1-4), thus indicating he was not an eyewitness to Jesus' life and teaching. However, the author of John claims that he is an eyewitness and that his report is true: "He who saw it has borne witness; his witness is true, and he knows that he tells the truth" (John 19:35; cf. 21:24 and 1:14).

The oldest narrative in the Gospels is preserved in the Passion Narrative. That has been a well-established conclusion for decades. It results from observing that only the Passion Narrative presents a coherent narrative shared by Matthew, Mark, Luke, and John. This shared "synoptic" view seems to result from the need to clarify and proclaim, in Jerusalem among those who saw Jesus crucified, that the one crucified is the Messiah. The narrative describes Jesus' last week from his triumphal entry into Jerusalem through his crucifixion and burial. These traditions were written first and cover events when all the disciples and other eyewitnesses were present to observe and remember them; moreover, the occurrences were frequently well-known public events. Thus, with the Passion Narrative we have the most reliable historical traditions because they were written first, portray events when Jesus' followers were present, and were verifiable public occurrences.

The youngest traditions are in the infancy narratives (Matt. 1–2; Luke 1–2); that is, the stories of Jesus' birth were written last, and the disciples and Evangelists were obviously not present at these events. Moreover, these stories are almost always private events. Some scholars thus conclude that there is no history in the birth stories. Let us examine these traditions and see what history, if any, may lie hidden in them.

Genealogy

Only the late Gospels of Matthew (c. 85 C.E.) and Luke (ca. 90) present Jesus' genealogy, and the two accounts differ markedly. Scholars generally concur that it is impossible to remove the difficulties in Matthew's and Luke's genealogies and find history. In the genealogies there is no obvious evidence of early tradition or searching for historical answers. They were compiled to provide Jesus' credentials for being the Messiah: he is "the son of David, the son of Abraham" (Matt. 1:1); Jesus is the son of David and "the son of God" (Luke 3:38). Both Matthew and Luke add the concept of Jesus' virginal birth. As G. Vermes states in *The Nativity*: "The child thus produced is more and more perceived not just figuratively but literally as divine, a son fathered not by Joseph of the house of David, but by God himself through his Holy Spirit" (p. 165).

Matthew's and Luke's genealogies cannot be harmonized. Most striking is the fact that Matthew and Luke cannot agree on the name of Jesus' grandfather. Was it Eli (Luke) or Jacob (Matt.)?

What is important for Matthew and Luke is the theological proclamation (kerygmatic claim) of the genealogies. Working forward from Abraham at the outset of his Gospel, Matthew seeks to show that Jesus is the son of David and son of Abraham. Working backward from Jesus to Joseph, Luke is eager to stress that Jesus is the son of David and finally the son of God. Thus, Luke places the genealogy after the theophany of the baptism: "You are my beloved Son; with you I am well pleased" (3:22).

Was Jesus a Davidid, a descendant of David? There is archaeological evidence of Davidids in Jerusalem in the first century C.E., and Davidids must have been active in the Temple, since they have specific duties assigned them in the cult. R. E. Brown (*Birth*, p. 88) speculated that if Jesus was a Davidid, he would not have been from the royal line. The genealogies tell us about Christology and claims regarding Jesus' credentials for being the Messiah. Those who wrote and those who edited them are not motivated by objective historiography; hence, scholars are dubious that they preserve reliable history.

Birth

Where was Jesus born? Many readers of the New Testament think they know the answer. They quote Matthew: "Jesus was born in Bethlehem of Judea in the days of Herod the king" (2:1). Inquisitive readers will want to explore what Matthew says or implies in his subsequent chapters and what the other Evangelists report. They will want to know why Jesus is never called "Jesus of Bethlehem." They may remember method four: "All sources and data must be included." By following this scientific method for obtaining answers to questions, it becomes apparent that five cities or villages are conceivable as Jesus' place of birth.

1) *Bethlehem.* The author of Matthew reported that "Jesus was born in Bethlehem." That statement has answered the question of Jesus' birthplace for most Christians and Jews for almost two thousand years. We learned in chapter 2 that an informed answer to any question requires that all data should be examined and that evaluating the theological tendencies of an Evangelist is essential to consider before discerning the most likely answer.

Matthew's theological agenda is obvious in his second chapter. More than any other Evangelist, he seeks to prove that Jesus is the Messiah because of the fulfillment of prophecies found in the Old Testament. Thus, he adds the statement that Jesus must have been born in Bethlehem because of prophecy: "O Bethlehem in the land of Judea ... from you shall come a ruler who shall govern (shepherd) my people, Israel" (Matt. 2:5 from Mic. 5:1-3). If Matthew was so influenced by Micah 5, then perhaps he had not examined the historical accuracy of his claim. Thus scholars conclude, probably correctly, that he had obtained information about Jesus' place of birth not from inductive exploration of historical data, but from a deduction based on prophecy.

Matthew's account of Jesus' birth has the following unique features. Only he reports the visit of the wise men; and that episode seems to fulfill Micah 5:1-3 (2:1-12). Only he mentions the flight to Egypt; and that account seeks to prove the prophecy of Hosea 11:1 (2:13-15). Only he describes the massacre of the infants (2:16-18), and the return from Egypt to Nazareth (2:19-23 [cf. Luke 2:39]); both convey echoes of Moses' infancy and the Exodus. Matthew's theological emphases are evident: Jesus is the Messiah because his life fulfills prophecy, and he is worthy to be "king" because of his royalty (or kingship) and wisdom (like Solomon).

Luke also reports that Jesus was born in Bethlehem (2:4-7). How has Luke's theological emphasis shaped the story of Jesus' birth? Only Luke adds the following episodes: the announcement to Zechariah (1:5-25), Mary's visit to Elizabeth (1:39-45), the Magnificat (1:46-56), the birth and circumcision of John the Baptist (1:57-66), the Benedictus (1:67-80), the birth of Jesus during the census (2:1-7), the announcement to the shepherds (2:8-20), Jesus' circumcision and presentation in the Temple (2:21-40), and Jesus' precociousness in the Temple (2:41-52). Luke's heightened interest in "history" and women, fondness for poetry, sensitivity to the plight of ordinary people, and focus on Jerusalem and the Temple are evident in these passages.

The historian is suspicious of the accuracy of Luke's use of a Roman census to date and locate Jesus' birth. Such a census is not supported by the known habits of officials during the Roman Empire. It is impractical that all who were to be taxed would know precisely where they were born and were able to return there for taxation. Luke may have confused a census under Quirinius in 6 C.E. with Jesus' earlier birth (see *Corpus Inscriptionum Latinarum* 6687).

Neither Matthew nor Luke knows of a Jesus of Bethlehem. Both emphasize that Jesus is "from" Nazareth. After his version of the infancy narrative, each Evangelist forgets about Bethlehem as Jesus' birthplace and turns attention to his connection with Galilee, especially Nazareth, which is "his own country" (Matt. 13:54, 57) and where he "had been brought up" (Luke 4:16). While many New Testament experts understand such passages to undermine the historical credibility of the earlier report that Jesus was born in Bethlehem, some claim that Matthew and Luke are simply explaining where Jesus spent his youth.

There is more discrepancy in the infancy stories than elsewhere; hence, many will ponder how much of the Bethlehem tradition has been shaped by faith. Such reasoning is well-founded, since the early followers of Jesus believed he was a descendant of David (see Rom. 1:3). If Jesus was believed to be the King of the Jews, then the early compilers of tradition surely knew that David was consecrated king in Bethlehem (1 Sam. 16:1-13). According to Luke, Joseph (Jesus' father) comes from the house of David and goes to "the City of David," which is Bethlehem (2:4, 11).

The textual expert will emphasize that only Matthew and Luke preserve the infancy narratives and that these are considerably different. The historian will point out that the appeal to prophecy makes suspect historical claims. These and other arguments are usually brought forth to reject Jesus' birth in Bethlehem.

The theologian may think that Jesus may have been born in Bethlehem, and then prophecy later was quoted to emphasize the theological significance of that fact. A theologian may want to stress that it is impressive that both Matthew and Luke, who are astoundingly independent of each other, claim that Jesus was born in Bethlehem. These scholars have a significant voice, and they make a valid point: theological explanations do not necessarily undermine historical claims.

In pondering where Jesus was born, light is supplied by one of my Roman Catholic students in Rome's Gregorianum. He wrote, "If we try to understand Matthew's mentality, we come to know that Matthew has a special intention and motivation for his writings. He strives to inform his readers that Jesus fulfilled everything that is written in the Old Testament. So he claims that Jesus was born in Bethlehem to fulfill Micah 5:1. John and Mark, in contrast, are more coherent in their teachings and theology than Matthew, so it seems to me that Nazareth is the most probable place of Jesus' birth." To what extent did this student show amazing honesty with history without sacrificing theology and Christology?

An examination of early Jewish texts indicates that the Messiah may be born in Bethlehem or elsewhere. He may even come directly from heaven or some other region. Certainly, the Messiah does not have to be born in Bethlehem. He may even arise out of the sea. Note this Jewish thought about the Messiah; it was composed about the same time as Matthew and Luke:

> After seven days I dreamed a dream in the night; and behold, a wind arose from the sea and stirred up all its waves. And I looked, and behold, this wind made something like the figure of a man come up out of the heart of the sea.... Then in great fear I awoke; and I besought the Most High ... "show me also the interpretation of this dream...." He said to me, "Just as no one can explore or know what is in the depths of the sea, so no one on earth can see my Son or those who are with him, except in the time of his day." (*4 Ezra* 13; *OTP* 1:551-53)

This Jewish author, as Matthew and Luke, perceived God's Son to be the Messiah, as he indicates elsewhere in this masterpiece.

2) *Bethlehem of Galilee.* Jesus spent his youth and public ministry in Lower Galilee, leaving Nazareth for Capernaum. It is conceivable that Jesus may have been born in Bethlehem of Galilee (as Chilton imagines in his *Rabbi*); it is an early Roman site. This little village is in the hill country north of the Bet Netofa Valley

and south of the mountains of Naphtali. This suggestion for Jesus' birth helps explain the Galilean and "Bethlehem connection"; but it breaks the theological link for it. That is, descent from David is not evident with Bethlehem of the north.

3) *Nazareth*. Historians are usually convinced that if a case can be made for Jesus' birthplace, the most likely site is Nazareth in Galilee. There are five reasons for this insight. First, Jesus is known as "Jesus from Nazareth," though the preposition "from" is often not represented in translations. The preposition with a following genitive is most likely a genitive of origin in Mark 1:9: "Jesus came *from Nazareth [apo Nazaret] of Galilee.*" If Jesus came from Nazareth, he may have been born there. Second, again it is imperative to stress that Jesus' identity is always with Nazareth (*passim*); he is never called Jesus of Bethlehem. Third, according to the earliest Evangelist, Mark, Jesus' hometown is Nazareth: "And he [Jesus] went away from there and came to his own country [= Nazareth]" (Mark 6:1). The Greek translated "to his own country" is the accusative of *patris*, which denotes the home of one's father. This poetic form usually indicates "native town, home-town, and fatherland." Fourth, the Evangelist John reports that Philip told Nathanael: "We have found him of whom Moses in the Law and also the prophets wrote, Jesus, the son of Joseph, the one from Nazareth." Nathanael replied to him: "Is it possible that anything good can come out of Nazareth?" (John 1:45-46). This statement implies that Jesus is from Nazareth; that is, he most likely was born in Nazareth. Nicodemus is unable to reply to the charge that Jesus cannot be a prophet or the Messiah, because no prophet is to come from Galilee, which includes Nazareth (John 7:52). Fifth, Matthew reports that the crowds exclaim, "This is the prophet, Jesus, the one from Nazareth of Galilee" (Matt. 21:11). All these passages are best explained, according to most scholars, by the assumption or conclusion that Jesus was born in Nazareth.

4) *Jerusalem*. It is conceivable that Jesus may have been born in Jerusalem for four reasons. First, archaeologists have found evidence only here of descendants of David, and Jesus is a descendant of David, according to the Evangelists (viz., Matt. 1:1, 20). Second, Jesus' relatives, Elizabeth and Zechariah, live just west of Jerusalem (viz., Luke 1:39-45). Third, Jesus is shown frequenting Jerusalem, and he receives his bar mitzvah in Jerusalem (Luke 2:41-42). Fourth, Jesus' family is known to be living in Jerusalem after the crucifixion (esp. Acts 1:14; 12:17; 15:13; 21:17-18). None of these points indicates the town or city of Jesus' birth, and no Evangelist develops the possibility that Jesus was born in Jerusalem, which could strengthen his credentials for being Davidic and messianic.

5) *Capernaum*. It is conceivable, although unlikely, that Jesus was born in Capernaum, a small fishing village on the northern shores of the Sea of Galilee. Mark 2:1 states that Jesus "returned to Capernaum" and that some heard that "he was at home [*en oikō*]." Does this statement suggest that his hometown, Capernaum, is also Jesus' place of birth? Matthew does call Capernaum "his own city" (9:1). Does that verse indicate that "his own city" is where he was born?

In Mark 2:1, the use of the dative case in Greek, which means "at home," merely means Jesus was back in his home. It does not suggest the house in which he had been born. Matthew 9:1 most likely, in light of the full New Testament evidence, denotes where Jesus dwelt at that time. According to Matthew 4:13, Jesus left Nazareth and descended to the coast of the Sea of Galilee; there he lived in

Capernaum. This city does not appear in the infancy story. Most likely, the mention of this town is colored by the Evangelists' narrative rhetoric; it thus denotes Jesus' place of residence (cf. Luke 5:17-19).

6) *Unknown.* Many New Testament experts are convinced that Jesus' place of birth is unknowable. They point out that the earliest parts of Jesus' life were probably last written and thus farthest away from eyewitnesses. That means the Evangelists and even the disciples were not eyewitnesses.

The infancy narratives seem divorced from the story of Jesus. They have the character of prefaces later added to the form of the gospel. They are not in the earliest Gospels, Mark and John, and they are not mirrored in Paul's earlier letters. It appears likely that during Jesus' ministry, no one, not even the disciples, seems to know about any miraculous birth (Mark 6:1-6; Matt. 13:54-58; Luke 4:16; John 4:44; 6:42).

An interesting question for Christians is whether Jesus can still be hailed as the Messiah or the Anointed One of God and not have been born in Bethlehem. Jesus' birth was not crucial to the kerygma (the early proclamations about Jesus Christ developed and announced in Jerusalem). The place of Jesus' birth does not help explain the problem confronted by Jesus' earliest followers in Jerusalem: why was Jesus crucified as a public criminal? Jesus' divinity—Sonship and messiahship—is grounded by the earliest Evangelist, Mark, in events when he had become an adult; that is, in theophanies (God's declarations). Most important, Jesus' divine relationship was announced through God's declaration at the Jordan when he was with John the Baptizer (Mark 1:11; cf. John 1:32) and by John's declaration.

Conclusion. The birth narratives, or infancy gospels, are found only in Matthew and Luke; and these are late gospels that depend on Mark and other early sources. The two accounts are motivated by the desire to show how Jesus' life proves prophecy, are highly charged theologically, and are vastly different. The theological affirmations that Jesus was born in Bethlehem do not prove that Jesus could not have been born there; but they do cloud the issue. It is certain that the Gospels point to Jesus' birth somewhere in the Holy Land. The theologian may be impressed by the Gospel of John, and stress that Jesus is from above and so transcends localities.

A careful and informed methodology demands that we not select one or two passages to produce a pleasing answer. We must *look at all the evidence.* In seeking answers to historical questions, we should study carefully and reflectively our earliest and independent sources, Mark and John. In seeking answers about Jesus' place of birth and in examining the early accounts of Jesus' birth, we should avoid two distorting myths: the ancient one that blindly follows the miraculous and the modern one that categorically denies the supernatural.

Jesus' Youth

The New Testament Apocrypha and Pseudepigrapha preserve many legends concocted to explain Jesus' youth. Tales have him studying in Egypt so he may learn the mysteries and medical knowledge associated with the pharaohs. Other legends describe Jesus studying in India to obtain spiritual insights from the ancients. Additional legends, also much later than the intracanonical Gospels, portray Jesus traveling to Spain so he may be associated with the alleged silver mines of Joseph of Arimathea. Many infancy gospels have been composed; almost all are fanciful. In the extracanonical *Infancy Gospel of Thomas,* Jesus is depicted making sparrows, then slapping his hands so that they may fly away. Note this account of Jesus' youth, preserved in the early *Infancy Gospel of Thomas* 11:

> When he was six years old, his mother gave him a pitcher and sent him to draw water and bring it into the house. But in the crowd he stumbled, and the pitcher was broken. But Jesus spread out the garment he was wearing, filled it with water and brought it to his mother. And when his mother saw the miracle, she kissed him, and kept to herself the mysteries which she had seen him do. (Elliott, *The Apocryphal Jesus,* p. 23)

Why are these ancient authors (and modern writers) so fascinated with Jesus' youth? The Evangelists have left "a narrative vacuum," and many have attempted to fill it. Only Luke reports that Jesus was in the Temple when he was twelve, apparently for his bar mitzvah (2:42), and that he began his public ministry when he was "about thirty years of age" (3:23). What did Jesus do from age twelve to thirty? The Evangelists supply no information. From twelve to thirty then are "Jesus' silent years," which does not denote he was silent. It means the Evangelists remain silent about what Jesus did during those years.

When Jesus appears as a public teacher, it is clear that he knows Hebrew and is gifted linguistically. How did Jesus obtain such understanding and learning? The supernaturalists, of course, can reply that God taught him. And there is evidence that Jesus spent all night, praying to God, and being obsessed with God (Luke 6:12). The historians will explain that Jesus was obviously a genius, and that he probably spent his youth studying and reading the scriptures. He had memorized much of it, especially Isaiah, Jeremiah, and the Psalms. His conversations with learned Jews, perhaps Pharisees and Essenes, stimulated and enriched his interpretations of Torah and related writings.

Jesus apparently grew up in Nazareth with four brothers—James, Joses, Judas, and Simon—and sisters, but we are not told their names or number (Mark 6:3). Before his public ministry, Jesus joins John the Baptizer, perhaps his cousin or half-cousin, in the area of the Jordan, and apparently also led a baptist movement (John 3:22–4:3 [see chap. 6]). During his youth, if his language and parables are any indication, Jesus was interested in farming in the Lower Galilee and fishing on the Sea of Galilee. He seems to have been self-taught, since he is not traditionally linked with a famous rabbi. Christians tend to believe that Jesus' wisdom came directly from God, perhaps through reading God's Word, the Torah, and listening to the Creator.

Was Jesus a *Mamzer*?

These reflections lead to interesting questions: What relation did Jesus have to his alleged father, Joseph, and to his mother, Mary? What would those hostile to Jesus think about the claims that he was special, may have had a miraculous birth, and had a unique relation to God?

If Joseph died when Jesus was a boy, he could not be present later to defend Jesus against a charge of being illegitimate. We know these charges appeared during his life, and in Jerusalem, according to the Fourth Evangelist (John 8:41). As a Jewish male, only Joseph could provide trustworthy witness in a court of law. He alone could claim to be Jesus' real father. He was the only one who could prove Jesus' legitimacy to those who might question his parentage.

During the first century, some Jews claimed Jesus was born miraculously of a virgin (Matt. 1; Luke 2). In response, other Jews most likely claimed that this belief proved Jesus had no legitimate father and was therefore illegitimate. If Jesus was the son of a woman who had been raped by a Roman soldier (named Panthera in some Rabbinic accounts), many Jews would deem him a "bastard." In the New Testament itself there is evidence that some Judeans claimed Jesus was illegitimate, and Jesus did not defend himself. Note John 8:41; the Judeans said to Jesus: "We were not born of fornication." If Jesus was born of a harlot or "born of fornication," many Jews would have claimed he was illegitimate. Since Jesus had many enemies, some Jews would have sought ways to defame him, and one means was to categorize him as a *mamzer*.

For centuries scholars thought *mamzer* was a Hebrew or Aramaic noun that defined an illegitimate person (a bastard). Now in light of recent research into the languages of pre-70 Judaism, we know that the noun *mamzer* came to denote anyone who could not prove to the leading Jewish authorities that his or her parents were both fully Jewish, and that they were legitimately married when the person was conceived (cf. the traditions mirrored in MMT). We have changed our understanding of *mamzer* because of its use in pre-70 texts recently recovered, because of the increased demands for purification in Second Temple Judaism, and because of the priestly demands emanating from the Temple cult into all parts of ancient Palestine.

If Jesus was judged to be a *mamzer* by some legal authorities, perhaps only during the last years of his ministry, then some Jews would have considered him to be "an outcast." Thence, he would have been close to those he befriended: tax collectors, harlots, and people with leprosy. Perhaps such outcasts included Mary Magdalene. She may have been considered "an outcast" in the minds of some religious men. Both Jesus and Mary Magdalene were likely deemed unholy or unclean by some scribes and lawyers who would have consigned them to the outskirts or cracks (interstices) of society. These reflections into the dangers of illegitimacy in Second Temple Judaism cast illuminating light on Jesus' time, his ministry, and his possible relation with Mary Magdalene (see chap. 6).

Was Jesus a Carpenter?

Scribes, priests, and religious leaders usually pursued a trade. Paul, for example, was a tentmaker. Work was deemed honorable for Jews, but not for most Romans. Thus, it is fundamental to ponder whether Jesus had a trade.

According to Mark 6:3, some in Nazareth ask, "Is this not the carpenter, the son of Mary and brother of James and Joses and Judas and Simon, and are not his sisters here with us?" If this text represents historical knowledge, Jesus was a carpenter. Some early manuscripts represent "a variant reading": "Is this not the son of the carpenter and of Mary?" The variant should not be ignored; it is more

Semitic than the accepted text, since in its phrasing Jesus is the son of a man and not of a woman. The customary reading also seems late and to reflect a developed Mariology (reflections on and elevation of Mary).

Or is the variant clearly secondary? Has it appeared because some Greek and Coptic scribes did not want Jesus to have soiled his hands in some trade, let alone the sometimes pejorative life of a carpenter (which was not a trade chosen by the elite)? Or did the "Marcan variant" arise out of conflation with Matthew 13:55-56: "Is this not the son of the carpenter? Is not his mother called Mary? And (are not) his brothers James and Joseph and Simon and Judas? And are not his sisters all with us?" This passage reveals the difficulty in discerning what is the original text or less altered reading. It is possible that Matthew and Luke used a copy of Mark that had what is called a variant as their text.

One should not dismiss the evidence that Jesus was only the son of a carpenter (and not a carpenter himself). And any argument that sons always follow the professions of their fathers is misleading. To make the claim that Joseph was a carpenter and so Jesus must also have been a carpenter is methodologically unsound. It overlooks exceptions, and certainly, Jesus is often an exception in his society. Furthermore, Joseph, Jesus' father, seems to disappear early in Jesus' life. He does not appear in the Gospels after Jesus is in the Temple at age twelve. If he died when Jesus was young, then he would not have been present to teach him the trade of a carpenter.

There is one other obstacle before concluding that Jesus was a carpenter. The Greek word in Mark 6:3 is *tektōn*. The noun does not mean primarily "carpenter." It denotes anyone who is a "builder" or "craftsman." For example, note *Sibylline Oracle* 5.403-4, which was composed in Egypt sometime in the latter decades of the first century C.E. Here is the passage: "For among them no one carelessly praises a god of insignificant clay, nor did a clever *sculptor* make one from rock, nor worship ornament of gold, a deception of souls" (*OTP* 1:402).

The noun for "sculptor" is *tektōn*. The governing word in the above passage is "rock" (*petrēs*). A sculptor makes something from stone, rock, or marble. Thus, if Jesus was a *tektōn*, then he could have been one who made things from rock.

For weeks in Nazareth I helped excavate a first-century vineyard with a rock fence (or "hedge") and three towers (cf. Mark 12:1). My colleagues, some of whom were Jewish, often wondered out loud if Jesus or Joseph had helped build the rock fence and towers we were exposing.

Perhaps the most impressive evidence against Jesus being a carpenter is the observation that not once does he include in his graphic speech and parables any analogy from the carpentry shop. If speech indicates experience and occupation, then Jesus may have done some shepherding, farming, and fishing. The Evangelists depict Jesus fishing with his disciples and knowing where to catch the most and best fish (Luke 5:1-7; John 21:4-6).

What Was Jesus' Appearance?

In an hour-long BBC production, shown not only in Great Britain but also in the United States and elsewhere, attention was given to Jesus' appearance. A skull of a Jew, who lived near the time of Jesus, had been found in the Holy Land. Forensic archaeologists covered the skull with clay in the attempt to reveal some of the man's features. The purpose was to indicate the facial features of a particular Jew who lived near the time of Jesus. Unfortunately, journalists began to proclaim that the man looked like Jesus. On *Paula Zahn Live,* in December 2004, I had to clarify that the work on the skull was intended only to help govern our imaginations of an early Jew's face. Such reflections are crucial to help us imagine how Jesus may have looked. Jesus had Semitic features. His face was most likely dark brown and sun-tanned. He may have been between five feet five and five feet seven and weighed between 130 and 170 pounds. Such reflections are informed speculations governed by what we know about early Jews from archaeological research and studies of images on Titus's arch and elsewhere. Most likely the Evangelists did not describe Jesus' physical features because that was not important in proclaiming the good news about him.

In the first century no one needed to ask what Jesus looked like. Those who remembered him had no need to imagine his face or physical appearance. The kerygmata (the earliest confessional proclamations) had no need for such physical details.

In the Middle Ages the *Letter of Lentulus* was forged to provide a description of Jesus. In *Authentic Apocrypha,* I explained why this letter is a medieval forgery. In the much earlier *Acts of John* (88-89, 93), John recalls that Jesus "appeared to me, bald-headed but with a thick and flowing beard; but to James he appeared as a youth whose beard was just starting." Perhaps this record warns us that imagination often creates an image of Jesus.

Did Jesus Live for Some Time with Essenes?

With the discovery of the Dead Sea Scrolls, many concluded that Jesus was an Essene or learned much from them. Some romantic novelists imagine Jesus joined the Essenes when he was young and learned from them the art of healing and secret knowledge. This claim is frequently heralded as new and insightful.

The argument is certainly not new. The first to claim that Jesus was linked with the Essenes is Johann Georg Wachter (1673–1757). He made this assertion in 1713 in his *De primordiis Christianae (Concerning Primordial Christianity).* In the early eighteenth century, Karl Friedrich Bahrdt also claimed that the key to unlocking the mystery of Jesus is the Essenes. He suggested that both Nicodemus and Joseph of Arimathea were not followers of Jesus; they were Essenes. The Essenes had "secret members" in every facet of Jewish society, especially in the upper echelon. Jesus only appeared to die on the cross, but was resuscitated by Essenes who had ensured that Jesus had received medicines to endure beatings and the crucifixion. Jesus was restored to some health, after three days, by Essenes in a cave.

In the same century Karl Heinrich Venturini developed Bahrdt's imaginative history further, arguing that the Essenes began to instruct Jesus when he was a child in Egypt. Bahrdt's and Venturini's lives of Jesus were reactions to the purely supernatural approach of their contemporaries. However, as imaginatively insightful and often exciting as they are, these lives of Jesus are fanciful and shaped by the effort to explain all of Jesus' life from reason and rationalism. Albert

Schweitzer offered this opinion of Bahrdt and Venturini, whom he claimed offered the earliest imaginative lives of Jesus: "It is strange to notice how often in the [study of the life of Jesus] a few imperfectly equipped free-lances have attacked and attempted to carry the decisive positions before the ordered ranks of professional theology have pushed their advance to these decisive points" (*Quest*, p. 38).

Is the claim that Jesus lived for some time with Essenes insightful? No; the lives of Jesus by Bahrdt and Venturini are fictional. They are guided by an attempt to explain all miraculous events by the application of human reason.

Most scholars, rightly in my opinion, align some of the scrolls found in the Qumran caves (the Dead Sea Scrolls) with the most conservative and rigid branch of the Essenes. Although Jesus probably never visited Qumran, he did teach in the area precisely where Essenes lived, according to Philo of Alexandria and Josephus: on the borders of towns and villages throughout ancient Palestine. As we shall see in chapter 8, Jesus sometimes reacts to a peculiar Essene teaching and even seems to laud the Essenes for their dedication to Torah and God. Thus, Jesus was not guided by Essenes, did not receive secret mysteries from them, and did not live with them; but he seems to have been influenced by them, both negatively and positively (as we shall see).

Conclusion

This chapter focused on four questions. What have we learned or seen more clearly that helps us answer these questions?

10) *When and where was Jesus born?* Jesus was born during the time of King Herod; that would be sometime before 4 B.C.E. when Herod died. If Herod sought to kill boys of two years of age and younger, Jesus would have been born about two years before Herod's death. That would mean Jesus was most likely born about 6 (or even 7) B.C.E.

When one examines all the canonical evidence, it is impossible to be certain where Jesus was born. He may have been born in Bethlehem of Judea, but the vast amount of independent evidence (multiple attestation and coherence) indicates that Jesus most likely grew up and was born in Nazareth, the home of his "fathers."

11) *Is there historicity in the virgin birth, and did some judge Jesus to be a* mamzer? The virgin birth tells us more about the faith of Jesus' followers than about history. It is certain that myths and legends circulated during the time of Jesus and the Evangelists. In some of these myths, great men, including Alexander the Great and Augustus as well as Melchizedek, Noah, and Moses, had miraculous births caused by a god or God.

Joseph and Mary may not have been able successfully to prove to some Jewish authorities that they were fully Jewish, that they were married before Jesus was conceived, and that Jesus was their legitimate son. In fact, Matthew preserves traditions that would make such a claim by Joseph and Mary impossible: "When his mother Mary had been betrothed to Joseph, before they came together she was found to be with child of the Holy Spirit. And her husband Joseph, being a just man and unwilling to put her to shame, resolved to divorce her quietly" (Matt. 1:18-19). Thus, some Jews most likely judged Jesus to be a *mamzer*.

73

Jesus could not prove to demanding Jews that he was fully and authentically a Jew. One cannot offer a defense for oneself. A father in good standing with credentials is required to deflect the charge that a son is illegitimate. Joseph could not be present to provide such facts if he died early in Jesus' life, as many scholars have concluded.

12) *Did Jesus travel to a foreign land to obtain wisdom and the powers of healing, or did he live with Essenes to obtain these powers?* All the evidence we possess indicates that Jesus obtained his insights and knowledge from Judaism, which had long before him been influenced by all contiguous cultures. He did not have to travel to Athens or Alexandria to obtain wisdom from Greeks and Romans; such wisdom was already influential in early Jewish thought. He did not have to live with Essenes to obtain special knowledge or wisdom. Some Jewish experts have joined with Christian scholars to imagine that Jesus' obsession with God, his long hours of praying, his study of Torah, and his all-night sessions of meditation with God helped nourish his God-given genius (see Flusser's *The Sage from Galilee*).

13) *Is there any reliable history in the noncanonical gospels that helps us understand Jesus' youth?* In chapter 3 we saw that there are sources outside the New Testament that must be consulted in any attempt to understand the historical Jesus. *The Gospel of Thomas* must not be ignored or given special status in assessing Jesus' teaching and mind. However, it is also arduous to find reliable history in the apocryphal gospels, especially regarding Jesus' youth. As we perceived earlier in this chapter, these apocryphal accounts are almost always fanciful and products of Christological imaginations.

These insights pave the way for further questioning. Who was Jesus' teacher, or did he have one? Did he perform miracles? What can be learned about Jesus' years before he began his ministry in Lower Galilee?

CHAPTER 6

Jesus, John the Baptizer, and Jesus' Early Public Life

14) Was John the Baptizer Jesus' teacher?

15) Was Jesus married to Mary Magdalene?

16) Did Jesus perform miracles?

In this chapter we focus on Jesus' relation to John the Baptizer, and Jesus' life before and during his time at Capernaum. Luke reports that John the Baptizer and Jesus were related (Luke 1:36); perhaps they were second cousins. Jesus goes to see John where he is baptizing, perhaps at Bethany ("Place of the Boat") Beyond the Jordan, which is also Bethabara, which means "Place [or House] on the Other Side (of the Jordan)" (or "Place of the Ford").

John the Baptizer

In the first century C.E., the Jordan was a powerful river and dissimilar to the streams now running into the Dead Sea (due to irrigation and diverted water). According to John 1:28, on the eastern side of one section of the Jordan is a place called "Bethany Beyond the Jordan" (MSS P^{66}, P^{75}, and the early uncials) or "Bethabara" (MSS C^2, K, Old Syriac Gospels).

John 1:28 specifies that John the Baptizer was baptizing "in Bethany Beyond the Jordan." Bethany Beyond the Jordan or Bethabara is "Beyond the Jordan," which probably means on the eastern side of the Jordan River. The site is opposite Jericho. The Baptizer also moved around, baptizing in more than one place (cf. John 3:23).

John the Baptizer wrote nothing. His earliest followers, unlike those of Jesus, composed no "biography" of him. Sources for John the Baptizer are numerous (viz., Mk, J^1, Q, M, L, A, T, Josephus, and other later texts; see Tatum, *John the Baptist and Jesus,* chap. 2).

According to the Fourth Evangelist, Jesus was with John the Baptizer at Bethany Beyond the Jordan, and from there two of the Baptizer's followers left him to follow Jesus (John 1:29-42). Here priests and Levites, sent by the Pharisees in Jerusalem, came to John and asked him: "Who are you?" (John 1:19). He replied that he was not the Christ. They then asked him if he were Elijah (whose ascension is often associated with the place where John was baptizing) or the prophet. He answered that he was not either of these two.

Where is this place on the other side of the Jordan? Some scholars incorrectly think that the place is fiction created by the Evangelist John, but it has become obvious that the Evangelist habitually interpreted places known to him. Sometime after 200 C.E., Origen, who moved from Alexandria to Palestine, reported that he could not find a place called Bethany Beyond the Jordan; hence, he changed the reading in his New Testament text (*Comm. on John* 6.204; GCS 10.149) to Bethabara, since he knew that name from the Targumim and traditions that were later preserved in the Jerusalem Talmud. Eusebius of Caesarea Maritima (*Onom.* 58.18) reported that the place is on the west bank of the Jordan River. The sixth-century Madaba Map follows Eusebius and adds: "Bethabara, the place where St. John baptized." The Fourth Evangelist, however, apparently placed the site on the east bank of the Jordan River.

Can the site of Bethany Beyond the Jordan be located today? Two places have received recent support: the region of Bathanea (northeast of the Sea of Galilee [Riesner]) and Wadi al-Kharrar (Tell Mar Liyas) in Perea (ruled by Herod Antipas) on the eastern bank of the Jordan and opposite Jericho (Piccirillo). At the latter site, Piccirillo has discovered first-century *realia,* including pottery and remains of stone vessels for the Jewish rites of purification. More research needs to be focused on all pertinent sites, since Bethany Beyond the Jordan is problematic for biblical exegetes and geographical topographers, and churches commemorating the work of John the Baptizer appear on the western (Prodromos or Qasr al-Yahud) and eastern banks (Tell Mar Liyas) of the Jordan.

Did John Baptize Jesus?

This is the first question that confronts us as we seek to discern the relation between Jesus and John. The author of Mark presents a clear statement: "In those days Jesus came from Nazareth of Galilee and was baptized by John in the Jordan" (Mark 1:9; aorist passive, third person masculine; passive verbs are often reserved for Jesus). This is the earliest account, and the actor is clear: John baptized Jesus. Matthew seems to follow Mark's account: "Then Jesus came from Galilee to the Jordan to John, to be baptized by him" (Matt. 3:13). Though Matthew does not report that John baptized Jesus, the reader obtains the impression that John baptized Jesus (3:13-15).

Luke's framing of this account makes it impossible for John to baptize Jesus. Before Jesus' baptism (Luke 3:21-22), John is thrown into prison (Luke 3:19-20). Note these words immediately before the Lucan account of Jesus' baptism: "But Herod the tetrarch...shut up John in prison" (Luke 3:19-20). Since John is in prison, he cannot be in the Jordan to baptize Jesus. Luke does not report who baptized Jesus; he brings into focus his own theological emphases: universalism and prayer. Luke thus emphasized that Jesus was baptized "when all the people were baptized" and "when Jesus had been praying."

According to the Gospel of John, the Baptizer does not baptize Jesus. He is inferior to Jesus and was sent by God to witness to the Son. However, Jesus appears to be a follower of the Baptizer: "After this Jesus and his disciples went into the land of Judea; there he remained with them and baptized. John also was baptizing at Aenon near Salim" (John 3:22-23; see also vv. 25-26).

How do we evaluate all these conflicting reports, especially between Mark and Luke? Did John baptize Jesus? Yes; the criterion of embarrassment (Rule One) makes it clear that the earliest account is accurate historically. John baptized Jesus. This would have been an embarrassment to the followers of Jesus who would not convey the report that Jesus had been baptized by John. Jesus' followers have given us these accounts; and they were struggling against the followers of John the Baptizer. They are mentioned in Acts 19:1-7.

Polemics (Rule Two) also helps us discern the most probable answer. This criterion enables us to perceive two reasons why those who passed on this tradition might have wanted to deny it. First, for them, baptism was for remission of sin (Mark 1:4 and Luke 3:3 [cf. Matt. 3:6, but contrast Matt. 3:1-2 and John 1:23]), and they did not want to report that Jesus had sins that required baptism (see esp. the *Gospel of the Hebrews*). Second, to claim that John baptized Jesus would imply that John would be superior to Jesus, since a superior baptizes an inferior person. All these insights lead to one conclusion: John baptized Jesus, as Mark (and perhaps Matthew) reported.

Why was Jesus baptized by John the Baptizer? John was calling Israel to repent and to prepare for the coming and final act of God. He was in the wilderness, preparing the Way of the Lord (cf. Isa. 40:3). Jesus probably felt that God's final drama was about to transpire and thus went to be baptized by John, to prepare for this final act. Recall the report in Matthew: John the Baptizer came "preaching in the wilderness of Judea: 'Repent, for the kingdom of heaven is at hand'" (3:1-2).

The Baptizer: Jesus' Teacher

Many historians conclude that John was Jesus' teacher. Note the report of John P. Meier; he rightly perceives that John was Jesus' teacher and Rabbi:

> What do [we] mean by disciple? By definition, the very fact that Jesus left Nazareth, came to the region of the Jordan to hear John, and accepted his message to the point of receiving his baptism means that, in the broad sense of the word, Jesus became John's disciple. Besides being an eschatological prophet, and indeed because of that, John was also a spiritual master and guide who taught a particular ritual observance as a sign of beginning a new way of life. To that extent, by submitting to his message and baptism, Jesus became the disciple, the pupil, the student of this rabbi called John. (*MJ* 2:116)

What texts lead to this conclusion? According to Mark, Jesus comes to John and, after being baptized by him, probably spends time with him (Mark 1:1-11). Later, Jesus withdraws elsewhere into the wilderness (Mark 1:12-13). What may be implied by Mark is far more explicit in John. Note this passage: "Now a discussion arose between John's disciples and a Jew over purifying. And they came to John, and said to him: 'Rabbi, he who was with you beyond the Jordan, to whom you bore witness, here he is baptizing, and all are going to him'" (John 3:25-26).

The Fourth Evangelist preserves an old tradition that contrasts with his own theology and stress on Jesus' superiority to the Baptizer. This pre-Johannine tradition reported that Jesus had been with the Baptizer, and that he is now "baptizing." Furthermore, Jesus receives from the Baptizer his first two disciples: "The next day again John was standing with two of his disciples; and he looked at Jesus as he walked, and said, 'Behold the Lamb of God!' The two disciples heard him say this, and they followed Jesus.... One of the two who heard John speak, and followed him [Jesus], was Andrew, Simon Peter's brother" (John 1:35-40).

The site where Jesus met John the Baptizer most likely has spiritual significance. The Baptizer and Jesus baptize in the Jordan not far from the place where Joshua led the Hebrews into the promised land. The Evangelists and others most likely thought of this place as a symbol of how Jesus is a Joshua figure who leads the faithful again into the promised land.

The spot is also the traditional site for commemorating where Elijah went into heaven in a chariot; in other words, this is the place on earth where a door is open into heaven (the *axis mundi*). Here a dove could descend from heaven to Jesus. This cosmic event plays a role in each of the Gospels: "The heavens opened and the Spirit" descended "upon him like a dove" (Mark 1:10; cf. Matt. 3:16; Luke 3:22; John 1:32). The authors of Mark (9:13), Matthew (11:14; 17:12), and John (1:21, 25) reflect early traditions that the Baptizer was thought to be Elijah, who must return before the coming of the Messiah. Most likely, the Baptizer, who was influenced by Jewish eschatology and apocalyptic theology, taught Jesus how to feel the mystical presence of God. The Evangelists report that both the Baptizer (John 1:32) and Jesus (Mark 1:10) experienced revelations during their ministry in the Jordan Valley. Through prayer and meditation, the two sought to help inaugurate God's final act in history and warn against the coming judgment and wrath to be poured out on unfaithful Jews and those who had tormented Jews.

The Baptizer taught Jesus and gave him not only a refined perspective but also choice words. Notice how the Baptizer's words flow into Jesus' words and are sometimes identical:

Words Attributed to the Baptizer	Words Attributed to Jesus
You brood of vipers! Who warned you to flee from the wrath to come? (Luke 3:7)	You brood of vipers! (Matt. 12:34)
Bear fruits that befit repentance, and do not begin to say to yourselves, "We have Abraham as our father." (Luke 3:8)	If you were Abraham's children, you would do what Abraham did ... (John 8:39)
Every tree therefore that does not bear good fruit is cut down and thrown into the fire. (Matt. 3:10)	Every tree that does not bear good fruit is cut down and thrown into the fire. (Matt. 7:19)
He who has two coats, let him share with him who has none; and he who has food, let him do likewise. (Luke 3:11)	For I was hungry and you gave me food ... I was naked and you clothed me. (Matt. 25:35-36)
The Father loves the Son, and has given all things into his hand. (John 3:35)	For the Father loves the Son. (John 5:20)

Clearly, the pupil learned much from the teacher. As is clear, Jesus sometimes quotes his teacher, paraphrases his words, or echoes them.

Eventually, Jesus broke with the Baptizer and went into Galilee: "Now after John was arrested, Jesus came into Galilee, preaching the good news of God, and saying, 'The time is fulfilled, and God's kingdom is at hand; repent and believe in the good news'" (Mark 1:14-15).

Why did Jesus leave John and go to Galilee? The historian can only surmise an answer. Jesus may have believed that while many came to John, he should go to the many: "I was sent to the lost sheep of the house of Israel" (Matt. 15:24). The Baptizer interpreted Scripture to mean that one should be in the wilderness to prepare the Way of God (Isa. 40:3); Jesus may have felt that one should leave the wilderness—it is the place of preparation. Maybe Jesus' concept of time had shifted to a more imminent schedule for the end of time. The Baptizer stressed God's vengeance. Jesus emphasized God's compassion, forgiveness, and acceptance of all, especially those considered unworthy and outcasts of society (Jesus' emphasis is altered by the editing of his parables by Matthew; cf. Matt. 22:1-14; 25:11-12).

Jesus focused his ministry in a small section of Lower Galilee. He localized his teaching around Capernaum, Bethsaida, and Chorazin. These villages are located in a very small area on the northern shores of the Sea of Galilee. He may have entered the cities in Galilee of Ptolemais, Sepphoris, Tiberias, and Gamla; but there is no record of him entering them.

Why? One can only speculate. On the one hand, the New Testament does not mention most of the cities and towns noted in Josephus's works. On the other hand, perhaps Jesus' message was more suited to people in villages. He certainly was critical of the ruling classes, the wealthy, and the political figures such as Herod Antipas, whom he called a "fox," which is a very dangerous charge since kings and rulers were symbolized as lions (Luke 13:32). These elite resided in the cities. Jesus' message may have been more appropriate in rural settings. However, Jesus also cursed Chorazin, Bethsaida, and Capernaum (Q = Matt. 11:20-24; Luke 10:13-15). According to Q, Jesus performed many "mighty works" in these villages, but he lamented that the people in these villages did not repent.

The Lower Galilee and Jesus' Miracles

Galilee was reputed to be a place of miracle workers just before and during Jesus' time. We hear of miracles performed by many, especially by Honi, Hilkiah the Hasid, Hanan ha-Nehba, Hanina ben Dosa, and Eleazar the Exorcist. "Honi the Circle-Drawer [*ha-Meaggel*]" or "Onias" (Josephus, *Ant* 14.22) lived in the middle of the first century B.C.E. and was revered for his efficacious words and prayers. He was reputed to have performed miraculous works, which conceivably included miracles of hearing, and to have caused rain to fall (m*Ta'an* 3.8; j*Ta'an* 3.9 [8]; b*Ta'an* 23). Honi may have understood himself to be "a (or the) Son of God" (m*Ta'an* 3.8). He was stoned to death, outside Jerusalem, during the civil war between Hyrcanus II and Aristobulus II (see Vermes, *JJ*, p. 73).

Hilkiah the Hasid, the grandson of Honi, lived in the latter part of the first century B.C.E. He was reputed to be a miracle worker, but no healing miracle is attributed to him (cf. b*Ta'an* 23a).

Hanan ha-Nehba was also the grandson of Honi, and lived in the early decades of the first century C.E. (b*Ta'an* 23b). According to the Babylonian Talmud, he prayed for rain, and the Rabbis would send schoolchildren to beg him for rain. These children would often seize the hem of his cloak (cf. Mark 6:56).

Hanina ben Dosa lived in Galilee during the middle of the first century C.E. According to the Babylonian Talmud, he was a pupil of Johanan ben Zakkai, denied being a prophet, and is hailed by a voice from heaven: "The whole world is sustained for the sake of my son Hanina, and Hanina my son has to subsist on a *qab* of carobs from one Sabbath evening to next Sabbath evening" (b*Ber* 17b). Hanina was remembered as a wonder-worker, caused rain to fall, and healed many, including the sons of R. Gamaliel and R. Johanan ben Zakkai.

Other Jews are reputed to have the powers of healing. Eleazar the Exorcist lived about the same time as Hanina ben Dosa. Josephus reports that in the presence of Vespasian (the Roman general) and other soldiers, Eleazar pulled a demon through the nostrils of possessed individuals by employing a ring that held a root prescribed by Solomon (*War* 180–85; *Ant* 46–49). According to the *Prayer of Nabonidus* (4Q242), an anonymous Jewish exorcist healed Nabonidus of "the evil disease" and forgave his sins (cf. Mark 2:1-12), but this reputedly occurred centuries before Jesus.

Although Jesus should be perceived in light of these other Galilean miracle workers, the stories about his miracles are often different. The Evangelists report that Jesus' miracles were frequently preceded by prayer, then the sick person is cured. Only Jesus speaks on his own authority: "And a leper came to him [Jesus] begging him, and kneeling, and saying to him: 'If you will, you can make me clean.' Moved with pity, he [Jesus] stretched out his hand and touched him, and said to him: '*I will*; be clean.' And immediately the leprosy left him, and he was made clean" (Mark 1:40-42; emphasis added).

Miracles are attributed to Apollonius of Tyana, who died about 98 C.E. Some of his miraculous deeds are strikingly reminiscent of Jesus' healing miracles. Perhaps this similarity is due to the likelihood that his traditions were shifted from oral to written traditions long after the Gospels were composed and well-known. The main source for Apollonius's miracles is Philostratus's *The Life of Apollonius of Tyana,* and it dates from the third century C.E., containing stories that were popular in the second century C.E. Thus, Apollonius's miracles may be recycled Jesus traditions and Hellenistic myths (see Eusebius, *Against the Life of Apollonius of Tyana*). In *Wonders Never Cease,* E. Koskenniemi rightly shows why it is difficult to reconstruct the life of Apollonius and impossible to ascertain the function of miracles in his life.

Far more important than reports of Hellenistic wonder-workers far removed from Jesus' time and culture are the miracles associated with Galileans, already discussed, and other Jewish miracle workers near Jesus' time (the Rabbinic reports should be included, but not taken at face value). While some Rabbis are reputed to have been able to persuade God to send rain (esp. Eleazar and Akiba [both ca. 100], Judah the Prince, and Joshua ben Levi), certain Rabbis also allegedly performed healing miracles, even exorcisms. Rabbi Simeon ben Yohai (early second cent. C.E.) is reputed to have performed a miracle and cast a demon from the daughter of the emperor (b*Me'il* 17b). Most likely, Rabbi Yose the Galilean (ca.

130–40 C.E.) was known to have performed healing miracles. The prophets Elijah and Elisha are also reputed to have performed miracles, even raising the dead; hence, Jesus' miracles evoked many early traditions among his fellow Jews. More than one Jewish tradition should be remembered when imagining Jesus and his miracles.

The mighty works attributed to Jesus in the Gospels can be divided between nature miracles and healing miracles. The former point to Jesus and his elevated stature; thus, Jesus walks on water and can control storms. The attention is drawn to Jesus. These stories seem to develop out of myths and legends that were created in the post-30 community to laud and elevate Jesus.

The reports of Jesus' healing miracles often focus on the persons who need healing and their faith in Jesus' ability to heal them. Note how the spotlight is often turned to the one healed and the faith manifested in Jesus: "And he said to her, 'Daughter, your faith has made you well.'" (Mark 5:34; see also Mark 10:52). These healing miracles are now, in Jesus Research, rightly considered part of Jesus' historical life (viz., Meier, *MJ* 1:220).

Jesus' reputed healing miracles reflect some history and early traditions. Did Jesus perform healing miracles? Yes. Why? First, they make sense within Jesus' culture, and miracle workers are reputed to be localized in Galilee, where the traditions place Jesus' miracles.

Jesus' healing miracles are also probably historical because they are in many sources; thus, the principle of multiple attestation indicates that Jesus' healing miracles are historical. They are found in Paul (Rom. 1:4), Q, Mark, M, L, J[1], A (Acts 10:38), and also Josephus: "Jesus . . . he was one who wrought surprising feats" (*Ant* 18 [trans. L. H. Feldman]).

Equally important for discerning the historicity of Jesus' healing miracles is the observation that those who criticized Jesus affirmed that he performed healing miracles (polemical ambience). Those who opposed Jesus claimed that Jesus was able to perform healing miracles because he was in league with the power of evil: "But when the Pharisees heard it they said, 'It is only by Beelzebul, the prince of demons, that this man casts out demons'" (Matt. 12:24). The Pharisees thus witness to Jesus' ability to perform healing miracles.

Finally, the criterion of embarrassment indicates that Jesus performed miracles, and some of his followers found this to be unattractive (as it is to some theologians today). Early Jesus traditions indicate that Jesus' miracles were an embarrassment to Jesus' family; they wanted to bring him home. They thought he was performing miracles because he was possessed of a demon. Note this passage in Mark: "And when his family heard it, they went out to seize him, for people were saying, 'He is beside himself.' And the scribes who came down from Jerusalem said: 'He is possessed by Beelzebul, and by the prince of demons he casts out the demons'" (3:21-22, 31-34).

Likewise, some texts indicate that Jesus was disappointed that Jews and Gentiles were coming to him to be healed, or to see miraculous deeds, and not to hear his good news about God (Mark 3:7-12; Matt. 4:23-25). After healing many people in Capernaum, Jesus is sought by many. Jesus said to them: "I must preach the good news of the Kingdom of God to the other cities also; for I was sent for this purpose" (Luke 4:43).

First-century Jewish culture and traditions, and especially the adoration of Jesus, enabled healing to occur (cf. also the reference to the man who exorcised in Jesus' name; Mark 9:38). Some Jews believed the cosmos was inhabited by angels and demons (*Ant* 8.46-48; *Testament of Solomon*); this fact is illustrated by the references to exorcisms in some Dead Sea Scrolls (*Genesis Apocryphon, A Liturgy for Healing the Stricken* [11Q11], *Songs of the Master* [4Q510-11]). Some Jews contended that the latter days (the eschatological end of time) is characterized by miraculous healings (cf. *Jubilees* 23 and *Messianic Apocalypse* [5Q521]). Some contemporaries of Jesus believed that God did heal the sick, either directly or indirectly. Hence, sick persons who believed that Jesus, the quintessential charismatic (as Weber showed), could heal them. Why? Many of Jesus' contemporaries, and most likely Jesus also, imagined that the healings that accompanied his ministry signaled the dawning of God's Rule, the Kingdom of God, and the appearance of the end-time.

In assessing these traditions about Jesus' miraculous healings, we should not imagine that the author of our sources assumed a distinct category of divine action that can be called "a miracle" (cf. Eve, *The Jewish Context of Jesus' Miracles*, p. 244). Likewise, a miracle did not mean breaking some putative law of nature; this is a modern concept. As Aquinas and Augustine demonstrated, a miracle revealed God's present power (see H. van der Loos, *The Miracles of Jesus*, pp. 34-39).

In comprehending the importance of healing miracles in Jesus' life and mission, we should hold in balance two perspectives. On the one hand, in Jewish sources, especially Josephus, Rabbinics, and the Pseudepigrapha (esp. *Test. Sol.*), miracles are attributed to holy men (*ḥsid*). This fact indicates that the historical Jesus should be conceived within the categories of holiness.

On the other hand, the Righteous Teacher of Qumran and Hillel the Elder—both of whom were considered men of exceptional power and holiness—never performed miracles and were not heralded as miracle workers. John the Baptizer, despite his significance and prominence, was not remembered as having performed miracles. While some parallels can be found to Jesus' healing miracles, we should not forget that this aspect of his life was something unusual and, at least to many Jews, signaled God's power breaking into present history.

Jesus' Family and His Relation to Mary Magdalene

When we observe that the Baptizer was related to Jesus, we might question to what degree the Palestinian Jesus Movement was a family movement. His mother and his brothers go with him to Capernaum (John 2:12). Jesus' brothers seem important in this new Jewish movement (John 2:12; 7:3, 10; 20:17; 21:23; 1 Cor. 9:5). Jesus' brother James is reputed to have seen the resurrected Jesus (1 Cor. 15). Jude is Jesus' brother (Mark 6:3), and some scholars conclude that parts of the Epistle of Jude may derive from him.

Early church traditions add more information about Jesus' family. At least the first two bishops of Jerusalem are Jesus' relatives: James and Symeon (Eusebius, *HE* 4.5.3-4; 5.12.1-2; and Epiphanius, *Pan* 66.21-22). Symeon (Simon) was the son of Clopas. The latter and his wife seem involved in the Palestinian Jesus Movement, and he is reputed to have been Jesus' cousin (cf. Hegesippus

[Eusebius, *HE* 4.22]). Hegesippus also reported that Jude's grandsons (or sons), Zoker and James, were the head of the Jesus Movement during the time of the Emperor Domitian (Eusebius, *HE* 3.17-18). Early traditions outside the New Testament contain the report that Judas Thomas was Jesus' twin brother (*Acts of Thomas* and *Book of Thomas*), and some scholars contend that Jude, Jesus' brother, is the Apostle Thomas (H. Koester).

The Palestinian Jesus Movement was also characterized by martyrdoms. Within the Jesus Clan are the martyrdoms of the Baptizer, Jesus, and James (Jesus' brother), as well as Symeon. Zoker and James were released by Domitian because they were simple folk. During the persecution of Christians by the Emperor Decius (250–51), a certain Conon claimed to be from Nazareth and to belong to Jesus' family (*Acts of Conon* [ed. H. Musurillo in 1972]). Outside the family clan are Stephen, Peter, and Paul, and others not recorded or mirrored in the New Testament. Discipleship was costly, as Dietrich Bonhoeffer urged, and as recorded as a Jesus saying by Mark: "If any want to become my followers, let them deny themselves and take up their cross and follow me" (Mark 8:34 NRSV).

Was Jesus married? Clearly, there is no proof in the Gospels that Jesus was married. Many Christians would stress that Jesus could not have been married because he was divine.

New Testament theologians would point out that perhaps Jesus' marriage might have been suppressed by the claim that he was the bridegroom of the community he was forming with God's help (John 3:29; Matt. 9:15; 25:1-13). The historian and sociologist might stress that since almost all Jews were married, and Jesus was a devout Jew, he was most likely married (see Phipps).

If there is a text that might have once mentioned Jesus' marriage, it could be the wedding at Cana (John 2). Jesus' mother is present and has authority, suggesting one of her children is being married. Jesus seems oblivious to the fact that the celebration is about to become an embarrassment, since the wine has been exhausted. Why did he not observe this fact? Why does Jesus' mother remain anonymous? Why does she have to instruct the servants to obey him? Why is Jesus portrayed so poorly in this story?

Who is the bridegroom? Why is the bridegroom (and bride) not identified? Why is the bridegroom scolded for what Jesus has done?

Why is the story so edited that even Jesus' brothers are removed from the scene? They must have been present, since they leave the wedding and Cana with Jesus (2:12). Before its editing by the Evangelist, the story of the marriage at Cana may have preserved a tradition that Jesus was being married. The Fourth Evangelist most likely would have edited this tradition to make the point that Jesus is the bridegroom of the new community being formed (John 3:29). It is also possible that a brother or sister of Jesus is the one being married in Cana.

Some Christian theologians would consider it blasphemous to consider Jesus was married. Other Christian theologians would claim the failure to explore such possibilities reflects Docetism, the heretical belief that Jesus only "appeared" to be human but was actually a being of celestial substance (cf. *The Acts of John*). Biblical theologians might urge us to ponder this question: If Jesus were not married, did he break the first commandment in the Bible: "So God created humankind in his image ... God blessed them, and God said to them, 'Be fruitful and multiply ...'" (Gen. 1:27-28)?

Jesus leaves Nazareth and Cana. He goes to Capernaum with his mother, brothers, and disciples (John 2:12). There he begins a ministry to help his fellow Jews and to proclaim the good news from God that God's Rule (the Kingdom of God) is beginning to break into the present (see chap. 8).

Conclusion

This chapter focused on three questions.

14) *Was John the Baptizer Jesus' teacher?* We saw reasons why the answer is probably yes.

15) *Was Jesus married to Mary Magdalene?* There is no evidence in the New Testament that Jesus was married; but such evidence could well have been edited out of his story. Such information would be irrelevant for the kerygma and might have been too obvious for his followers. As a faithful Jew, he might have been married, as were almost all Jews.

Jesus may not have had a father to help with the needs of marrying, and he may have been too preoccupied with performing the tasks that he felt were necessary to proclaim and prepare for God's coming Rule. He may have been intimate with Mary Magdalene, but that could be purely spiritual. She may have been attracted to him because of spiritual reasons, if we can trust the New Testament. It is conceivable that the wedding at Cana may have once preserved a wedding of one of Jesus' relatives, perhaps his own; but we can never know since the account is so heavily edited to bear the message of the Fourth Evangelist.

16) *Did Jesus perform miracles?* Yes, the literary form of these accounts, along with the criteria of multiple attestation and polemical ambience, indicates that none of Jesus' contemporaries seems to have doubted that he was able to and did perform healing miracles. His opponents did not deny that Jesus performed miracles; they judged that he did so because he was in league with Satan (Beelzebub). Josephus also reports that Jesus performed miracles.

That Jesus performed miracles—and especially on the Sabbath—caused him to be feared by some priests in authority. Why? Most likely, these priests knew that such actions challenged their authority and were performed on the Sabbath against the rules that they had developed recently in Jerusalem. The leaders in Jerusalem would be hostile to any person with charismatic bearing and an enthused following. Obviously, some regional tension between Lower Galilee and Judea helped lead to the problems Jesus encountered in Judea (cf. Mark 14:70; John 7:52). Many of those in authority in Judea, like the Hasmoneans earlier, felt the Galileans were inferior to Judeans (recall how Simon, the Hasmonean, took Galilean Jews to Judea [1 Macc. 5:23] and how King Aristobulus conquered the region [*Ant* 13]). That regional tension had festered for a thousand years before the first century C.E.; it probably even antedated the division of the Land into Israel of the north, and Judea of the south, in the tenth century B.C.E. (even though archaeological research reveals almost total abandonment of Galilee after the eighth century B.C.E.). It is wise to ponder to what degree Jesus' message was shaped by such old Israelite traditions.

CHAPTER 7

Jesus and Archaeology

17) How and in what significant ways is archaeology important for Jesus Research?

18) What are the most important archaeological discoveries for Jesus Research?

19) Was Jesus a peasant?

Caveats and Proper Perception

At the outset, it seems imperative to clarify some caveats and the proper perception of the purpose of archaeology for Jesus Research. These two disciplines have been sadly divorced from each other.

Those dedicated to Jesus Research have tended to avoid archaeology for four main reasons. First, Jesus Research is practiced by scholars trained in the New Testament and theology, but archaeologists are scientists trained to excavate the remains of ancient civilizations. Second, the study of the historical Jesus has often been connected since 1835, at least, with an attempt to comprehend the man who has generated faith in him; but archaeologists are not trying to find a foundation for faith. Third, Jesus Research and archaeology are based on entirely different methodologies. The former is focused on texts and is fundamentally exegetical; the latter is focused on balks, pits, and stratifications left by generations of people who lived, and left objects for interpretation, at a specific site. Fourth, entirely different questions are being asked. Experts in Jesus Research ask one focused question: what can be known historically about Jesus? Archaeologists sift debris from the past and ask this question: how do these remains from the past help us reconstruct the lives and cultures of those who lived here?

Frequently, too much is asked of archaeology and the archaeologists. Journalists have misrepresented their work, claiming that a new find shores up the Bible—as if sacred scriptures need any such support.

Archaeologists should not be expected to provide answers to the questions usually arising when thinking about the historical Jesus. They can clarify the setting in which Jesus lived and in which his thought developed, often providing manuscripts or inscriptions that reveal the precise meaning of a word in the New Testament that has bewitched specialists. They can supply an invaluable service: improving necessary historical speculations and imaginations so that Jesus' life and thought are shaped not by modern experiences and perceptions, but according to life and thought in Galilee and Judea before 70 C.E. Archaeology does not prove faith; but while fundamentally indifferent to faith, it may improve faith (see *AF*).

If interpretation of texts must be defined by contexts, then archaeology is fundamental in Jesus Research (see *Archaeology*). Only archaeologists can display the sociological contexts of the New Testament texts. Scholars expert in Jesus Research begin with texts that point to a man who left the hills of Lower Galilee and eventually entered world history. Archaeologists begin with picks and move to trowels and light brushes; they demonstrate, if unintentionally, that much of the story in the Gospels is not narrative created for theology. They reveal real places and objects that shift the perception of those dedicated to Jesus Research from a myopic focus on Greek texts to their original Semitic contexts.

Recent Archaeological Discoveries Imperative for Jesus Research

After 1967, Israeli archaeologists began to excavate Jerusalem in a professional and systematic way. The burning of the Temple in the first century became evident to me as a young scholar living in Jerusalem. I was able to scoop up tiny charred timbers from the conflagration of 70 C.E. and place them in a jar. The burning of the Temple is no longer only a story one confronts in Josephus and the New Testament.

The Huldah Gates in Herod's southern retaining wall of the Temple Mount were identified, and the pre-70 monumental steps leading up to the Temple are now exposed. One can now graphically imagine how Jesus and his disciples entered the Temple. Nearby pre-70 *mikvaot* were identified. As a devout Jew, Jesus most likely purified himself in one, or more, of these before he went up into the Temple to pray, worship, or teach.

Greek inscriptions from the Temple had been recovered before 1967. These warned *Goi* (non-Jews) not to proceed further into the Temple. On the western upper hill, the remains of a woman's arm were found. She died in a palatial dwelling in the Upper City. The house had belonged to a famous priestly family named Kathros. The Rabbinic references to the unjust weights used by this priestly family (t*Minhot* 13.21) add historical dimensions to Jesus' outrage against the money-changers in the Temple. Jews now often join with Christians in talking about corruption in some aspects of the Temple cult.

First-century sewers are now exposed and identified. Josephus described how women and children hid in them, fleeing Roman soldiers. Evidence of a massive fire is present in many rooms not seen by human eyes since 70; in one of them dark burns are obvious. Had the wall been burned by a large caldron cast over the Jerusalem walls by a Roman catapult? Evidence of conflagration marred once elegant mosaics. Archaeologists uncovered a floor with charred timbers that seemed to be smoldering two thousand years later. Jesus' prediction of such destruction in Mark 13 is certainly edited Jesus traditions, but he most likely felt those who wanted to fight against the Romans would bring disaster.

Within the walls of Old Jerusalem, the debris left from the first Jewish War

(66–70 C.E.) sealed an ancient world. Beneath the thick layer of destruction lay a world long lost. In this hermetically sealed time capsule were traces of the Jewish culture that Jesus knew. What shaped his mind and life could now be seen; and it could be touched. We were invited now, for the first time in two thousand years, to enter a world that we could not have previously imagined. It was the world Jesus had known.

What was recovered? How do archaeological discoveries help us reconstruct Jesus' world and improve our understanding of his life and message?

Realia (Real Objects) from Jesus' Time and the Culture He Knew

Realia from the time of Jesus have been recovered in Jerusalem, Jericho, Qumran, desert caves, Masada, Caesarea Maritima, Caesarea Philippi, and throughout Lower Galilee. Among the most impressive pre-70 *realia* for Jesus Research are the following (most of them have been published):

bronze tweezers

bronze Jewish coins

wine amphorae

wooden furniture

bronze and marble statues

marble busts

wooden combs

bronze spoons and ladles

oil fillers of various sizes

clay cooking pots, bowls, and cups

hand-mills for grinding grain

remains of dates and wheat

glass vessels and *unguentaria*

iron-studded sledges

fish hooks

a wooden boat

wooden and bronze plows

remains of ovens

olive presses and stone weights

paved streets

a woman's black-braided hair

nails from sandals

loom weights

alabaster and clay inkwells

bronze lion-faced chest clasps

inscriptions

ossuaries with bones

bronze and iron swords

stone ballistic missiles

charred timbers

layers of ash

gold, silver, and bronze Roman coins

a gold cube

elegant cooking ware (*terra siglatta*)

elegant mosaic floors with decorations

stone pillars with capitals

gold, silver, and bronze jewelry

wooden cosmetic bowls and dishes

bronze and clay lamps of various sizes

iron and bronze cooking pots

bronze and iron arrowheads

bronze incense shovels

menorahs inscribed on various objects

stone dice

wooden comb-rakes for harvesting

weights for a fishing net

stone and lead anchors

a wooden broom or rake

remains of pottery kilns

oil presses

walls and gates

leather sandals

bathhouses

woven cloth for clothes

bone styluses

leather, papyri, and copper scrolls

shards with the alphabet

mikvaot (ritual cleansing baths)

iron and bronze knives and sickles

bronze spear points

blackened walls where a fire bomb hit

stone tables, bowls, and cups

Our Gospels are texts that need a context; hence, these *realia* from Jesus' time help us understand his culture and the contextuality of the "texts" that derive, somehow, from him. We now can see what was in Jesus' mind when he mentioned a sword; it was made of bronze or iron. We can see the type of silver and bronze coins he mentioned but never described. We can hold lamps and vessels for replenishing the oil in the lamps.

The recovery of stone vessels—demanded by the "new" Jewish laws for keeping the contents pure and/or the Jewish rites of purification—along with the numerous *mikvaot* defines a historical and sociological context. Some powerful priests in Jerusalem were raising the standards of purity, extending to all Jews the purity standards that for centuries had been preserved for priests, and constructing barriers within Judaism among all strata of society. Recall that Jesus' instruction regarding purity had been prompted by hostile charges brought by Pharisees and scribes "who had come from Jerusalem" to entrap him (Mark 7:1).

The *mikvaot* remind us of the exaggerated importance devoted to being pure, a preoccupation that often began to mar Early Judaism during Jesus' time. The *mikvaot* and the stone vessels—both now found not only in Jerusalem but in Lower Galilee where Jesus taught—stimulate us to ponder Jesus' concept of purity.

What makes one defiled or impure? Many Jews now join Christians in seeing the wisdom in Jesus' teaching that impurity is not preoccupation with obtaining stone vessels or building *mikvaot* so as to keep oneself "pure." Impurity is defined by what is within oneself; hence, what comes out of a person: "Hear me, all of you, and understand: there is nothing outside a man which by going into him can defile him; but the things which come out of a man are what defile him" (Mark 7:14 RSV).

Physical Descriptions in the Gospels and Archaeology

Houses. In Capernaum, houses from Jesus' time have been unearthed. The walls are too thin to support tile roofs. Evidence of wooden beams proves that the roofs were thatched. Thus, far more reliable is Mark's account than Luke's alteration of a well-known story. Mark describes how four men removed the roof and then lowered their sick friend down to Jesus to be healed (Mark 2:1-12). Luke describes the house incorrectly, adding that men went up on the roof and let down the paralyzed man "through the tiles" of the roof (Luke 5:19). There were tiles in Jerusalem, Rome, and Pompeii, but not in Capernaum. Archaeological research in Capernaum brings us into Jesus' own world and helps us to image the stories of his life and teaching.

Sleeping quarters. The houses in Capernaum had only one bedroom. That means all members of a family slept in the same room and perhaps in the same bed. Anthropologists and sociologists will point out the lack of privacy in such a bedroom, and the likelihood that sometimes one awoke to find that an elderly relative had died in the night. Archaeological discoveries about sleeping quarters remind us of the story of Enoch who had been "sleeping together with" his grandfather (*1 En.* 83:6). We finally may imagine Jesus' advice that the final day will dawn with two being in one bed (Luke 17:34), and the reference to a person who is awakened at midnight and has been sleeping in bed with his children (Luke 11:7). Our interpretation of Jesus' message needs to be informed by images of his own time and not in light of houses today with four bedrooms.

A wooden fishing boat. A wooden boat, found in the mud on the western shores of the Sea of Galilee, dates from Jesus' time. The boat was designed for fishing. The top of the sides was precariously close to the water level, but this design made it easy for fishermen to cast and retrieve nets. Studying this boat reminds us of the danger of sinking from the storms that suddenly arise on the Sea of Galilee. Again, we have a better context to understand a text: "And a great storm of wind arose, and the waves beat into the boat, so that the boat was already filling. But he [Jesus] was in the stern, asleep on the cushion; and they woke him and said to him, 'Teacher, do you not care if we perish?' " (Mark 4:37-38 RSV).

Tombs. The Evangelists describe the tomb in which Jesus' corpse was placed. The tomb had a large stone that would roll in front of the entrance to seal it. First-century tombs with rolling stones in place (*in situ*) can be seen outside the present walls of Jerusalem. Standing above these tombs and peering past the stone that is moved to the side of the entrance, one can image the Beloved Disciple bending down and looking inside Jesus' tomb (John 20:4-5).

Bathhouses. Bathhouses from Jesus' time have been found in ancient Palestine. These often have a courtyard (*palaestra*), dressing room (*apodyterium*), cold-water room (*frigidarium*), warm-water room (*tepidarium*), and steam room (*caldarium*). Remains of mosaics and stucco, even frescoes, indicate opulence (esp. at Herod's Masada and the Herodian villa called Ramat Hanadiv). A bronze scraper (*strigilis*) found in or near Jerusalem helps us imagine how a gladiator, and others, would pour oil on the skin and with the *strigilis* remove sweat and dirt, thus providing some cleansing before the discovery of soap.

Archaeologists have revealed extremely elaborate homes and rooms in Upper Jerusalem, the slope west of the Temple, as well as monumental staircases and bridges into the Temple. The evidence of such wealth brings to mind the gulf between the affluent and the poor, who usually leave no traces. We hear with more informed imagination Jesus' prophecy that we shall always have the poor with us (Mark 14:7).

Synagogues. The Gospels contain numerous references to Jesus' teaching in synagogues in many villages of Lower Galilee: "And he went throughout all Galilee, preaching in their synagogues and casting out demons" (Mark 1:39). While remains of pre-70 synagogues have been discovered in Judea in Masada and the Herodium, and in the Golan at Gamla, no building that is a pre-70 synagogue has been found in Galilee. Many scholars have concluded, perhaps prematurely, that synagogues before 70 in Galilee were not buildings designed as synagogues. They were simply houses in which Jews gathered together (the meaning of the Greek *synagogos*). On the one hand, we must not think about Jesus teaching in a basilica like the white-marble late fifth-century synagogue in Capernaum. On the other hand, Jesus taught in houses, in the open fields, beside the lake, and perhaps in buildings that were built to be synagogues. The Theodotus inscription as well as a reference to repairing a synagogue proves that in some places, during the time of Jesus, a synagogue was a building designed as a synagogue (see Kloppenborg in *Archaeology*).

Pagan temples. Romans and members of the Herodian Dynasty built pagan shrines and temples in Palestine during Jesus' time; but they were always on the outskirts of Lower Galilee or Judea. Many of these places are not associated, according to the Gospels, with Jesus' life. No pagan temples have been found in Lower Galilee, where Jesus centered his ministry, but a temple to Augustus has been unearthed in Golan on the major road from Tyre to Damascus. Perhaps it was here, which is near "the villages of Caesarea Philippi" (Mark 8:27), that Jesus asked his disciples, "Who do men say that I am?" (Mark 8:27). If Jesus imagined he might be God's son, then the Temple of Augustus would be an ideal place to seek his disciples' understanding, since Augustus was being hailed as God's son.

Archaeology and Jesus' Deeds

According to the Gospel of John, Jesus exits the Temple in Jerusalem and sees a man who had been born blind (John 8–9). Jesus heals him and instructs him: " 'Go, wash in the pool of Siloam' (which means Sent). So he went and washed and came back seeing" (John 9:7 RSV). Too many biblical theologians have concluded that this is pure story. There is no history involved, because no Pool of Siloam from Jesus' time is known, and because Jesus is portrayed as one Sent by God by the Fourth Evangelist.

In the past few years, archaeologists have unearthed the Pool of Siloam from Jesus' time. It is the largest *mikveh* (ritual bath) found in ancient Palestine. It was a *mikveh* in which those who wished to enter the Temple, and had already bathed, would immerse themselves and become ritually pure. Most likely, when Jesus asked the blind man to "wash" in the Pool of Siloam, he was challenging the priestly interpretation of purity. According to some priests, the man would have made a *mikveh* unclean; he had spit and clay dirt on his eyes (John 9:6). Again, archaeology has provided the means to see some history in a Johannine story, and warn us not to dismiss the Gospel of John when studying the historical Jesus.

Archaeology and Jesus' Sayings: The Parables of Jesus

Numerous times I helped excavate an area of Nazareth that is about a ten-minute walk from the heart of Nazareth in Jesus' time. On the slopes of a hill, I helped discover stone fences, sloped areas for a vineyard, a wine press, and three towers. These towers perplexed each of us who was excavating the area. Now, for the first time, we know that vineyards beside Nazareth had stone fences (created by a craftsman [a *tektōn*]), wine presses, and even towers. A well-known parable and what were assumed to be unnecessary details bring us into the world known by Jesus and his followers: "And he began to speak to them in parables. 'A man planted a vineyard, and set a hedge [a stone wall] around it, and dug a pit for the wine press, and built a tower'" (Mark 12:1). The details are impressive and suggest that this parable may derive from one who was an eyewitness and may have heard the parable. Archaeological excavations in Nazareth help provide the context of a text and remind us that apparently irrelevant details, such as a tower in a vineyard, may be meaningless to us but were probably meaningful to those who heard Jesus' parable. Once again, we should be more reluctant to dismiss the importance of eyewitnesses behind the edited Gospel texts.

The Passion of Jesus and Archaeology

Jesus' Passion (his last week of suffering) concludes Jesus' earthly life. It begins just before he enters Jerusalem, on Sunday; it ends when he is buried, on Friday. This story is one of the most historical accounts. It is well attested (multiple attestation), it is full of details that were embarrassing to Jesus' followers, and it recounts events that were publicly observed by many in Jerusalem, including those who heard Peter's speeches after 30.

Nineteen events are found in Mark's chronology of these events:

1) 10:32: Jesus and the disciples are "on the road, going up to Jerusalem."

2) 10:35-37: James and John, the sons of Zebedee, ask to sit beside Jesus in seats of honor when God establishes his Rule.

3) 10:46-52: Jesus' group ascends from Jericho to Jerusalem.

4) 11:1-10: Jesus' triumphal entry into Jerusalem (Palm Sunday).

5) 11:15-19: The cleansing of the Temple.

Jesus' death is sought by the chief priests and the scribes.

Crowds were "astonished by his teaching."

Jesus and his group "leave the city" (perhaps to go to Bethany; cf. 11:11).

6) 11:27-32: In Jerusalem and the Temple again, Jesus' authority is questioned by "the chief priests and the scribes and the elders."

7) 13:1-2: Massive stones impress Jesus' disciples: "Look, Teacher, what wonderful stones and what wonderful buildings" (massive stones are now visible); 13:2: Jesus predicts the Temple's destruction.

8) 14:1-2: Two days before the Passover (the Feast of Unleavened Bread), the chief priests and the scribes seek to arrest Jesus.

9) 14:3-9: Jesus is anointed in Bethany.

10) 14:10-11: Judas Iscariot goes to the high priests to betray Jesus.

11) 14:12-21: Jesus celebrates Passover with his disciples.

12) 14:22-26: The Last Supper and exit to the Mount of Olives.

13) 14:27-42: Peter's denial foretold and Jesus' prayer in Gethsemane.

14) 14:43-50: Jesus' arrest.

15) 14:53-65: Jesus before the high priests, elders, and scribes.

Charge against Jesus: he would destroy the Temple (does not stick).

Jesus' confession: he is the Christ, the Son of the Blessed.

The high priest declares blasphemy.

Jesus is beaten.

16) 15:1-15: The high priest's group takes Jesus to Pilate.

(Gospel of John: Annas was the father-in-law of Caiaphas, the high priest.)

17) 15:21: Simon of Cyrene, who had come from the country, the father of Alexander and Rufus, is forced to carry Jesus' cross.

18) 15:22-32: Jesus is crucified on Golgotha.

19) 15:42-47: Jesus' corpse is buried in a rock-hewn tomb. Joseph of Arimathea

seems in charge. A linen shroud is put on the corpse, and a stone is rolled before the door of the tomb.

How much history is evident in these nineteen elements in the Passion Story? How can archaeology and topography help us search for an answer to this question? Although archaeology cannot prove the history of an account, nine archaeological discoveries help indicate that places and persons mentioned and described in Jesus' Passion Narrative are not fictitious elements.

1) *Steps to the Temple.* Jesus' actions in the Temple and his altercation with the money-changers come more vividly to mind as one examines, and even walks on, the paved steps that lead up into the Temple. These steps are Herodian; that is, they were placed there sometime before 30 C.E. by the builders of Herod the Great.

2) *The Temple.* Jesus frequented the Temple and taught in the porticoes. The Temple has been destroyed, yet one can see the Temple's massive retaining walls constructed by Herod's architects. The most famous and impressive section of the retaining wall is the Wailing Wall where Jews now congregate daily to bewail the loss of the Temple.

3) *Pilate inscription.* The historicity of Pilate was never doubted by experts. Now his title is clear, despite the misrepresentations found in Josephus. A stone inscription found in Caesarea Maritima mentions "Pontius Pilate" and his title: *prefectus* (that is, prefect).

4) *Caiaphas ossuary.* Caiaphas was appointed high priest by Valerius Gratus (15–26). Caiaphas served as high priest for nineteen years (18–36), and must have been able to achieve remarkable compromises with the Romans, since most high priests barely lasted one year (including the three just before Caiaphas). He is the high priest who condemned Jesus and sent him to Pilate (John 18:13). His family's tomb and an ossuary bearing his name, Joseph Caiaphas, were found south of Jerusalem's southern walls.

5) *Annas's tomb.* Annas ben Seth (Ananus) was appointed by Quirinius, and served as high priest from 6 to 15 C.E. He was the father-in-law of Caiaphas (John 18:13). Annas's elegant tomb has been identified south of Jerusalem's Dung Gate.

6) *Remains of a crucified man.* The heel of a Jew named Jehoḥanan was found in a tomb north of Old Jerusalem. He had been crucified about the time of Jesus' crucifixion. The spike remains attached to his ankle with parts of the plaque that held him firmly to the wooden cross. An examination of the bones brings poignantly to mind the horrors of crucifixion.

Jehoḥanan's bones had been collected and placed in an ossuary (a bone box). This discovery also proves that one who had been crucified could have received an honorable burial, and not been thrown into a quagmire, as too many have claimed over the centuries. Archaeological research has shown that Jesus' burial, as described in the Gospels, follows Jewish customs. He was buried before sunset on the day he died, he was wrapped in a linen garment, and he was placed in a tomb cut out of rock with a stone rolled in front of it (similar tombs are visible outside the walls of Jerusalem).

7) *Ossuary of Simon of Cyrene.* An ossuary, from the time of Jesus, bears the names of Simon and Alexander. It was found in a tomb characterized by names unfamiliar to Jews living in Jerusalem; but they are familiar to those in Cyrene,

North Africa. Archaeological research indicates that this ossuary may have once held the bones of the man who carried Jesus' cross and those of his son. At least the son was probably known to Mark and his community: "And they forced a passer-by, Simon of Cyrene, the father of Alexander and Rufus, having come from the field, to carry his cross" (Mark 15:21). Since the Evangelist Mark identifies Simon of Cyrene as "the father of Alexander and Rufus," it is likely these men were known to Mark and those for whom he directed his Gospel. Perhaps the ossuary of Simon and Alexander has been recovered.

8) *Golgotha: the rock that was rejected.* Archaeologists have discovered that Golgotha, the massive stone outcropping inside the Church of the Holy Sepulcher, was outside Jerusalem in 30 C.E., but within it by 44 C.E. It is a fist of stone that was rejected by those who quarried this area during the seventh century B.C.E. Centuries later, most likely the site had become a garden on the main road leading into Jerusalem from Jaffa. Most experts conclude that this stone is indeed Golgotha. Since crucifixions were always outside the walls, the tradition that Jesus was crucified on this massive stone most likely antedates 44 when it was incorporated within Jerusalem's walls. Recall the tradition in Hebrews: "So Jesus also suffered outside the gate" (Heb. 13:12). One now might read the early kerygma with a new perspective. Before the high priestly family, including Annas and Caiaphas, Peter is reputed to have claimed:

> Rulers of the people and elders ... be it known to all of you, and to all the people of Israel, that ... Jesus Christ of Nazareth, whom you crucified, whom God raised from the dead, ... This [Jesus] is the stone which was rejected by you builders, but which has become the head of the corner [Ps. 118:22]. And there is salvation in no one else. (Acts 4:8-12)

9) *A tomb with a rolling stone.* A tomb alleged to belong to Herod's family is located on the slopes of the Hinnom Valley to the west of Jerusalem's walls. Most impressive is the stone situated in a chiseled slot. One can easily imagine how the round stone could be rolled to close the entrance of the tomb. Other pre-70 tombs around Jerusalem also fit the description of Jesus' tomb.

Many who study these nine aspects of Jesus' Passion are amazed how much archaeology has helped clarify the history in the story. Pilate, Caiaphas, Annas, the remains of a crucified man, Simon and his son, the place of Golgotha, and tombs with rolling stones are not simply fictional aspects of an ancient story.

Now, we know with some certainty what are the historical elements in Jesus' Passion. They are as follows:

- Envoys sent out from Jerusalem probably spied on Jesus.
- Some of Jesus' Twelve expected a messianic revolution.
- Jesus' entrance into Jerusalem with crowds aroused concern among all who were entrusted with peace in Jerusalem.
- Jesus' action in the Temple sealed his fate.
- Caiaphas and Annas probably questioned him.
- Pilate condemned Jesus to be crucified.
- Simon of Cyrene carried Jesus' cross after that became impossible for Jesus.

93

• Roman soldiers completed the crucifixion at Golgotha.
• Jesus died before the beginning of the Sabbath.

Archaeology and So-called Peasantry in Lower Galilee

Many scholars who are specialists in Jesus Research concur that Jesus was a peasant. Some of them are influenced by J. D. Crossan, who wrote a major book, *The Historical Jesus: The Life of a Mediterranean Jewish Peasant* (1991).

To presume that one can talk about a "Mediterranean peasant" is misleading. First, not one but many cultures were defined by the Mediterranean. Second, archaeological work in Lower Galilee reveals only two cities—Jotapata and Gamla—that permit us to talk about the economic stratification of pre-70 Galilean society. Neither suggests that we should imagine peasants. Far better is the concept of farmers. If Jesus had been a carpenter, as Mark 6:3 indicates, then he was not a peasant. Today, a "peasant" denotes one who is impoverished; originally, in fifteenth-century France (*paisant* is the origin of "peasant") the term "peasant" denoted one who worked the countryside, and then the term was related to Feudalism.

Many Jesus Research Scholars rightly now shun the assumption that Jesus was poor. No Gospel clarifies Jesus' economic status, but he is never portrayed working for a living, and his family is not depicted as impoverished. Jesus must have enjoyed free time to study and think. That would mean he did not exhaust himself laboring in the field or fishing on the Sea of Galilee.

Is it a remnant of Romanticism to imagine that Jesus was a peasant? None of Jesus' Twelve were peasants or poor. Some were almost wealthy, including Matthew, Peter, Judas, and the sons of Zebedee (remember that Zebedee had two grown sons and at least two hired fishermen). It thus does not seem wise to portray the historical Jesus as a peasant. In contemplating Jesus' life, especially his youth, it is best not to label him a peasant.

Conclusion

How then does archaeology clarify our perception of the historical Jesus? Excavations help us imagine Jesus in first-century settings like Capernaum, since buildings and streets from his time have been excavated. The walls of the buildings would most likely support only thatched rooms, as indicated by Mark (chap. 2), so Luke incorrectly imagined tiled roofs in Capernaum (chap. 5).

Archaeological research has revealed *mikvaot* and stone vessels. Almost always these begin just before Jesus was born and disappear about 70 C.E. These indicate a growing preoccupation with purity and impurity and make apparent that only the wealthy could afford such architectural features or elaborate stone vessels for holding grain. These features of Jewish life before 70 help us understand Jesus' concerted efforts to combat the ever increasing rules for purification that he and his contemporaries experienced.

Archaeologists have provided data for imagining Jesus' thought and parables. Past errors of interpretation can be corrected. For example, the Parable of the

Young Women (Matt. 25) comes to life when we no longer imagine that Jesus is referring to a lamp like one associated with Ben Franklin, which could supply light for ten hours, and perceive Jesus' reference to a small lamp, which could produce light for less than an hour. We can also avoid referring to a "flask," which often denotes a whiskey flask, and imagine an oil filler that would enable a young woman to replenish her lamp and avoid being in the dark.

Most important, archaeology provides the context for texts, without which a passage can mean whatever a reader might want or nothing at all. This method, which includes the recovery of pre-70 scrolls, provides the best avenue for entering into the world of Second Temple Judaism. The pure literary approach to the historical Jesus becomes corrected with reminders of life lived long ago.

Three questions were the focus of this chapter. Let us now see how they might be answered. We have observed that archaeology is imperative in helping us to perceive the context of Jesus' life and thought. Perhaps the most important archaeological discoveries pertain to the Passion Narrative, since numerous discoveries indicate the historicity of the main players and places in that account. Since archaeology does not disclose evidence of peasants in Lower Galilee, it is unwise to assume, or to perpetuate, the idea that Jesus was a peasant. Finally, archaeology cannot prove the accuracy of historical accounts; it can, however, enlighten our reflections upon them. Archaeology is essential for attempts to reconstruct Jesus' time and his own life and thought.

CHAPTER 8

Jesus' Proclamation of God's Rule (the Kingdom of God) and His Parables

20) What was Jesus' fundamental message?

21) When did Jesus imagine God would inaugurate his Rule?

22) What term did Jesus use for God?

Jesus' Fundamental Message

It has become clear to the leading scholars that Jesus thought his primary mission was to declare the coming Kingdom of God or, better, God's Rule. In "The Eschatology of Jesus," Dale C. Allison astutely reports: "Indeed, many are convinced that much of Jesus' message can be fairly characterized as apocalyptic eschatology" (*Encyclopedia of Apocalypticism* I, p. 267). As we shall soon see, that does not mean, as some theologians fear, wanting solutions to preoccupying concerns, that Jesus taught an imminent eschatology.

Jesus inherited some of his thought and the urgency of the day from his teacher, John the Baptizer; and both of them lived within the world of Judaism that produced the major apocalypses, namely, *1 Enoch, 2 Baruch,* and *4 Baruch.* Jesus imagined God's Rule as breaking into the present; hence, for him, the primary task is to prepare for God's Day and God's Rule.

The Evangelist Mark presents his summary of Jesus' message. Most scholars rightly judge that Mark, who may represent Peter's eyewitness, has accurately summarized, in his own language, Jesus' central message: "And after John [the Baptizer] had been arrested, Jesus came into Galilee, proclaiming the Good News from God, and saying, 'The time has been fulfilled, and God's Rule has come close. Repent, and believe the Good News'" (Mark 1:14-15).

How Do We Know That Jesus' Fundamental Message Is the Dawning of God's Rule?

Five methods help us see that Jesus' major task was to proclaim God and God's coming Rule. (1) *Multiple attestation:* almost all sources of Jesus' sayings independently report that he proclaimed the coming of God's Rule (e.g., Mk, J, Q, M, L). Jesus' claim that God's Rule is coming is also indicated by its appearance in multiple forms (esp. in the Lord's Prayer, dominical sayings, and parables).

(2) *Coherence:* Jesus' proclamation of God's Rule coheres with what we have learned already about him. For example, he refused to be categorized as a miracle worker and claimed to be the Proclaimer of God's Rule. (3) *Theocentric:* the authenticity of Jesus' Kingdom of God proclamations is typical of him and distinct from his followers' more Christocentric perspective. (4) *Jesus' Jewishness:* Jesus, as a faithful and devout Jew, focused on God and God's Rule; this idea appears in Aramaic (*mlkwt' d'lh* means Kingdom of God or, better, God's Rule). (5) *Ripple effect:* remember how expanding and concentric ripples lead back to one spot where a rock had been cast into the water? Likewise, all evolving Jesus traditions point back to Jesus as the one who proclaimed God's Rule.

How Unique Is Jesus' Fundamental Message?

New Testament scholars (e.g., N. Perrin) have claimed that the concept of God's Rule (or the Kingdom of God) was not found within Judaism; hence, the thought was unique to Jesus. These scholars were not adequately informed of early Jewish thought. God's Rule (or the Kingdom of God) appears in numerous Jewish documents that antedate Jesus (see *ANRW* 25.1 [1982]: 451-76). For example, the expression "the kingdom of our God" is found in a pre-70 Jewish hymnbook that was composed in Jerusalem:

> Lord, you are our king forevermore,
> for in you, O God, does our soul take pride.
> How long is the time of a person's life on the earth?
> As is his time, so also is his hope in him.
> But we hope in God our savior,
> for the strength of our God is forever with mercy.
> And the kingdom of our God is forever over the
> nations in judgment. (*Pss. Sol.* 17:1-4; Wright in *OTP* 2:665)

This Jew, roughly contemporaneous with Jesus, shared a hope associated with Jesus. It was in "God our savior." He will bring in "the kingdom of our God," and it will last "forever."

The Time of the Coming of God's Kingdom

The key question about Jesus' proclamation of the coming of God's Rule concerns the time of this cataclysmic event. In *The Quest of the Historical Jesus* (originally published in German in 1906), Albert Schweitzer argued that Jesus stressed a thoroughgoing eschatology. Jesus looked to the future for God's Rule. In *The Parables of the Kingdom* (1935), C. H. Dodd argued that Jesus held a "realized eschatology"; that is, Jesus believed that God's Rule had dawned in his own time. Dodd later lamented he had coined a misleading term; eschatology cannot be "realized" in the present. A far better expression is "realizing eschatology." This brings out the verbal dynamic: God's Rule is actively dawning in the present.

M. J. Borg in *Jesus: A New Vision* concludes that Jesus' message was not eschatological. While Dodd overreacted to Schweitzer's extreme position, Borg rightly calls for a nuanced definition of *eschatology*, warning against finding a Jesus who was obsessed with a far-off future. It is apparent that *eschatology* often has not been defined or has been poorly defined.

Defining eschatology. Eschatology is composed of two Greek nouns: *eschatos,* which means "last," and *logos,* which means "reflections upon." Thus strictly speaking, eschatology would mean an understanding of the last things, the last days before the dawn of a new era, or the last times in the present age. As we know from studying the Jewish apocalypses, such as Daniel, *1 Enoch, 2 Enoch, 4 Ezra,* and *2 Baruch,* apocalyptic eschatology is often wedded with morality and Wisdom, so that the seer intends to focus on the importance of the present and being right with God.

Jesus' eschatology does not mean a preoccupation with the end of time. It does not mean a focus on what has not yet happened. As is clear in most of his parables, for Jesus, eschatology means a focus and emphasis on the present, because the time is ripe for spiritual discernment and moral responsibility. The present is the time to open eyes and see those who have been marginalized or castigated as inferior, unworthy, or impure. Thus, Jesus called for the immediate emancipation of women, *mamzerim* (those who could not prove to authorities that they are fully legitimate Jews), people with leprosy, and people who cannot walk or see or have other physical or mental disabilities.

Jesus experienced a realizing eschatology. As the dawning of a new day precedes the rising sun, so Jesus thought about the breaking into the present of God's future day. His teaching is often a mixture of realizing eschatology and futuristic eschatology (as in Qumran's *Thanksgiving Hymns*). Examples of texts that are Jewish and somewhat contemporaneous with Jesus, and embody a mixture of imminent and futuristic eschatology are the following:

> But when Rome will also rule over Egypt
> ... then indeed the most great kingdom
> of the immortal king will become manifest over men.
> (*Sib. Or.* 3.46-48 [second cent. B.C.E.]; *OTP* 1:363 [Collins])

> Then his kingdom will appear throughout his whole creation.
> Then the devil will have an end.
> Yea, sorrow will be led away with him.
> (*Test. Moses* 10:1 [first cent. C.E.]; *OTP* 1:931 [Priest])

Jesus' eschatological message fits neatly within the Judaism he knew. As B. Chilton states in *Pure Kingdom*: "In that his vision included a hope for the future, it was irreducibly eschatological" (p. 142).

Jesus' disciples misunderstood his eschatology: "They supposed that God's Rule was to appear immediately" (Luke 19:11). Jesus is portrayed correcting their misunderstanding (Luke 19:11-27), and warned that the full dawning of God's Rule would not be immediate. For example, in the Parable of the Young Women (Matt. 25), Jesus warned that his followers must be prepared to wait patiently for the arrival of the Coming One.

Did Jesus Know When the Hour of God's Rule Would Dawn?

The crucial text for answering this question is Mark 9:1. Here is my translation: "And he said to them, 'Truly, I say to you, there are some standing here who will not taste death before they see that God's Rule has come with dynamic-power [*en dunamei*].'" Apparently, Jesus thought that some of those standing beside him would not die until they saw God's Rule coming in full eschatological power. This saying is authentic to Jesus. It is *embarrassing*; Jesus is portrayed as ignorant about the time of God's Rule. The verse was edited by Matthew and Luke to remove the embarrassment; both of them rewrote the saying so that it was fulfilled in Jesus' lifetime. Mark 9:1 also is authentic to Jesus because it *coheres* with Jesus' emphasis on the urgency of the times. At times, Jesus felt that God was so close that God's Rule was imminent; note these examples:

> I watched Satan fall from heaven like a flash of lightning. (Luke 10:18)
> But if it is by God's finger that I cast out the demons,
> then God's Rule has come upon you. (Luke 11:20; cf. Matt. 12:28)

The astounding miracles surrounding Jesus' message would have convinced many that the time was pregnant for the fulfillment of God's promises. For the present purposes of an essential guide, only one other verse in Mark will be brought under the microscope. Here is another saying attributed to Jesus: "But of that day or that hour no one knows, not even the angels in heaven, nor the Son, but only the Father" (Mark 13:32).

Many New Testament scholars (e.g., Perrin, Conzelmann) concluded that this saying cannot go back to Jesus and was created by his followers. Why? They contend that the reference to "the Son" reflects the kerygma of the Palestinian Jesus Movement after 30 C.E. and is not found in Second Temple Judaism.

The New Testament experts who concluded that the concept of the Son of God must be a Christian creation did not comprehend and understand Second Temple Judaism. But the concept of son, or Son, of God is not a Christian creation. It develops out of the concept of Israel being God's firstborn son (Exod. 4; Hos. 11), and the king being enthroned as God's son (Ps. 2). This concept developed within Second Temple Judaism so that the concept of God's Son evolved (see Hengel). The term "Son of God" appears in a Qumran text. For example, note the following passage: "He will be called Son of God, and they will call him Son of the Most High. Like the sparks that you saw, so will their kingdom be" (*An Aramaic Apocalypse*; 4Q246 col. 2). According to this apocalypse, some eschatological figure will be hailed as "Son of God" and "Son of the Most High."

The major reason against the authenticity of Mark 13:32 is removed by the discovery of the concept "the Son" of God within pre-70 Judaism. Now we need to explore the next issue: is that verse authentic to Jesus?

The saying in Mark 13:32 is probably authentic for numerous reasons. (1) It *attributes ignorance to Jesus,* and this attribution is unthinkable for his followers. They would never have imagined that the Son, Jesus, did not know the day or the hour of the coming of the Son of Man "with great power and glory" and the dawning of God's Rule. (2) The saying *is also embarrassing to Jesus' followers* who preserved it; it makes Jesus ignorant. (3) The saying *fits into the thought world of Second Temple Judaism*. A passage in *4 Ezra* is crucial for understanding Mark 13:32. According to this Jewish apocalypse, composed a few decades after the burning of the Temple in 70 C.E. but preserving much pre-70 Jewish thought, Uriel, the archangel, must confess that he does not know the time (*sed nescio; 4 Ezra* 4:42). In two first-century texts, Mark and *4 Ezra,* we are told that an angel, and even an archangel, is ignorant.

Mark 13:32 seems to indicate that only God knows the time of the fulfillment of God's Rule. Jesus apparently claims that only God knows the time of the end. Such admission does not fit with the creative energies in the kerygma; but it is coherent with the many expressions of humility on the part of Jesus: "Truly, truly, I say to you, the Son by himself can do nothing, but only what he might see the Father doing" (John 5:19; cf. Q [Matt. 12:42 and Luke 11:31]).

Could both Mark 9:1 and Mark 13:32 be authentic to Jesus? Yes; we should not expect Jesus to be a systematic theologian, or one who was not human. Surely, the historian is not the only one who can imagine a first-century prophet at times thinking that God's Rule was soon to be fully present and at other times pondering that only God knows that time.

Thus, we have seen that Jesus' message is eschatological. He saw the pregnancy of the present, calling all to be prepared for God's Rule, the Kingdom of God, which was beginning to dawn in the present and at times appeared imminent to Jesus.

Jesus' Parables

Jesus' proclamation that God's Rule was imminent is characteristically expressed in parables. We shall now explore three consecutive issues: (1) the parables and Jesus' creativity, (2) defining a parable, and (3) Jesus' parables and God's Rule.

1) *The parables and Jesus' creativity.* One of the fruits of scholarly research is the conclusion that Jesus' favorite means of teaching was in parables. While parables are foreshadowed in the Old Testament (cf. 2 Sam. 12:1-7), and while parables may be present in some Jewish apocryphal works (viz., 1 *En.* 37–71; *Apocryphon of Ezekiel*) and somewhat infrequent in Rabbinics (cf. Flusser and Young), it is clear that Jesus' creativity is evident in his parables. While one has to search for parables in Rabbinics, they abound in words attributed to Jesus. He made them his major means of teaching. In Jesus' parables we find the stamp of a poetic mind that saw how major truths could be conveyed as stories that are real to human life in pre-70 Lower Galilee.

Jesus spoke in parables. They are *multiply attested* (Mk, Q, M, L, Jn [chap. 15], and *Gos. Thom.*). The kerygma of the thirties and forties is *dissimilar* to Jesus' parabolic sayings. It is not conveyed via parables; hence, one should not imagine that this form of speech was attributed to Jesus by those who did not use it. The theology and message of the parables are *coherent* with what is discerned as authentic to Jesus by other means. Thus, Jesus did not invent parabolic speech; he chose and emphasized this pictorial way of expressing his ideas; sometimes he used the parables to portray an aspect of God's Rule.

Two dangers must be avoided in studying Jesus' parables. First, some Jewish parables have been incorrectly attributed to Jesus, as in the *Apocryphon of Ezekiel*. Different forms of this document exist; one is in Rabbinics and another is in the writings of an early church scholar. Second, Matthew and Luke heavily edited Jesus' parables found in Mark (esp. in the Parable of the Banquet; cf. *Gos. Thom.* 64), so we need to be alert to the alteration of Jesus' words by all who transmitted them.

2) *Defining a parable.* Jesus' parables are stories that reflect the daily life of Galilean farmers and fishermen, housewives and poor women. These stories are deeply theological, illustrating the nature of God's Rule, and often critiquing societies' hierarchy and the attitude of those in authority (including fathers and merchants). When Jesus spoke in parables, he presented his thoughts simply, directly, imaginatively, and pictorially. Sometimes, a parable has one point of comparison. Jesus' parables are not allegories, but some have allegorical features. All in a parable is usually true to normal life and nature. The parables are works of art that invite one to enter an imagined world; they represent a remarkable realism. Jesus could have said benevolence should not be ostentatious (as C. H. Dodd wrote), yet few would have remembered such an abstract thought. So, Jesus said, "[W]hen you give alms, blow no trumpet before you" (Matt. 6:2). Jesus used language that was real, pictorial, instantly comprehensible, and easy to remember.

Many parables are attributed to Jesus by Matthew, Mark, and Luke; and some seem reflected in the Gospel of John (cf. John 15:1-8). Two parables allegedly taught by Jesus are found only in the *Gospel of Thomas*: the Empty Jar (Log. 97), which has a Palestinian ring to it, and the Powerful Man (Log. 98). These two parables may derive ultimately from Jesus; they should not be excluded from a study of Jesus' parables. Many parables in the *Gospel of Thomas* do not have the allegorical additions supplied by Matthew and Luke; hence, they may not derive from these Gospels. This "apocryphal" gospel stimulates thought on how many of Jesus' parables are permanently lost as his voice was drowned out by the silencing of traditions.

3) *Jesus' parables and God's Rule.* Jesus' major concern—the proclamation that God's Rule is now dawning—shapes some, but not all, of his parables. The Greek word *historia* gives us "history" and "story." Our history is our story. For millennia, humans have expressed the need to think in terms of narrative that focuses on their own peculiar story or history. The fundamental need of humans, after food, is to share drama and "story."

We meet ourselves when Jesus explains God's Rule by telling parables. When we listen to a parable, we are invited to enter into a world in which we imagine ourselves present. Inevitably, Jesus' pictorial imagery invites us to become involved and make a judgment that will unexpectedly include, inadvertently, a judgment on us by ourselves.

How Is Jesus' Method of Teaching Related to His Fundamental Message?

Jesus' authentic speech is pictorial. He urged his followers to pick up a cross and follow him. He warned that the log in our own eye may blind us to the speck in our friend's eye.

The parables are one of our most important sources for understanding Jesus' mind. He chose stories sometimes to declare the dawning of God's Rule. The parables represent a genius who saw abstract concepts in ordinary things. They reveal the image of one special mind. As C. H. Dodd stated, the parables "are the natural expression of a mind that sees truth in concrete pictures rather than conceives it in abstractions" (*ParablesD*, pp. 15-16).

Too often New Testament scholars forget how they began. They began recognizing Jesus' creative genius, but they end up too often denying any creativity to him.

Jesus was a genius, and he had unique thoughts. Most likely, Jesus was the greatest poetic genius in Second Temple Judaism. The confessional approach misses this historical fact. The polemical approach, which often balloons into a faith, blinds one to the fact. We must not allow the acids of critical research to leave us with an iconoclast who is both isolated from his fellow Jews and divorced from the Palestinian Jesus Movement (see Hays in *First Things*). On the one hand, Jesus was a product of his time and spoke in the language of his country. On the other hand, as with all geniuses, Jesus transcended his time and was amazingly creative.

Jesus taught his followers to imagine God's Rule with specific images derived from nature. Jesus' point is that God's dealings with humans are coherent with the way God controls nature and the cosmos. God's Rule is like a mustard seed; it begins tiny and ends large (Mark 4:30-32; *Gos. Thom.* 20). God's Rule must be received as a child would receive it, or one cannot enter it (Mark 10:13-16). It demands that one not be preoccupied about one's own future; one must be "rich for God" (Luke 12:13-21). It is like leaven that leavens the whole (Q [Matt. 13:33; Luke 13:21; *Gos. Thom.* 96]). It may be delayed, so keep your lamps full of oil so that your light does not go out in the darkness (M [Matt. 25:1-13; cf. Luke 12:35-38]). God's Rule is like a large fisherman who knew to keep only the large fish (*Gos. Thom.*). It will come when God is ready (Mark 4:26-29).

We have seen that Jesus' primary emphasis is the time when God will rule as king among his people on earth, and that sometimes Jesus used parables to clarify an aspect of God's Rule. In *Parables as Poetic Fictions,* C. W. Hedrick accurately summarizes the state of present research: "New Testament scholarship has, in the main, been quite positive about two aspects of the Jesus tradition: it affirms that the proclamation of the kingdom of God is an essential feature of the message of Jesus and that Jesus announced his message in 'parabolic' stories" (p. 7).

What does a study of Jesus' parables have to do with his eschatological views? In *The Parables,* D. O. Via points out that while the parables can offer us help in comprehending Jesus' eschatology, "more importantly, they are an independent and richer expression of the intention of his explicit eschatology" (p. 205). As D. C. Allison states: "Jesus' millenarian eschatology was, then, the revised religious story that became the context of his followers' experience" (*MillProphet*, p. 171).

Jesus' Word for God

In the Old Testament and at Qumran we find many words for God, especially *the Almighty, the Lord God,* and *Elohim.* Among the Galilean miracle workers and in Rabbinics, as well as in Jewish liturgy, we find God addressed as "Father," or *Abba.* That is Jesus' favorite word for God (see Jeremias, *Abba*).

uniqueness often resides not in a neologism; it usually is reflected in chooses and emphasizes. He chose and emphasized *Abba* as his special way of referring to God, who is creating now in time and space. This noun is used often by children, but their parents taught them to say "Abba." It does convey an intimate, close, and loving relation with the Creator. In the Garden of Gethsemane, Jesus prayed for deliverance, addressing the Infinite One as "Abba."

Jesus also taught his followers how to pray to God. He taught and showed them how to address God as "Father" (Luke) or "our Father" (Matt.). The early members of the Palestinian Jesus Movement used the word *Abba* and continued the practice of preferring this name for God. Jesus illustrated for his disciples how to focus on the "Father"—the one whose Rule defined his life and thought.

Conclusion

Jesus was inconsistent regarding the time of the coming of God's Rule. He knew and experienced the coming of God's Rule, feeling it present at times (Mark 9:1) and at other times not so far off. The consummation of God's Rule, however, and all the fulfillment of scriptural promises are unknown to him, and even to the archangels (Mark 13:32]).

We have seen that Jesus' authentic message was fundamentally eschatological. His parables and teachings, and the prayer he taught (the Lord's Prayer), contain the perspective that the present time is impregnated with the power of the end of time. Rather than draining the present of meaning, Jesus' proclamation charged the present with power and meaning. All time, past and present, was focused on the immediate present.

The attempts to understand Jesus' eschatology and discern the time of the fulfillment of God's Rule have myopically focused on the Greek New Testament text. Greek has a temporal sense of past, present, and future. Jesus perceived time in Semitic concepts: fulfilled time and unfulfilled time. Thus, Jesus imagined God's Rule as a mixture of fulfilled and unfulfilled time in the present. He could ponder a future action as fulfilled, as did the prophets when they perceived how God had completed a task that has not yet been experienced by humans (*perfectum futurum*).

Jesus was more like Aristotle than Plato. He was realistic and did not dream about another world of ideas. Jesus was thus closer to Jeremiah than to the dreamy apocalyptists. Hence, *realia* from his time and place help us connect to those who held what we can now touch: a coin of Caesar, a mustard seed, a sword, a tower in a first-century vineyard, and steps leading up into the Temple.

Now we can answer questions 20 through 22. Jesus' fundamental message was the proclamation that God's Rule was beginning to dawn during his lifetime. We have examined Jesus' conflicting comments about the time of the coming of God's Rule, suggesting that we should not portray Jesus as a consistent systematic theologian. Jesus' sayings contain tensions between a realizing eschatology and a futuristic eschatology. Jesus' favorite word for God, *Abba*, is found in pre-70 Jewish traditions and texts. As a devout Jew, Jesus emphasized that God is a loving Father who is close to those who call upon him.

Why then was Jesus crucified? Why would anyone be offended by Jesus' fundamental message and concept of Father? These questions lead us into our final chapter.

CHAPTER 9

Jesus' Crucifixion and Resurrection

*23) What led to Jesus' confrontation
with some of the leading priests?*

24) Who crucified Jesus and why?

25) Has Jesus' bone box (ossuary) been recovered?

*26) If Jesus' bones have been discovered,
is resurrection faith possible?*

27) Did Jesus rise from the dead?

We now approach the end of Jesus' life and the Passion. Why would anyone want to arrest and crucify a prophet who reputedly called on all to love one another as God loved them? J. P. Meier opined that Jesus' crucifixion by the Roman prefect is the "most central of all the enigmas" in Jesus Research (*MJ*, 3:646).

Some theologians have a clear and ready-made answer to all the above questions. Jesus suffered to fulfill scripture. He died because it was God's will that he would die. Jesus predicted that he, as the Son of Man, had come to suffer and die for the sins of the people. Evidence for this is readily at hand in the Gospels. It is a major theme of the Gospel of Mark.

New Testament theologians, however, have stressed that Jesus probably never thought he would be crucified, and the predictions of such a death, the claim that Jesus died according to God's will and to fulfill scripture, sound like the shaping of Jesus traditions by post-30 confessions and the experience of the risen Lord in the Palestinian Jesus Movement. These scholars point out that in Gethsemane Jesus asked for the "cup" to be removed from him. Historians stress that Jesus' last words were a cry of dereliction: "My God, my God, why have *you* (also) forsaken me?" (Mark 15:34). If these events are historical, they undermine the claim that Jesus wanted to suffer in order to fulfill scripture.

The disciples are lost for an explanation of Jesus' surprising death, and they express the loss of their hope. All this sounds plausible to the historian, and indicates that Jesus' predictions about his crucifixion may derive from the kerygma, especially when the predictions of his death and resurrection are couched in terms that mirror what actually happened, and most likely could not have been anticipated by Jesus (see esp. Mark 10:32-34). The predictions are thus *post eventum* statements; that is, the followers of Jesus created such narratives after 30 c.e. to explain the necessity of Jesus' horrible death. We shall begin with threads already woven into the preceding chapters.

Jesus' Confrontation with the Romans and Some Leading Priests

During his ministry in Lower Galilee, Jesus was asked many questions by scribes and Pharisees who had been *sent from* the sacerdotal aristocracy in Jerusalem (Mark 7:1-23). Tension was mounting against him from some powerful priests. There are three main reasons: (1) the concept of kingship, the proclamation of the imminent dawning of God's Rule, and his support from crowds; (2) his views on purity; and (3) claims made about him and his own high self-esteem.

1) *Jesus, the concept of kingship, and the crowds.* When Jesus was born, Herod (no descendant of David) was "the King of the Jews." After the death of Herod the Great and during Jesus' ministry, no king lived in the promised land. The Herodians as well as all priests sworn to keep peace in Israel would have reacted to Jesus' primary message: the in-breaking of the Rule of God in which God will be king. The political figures, including the influential priests, would have been even more incensed by Jesus' self-understanding. Either Jesus saw himself as the one who announced this Kingship, or he was God's representative in this new Kingdom. All political figures would have been alarmed by the many claims made by Jesus' followers that he was "the King"; for example, after he fed the five thousand, the crowds wanted to make him king (John 6:15). According to John, one of Jesus' disciples hailed him as "the King of Israel" (1:49). Jesus makes a kingly entrance into Jerusalem (Mark 11:9; Matt. 21:9; John 12:13). A crowd salutes him, casting branches on his way, and quoting a prophecy about how a mounted king would enter the Holy City:

> Rejoice greatly, Daughter Zion;
> Raise a shout, Daughter Jerusalem
> Lo, your king shall come to you.
> He is victorious, triumphant,
> Yet humble, riding on an ass,
> On a donkey foaled by a she-ass. (Zech. 9:9)

The Romans and the leading priests were no fools; they knew how to survive and to keep an eagle eye on any possible disturbances to the fragile peace in the eastern empire that was intermittently threatened by the Parthian armies. Many of these political figures would have remembered how Marcus Agrippa—and thus of the emperor's kingly family—left Jerusalem. He was hailed by the Jews, applauding and "strewing flowers" in his road (Philo, *On the Embassy to Gaius* 297). Jesus' entrance into Jerusalem was a similar demonstration.

During Jesus' triumphal entry, some would have imagined that Jesus was acting out the claim that he was the king sent by God. The Evangelists would have agreed. Before Pilate, a multitude reported that Jesus had claimed to be "Christ, a king" (Luke 23:2). Above Jesus' head was placed a plaque that declared he had been crucified because he, and his followers, claimed that he was "King of the

Jews." By this the Romans indicated that Jesus had threatened the power of the emperor and caused disturbances. Almost all in Jerusalem on that fateful Friday knew that Jesus from Nazareth had been crucified as a common criminal, a political insurrectionist.

It is clear that Jesus was accompanied by crowds. Sociologists would point out that to high priests and Roman officials, these crowds are mobs. Such scholars have stressed that the most dangerous and volatile social group is a crowd. A crowd has no tradition and no published agenda. And if the crowd has a clear leader, he (or she) is one who is energetically leading a mob and not one who is seated for discussion. The Romans did not need to read the books on the crowd that have been published by sociologists over the past fifty years; they had learned from a century of trying to control an expanding empire how dangerous, unruly, and insurrectionist is a crowd. It can become instantaneously a politically motivated mob. Perception of a crowd's danger was common coin in Hellenistic culture; for example, Philo of Alexandria referred to crowds as the "worst of evil polities" (*On the Creation* 171). According to the Gospels, Jesus was often framed by a crowd: "And when Jesus had crossed again in the boat to the other side, a large crowd gathered about him; and he was beside the sea" (Mark 5:21). Gathering crowds signaled to most authorities that Jesus could be a dangerous insurrectionist. Recall also the crowd that arrested Jesus: "And immediately, while he was still speaking Judas, one of the Twelve, came, and with him a crowd with swords and clubs" (Mark 14:43).

Did Jesus choose the Twelve? For decades I argued that the Twelve was a creation of the Palestinian Jesus Movement. I emphasized that Peter is always listed first. Then I wondered why Judas would be in that list, even in last place, if Jesus had not called into being the Twelve. That Jesus chose the Twelve to accompany him to Jerusalem now seems evident, because Judas is habitually mentioned as "one of the Twelve." Thus, Jesus most likely chose twelve men (cf. Mark 3:13-19a; Matt. 10:1-16; Luke 6:12-16; Acts 1:13). A charismatic prophet with twelve leaders may not be a crowd, but such a group would seem threatening in the volatile climate of Jesus' time and place.

When Jesus chose the Twelve, he had a political agenda, even if his revolution was primarily religious. The *Testaments of the Twelve Patriarchs* and other testaments attributed to the twelve sons of Jacob indicate the regnant importance of the Twelve Tribes of Israel. These tribes are to rule on earth when God restores the political autonomy to Israel.

I have found surprising two claims emphasized by scholars. First, they rightly point out that in Second Temple Judaism, the historian cannot distinguish between religious and political issues. Then, they continue by stressing that Jesus had no interest in politics and that his revolution was strictly religious.

It is best to be consistent. Jesus chose the Twelve; and there was some political agenda in his mind. That does not require assuming that Jesus thought about a militant Messiah (whether himself or another person). Shortly before Jesus was born, a Jew in Jerusalem authored the *Psalms of Solomon*. Under the inspiration of Isaiah 11, this Jew indicated that the Messiah will not need an army (a sword or horse); he will slay the enemies of the Jews with the sword of his mouth (*Pss. Sol.* 17:33-34). This hymnbook helps clarify that God's Messiah will be a political figure, but not necessarily a militant insurrectionist. Such nuances are required when reconstructing Jesus' intentions. He had a political agenda; but he was not imagining a military overthrow of the government. Recall a statement that probably is original to Jesus: "All who take the sword will perish by the sword" (Matt. 26:52).

Further evidence that Jesus probably imagined a political movement can be recovered. First, on the way up to Jerusalem James and John ask to sit on Jesus' right and left (Mark 10:35-37). Their request probably reveals that they expected Jesus to establish a new kingdom in which they would sit on thrones beside him.

Second, according to Luke, during the Last Supper, Jesus said to the Twelve the following:

> You are those who have continued with me in my trials; and I assign to you, as my Father assigned to me, a kingdom, that you may eat and drink at my table in my kingdom, and sit on thrones judging the twelve tribes of Israel. (Luke 22:28-30 RSV)

If any such sentiment would have leaked to the Romans and the high priestly group, they would have been convinced that Jesus was planning a coup.

Third, shortly after the crucifixion and resurrection, Jesus' disciples ask him: "Lord, will you at this time restore the kingdom to Israel?" (Acts 1:6). Fourth, in the Garden of Gethsemane, on Jesus' last night, his disciples had at least one sword. Fifth, earlier he said that two swords would be enough (Luke 22:38). Sixth, Jesus instructed his disciples to buy a sword (Luke 22:36). Seventh, he warned that he did not come to bring peace but a sword (Matt. 10:34). It is not clear whether these statements were meant metaphorically or literally; in either case they would have convinced the many powerful leaders that Jesus was leading a political movement.

While the previous statements about swords suggest a violent political movement, most of Jesus' sayings warn against a militant resistance to Rome and, most likely, should be given more prominence, especially in light of his nonviolent life. Some of these sayings of Jesus may be summarized now. First, Jesus warned that he who lives by the sword dies by the sword (Matt. 26:52). Second, he advised his followers not to retaliate but to turn the other cheek (Matt. 5:39; Luke 6:29). Third, on the street to Golgotha, he lamented: "For if they do this when the wood is green, what will happen when it is dry?" (Luke 23:31 [L]). The opaqueness and the interrogative nature of this saying indicate that it does not derive from the preaching in the Palestinian Jesus Movement. The words are probably authentic to Jesus. What did he mean? He meant that if they crucify the "green" wood (the nonrevolutionaries), what shall they do to the "dry" wood (the hotheads and zealots of the people)?

Though the just-cited Jesus traditions are blatantly contradictory, Jesus did not portray himself to be a political revolutionary or a militant Messiah, as imagined, for example, in *2 Baruch* and the Palestinian Targum (Gen. 49:10). Most likely, Jesus led a nonviolent anti-Roman movement that became very popular and dangerous to Romans and their quislings, the high priestly group. Jesus' attitude should not be considered unique. While philo-Roman sentiments can be found in early Rabbinics, many Jews considered Rome to be destructively arrogant (cf. *Sib.*

Or. 3). Shortly after Jesus' death, a Jew blasted the Romans for hating those who speak the truth (*4 Ezra* 11). Much later, a Jew compared Rome to a pig who thinks he is clean but "robs, steals, and plunders" (*Midrash Psalms* 80.6).

The historian can provide some insights that help explain the tensions now exposed. For Jesus, only God is King. Jesus announced the dawning of God's Rule. Jesus did not lead a popular uprising; he did not claim to be a warrior or a Messiah who had been sent to destroy Romans.

The historian also raises questions that are difficult to answer. Did Jesus expect God to act with eschatological and apocalyptic power to establish a new Israel? If Jesus envisioned his Twelve as heads of twelve tribes, what did he imagine would be his role? How much history is revealed in Mark 15: "And Pilate again said to them: 'Then what shall I do with the man whom you call the King of the Jews?' " (v. 12)? However one answers these questions, it is clear that, in contrast to the hotheads and the revolutionaries, Jesus "did not take jealous zeal as his point of departure for radical interpretation of the law, but the law of love (Lev. 19:18), which he made universally applicable" (Hengel, *Victory over Violence*, p. 49). R. Horsley also rightly portrays Jesus as the leader of a nonviolent and popular movement of resistance against Roman rule (*Jesus and Empire*).

2) *Purity.* In the preceding pages, we intermittently pointed out that Jesus challenged and rejected the priests' exaggerated definition of purity. The recovery of numerous stone vessels and *mikvaot*—to accommodate the Jewish rites for purification—are palpable proof of the new purity legislations devised by priests in the Temple just before and during Jesus' ministry. As the requirements for purity were increased, the ability of the average religious Jew to remain pure decreased.

Despite the suggestions of some distinguished scholars (e.g., E. P. Sanders), impurity implies danger and threatens the loss of all power. For example, the fear of impurity is placarded in a document that clearly antedates Jesus. It is the *Temple Scroll*, which represents more than the views of the Qumran Essenes. According to this document, a pregnant woman with a dead fetus brings danger to all near her. If she enters a house, it becomes unclean; within the house, all commodities in earthen vessels become impure and worthless (11QT 50). Jesus knew about the meaning attributed to stone vessels by the priestly establishment. He attended a wedding in a wealthy house with six stone jars that were designated for the Jewish rites of purity (John 2:1-12). Many years ago, the anthropologist Mary Douglas clarified that purity is related to liturgies and danger (see her *Purity and Danger*; also see Schmidt).

Resisting purity legislations meant danger for Jesus and his group. When Jesus rejected the newly devised purity laws, he undermined the priests' power, prestige, and purse.

Jesus' position on purity exacerbated his relations with the high priests, and that led to his "arrest," and finally being sent to Pilate. Jesus' attitude to the purity regulations being increased by the sacerdotal aristocracy in Jerusalem was one factor contributing to his death.

3) *Claims.* Jesus' own claims and the adoration given to him by many would have threatened all in power, Romans and priests. Jesus' ability to perform miracles would also have thwarted the authority of those in leadership positions.

Miracle workers and charismatics define the abode of God and the place where

God resides on earth (the *axis mundi*). That undermines all claims for the Temple to be the only "House of God." Did Jesus ever suggest a Jew could worship anywhere and not only in the Temple (as in John 4:21)? If so, he then openly challenged the Deuteronomist theology of the Pentateuch and enflamed the Jerusalem priests.

There is evidence that Jesus may have had a messianic consciousness; during his life, some Jews probably thought he was the Messiah. Jesus' imagining that he was the triumphant Son of Man would have disturbed Romans and priests. When he proclaimed the eschatological dimension of God's Rule, those in authority would have been offended and challenged. If he claimed, or imagined, to be God's Son, then priests would consider this blasphemy. While his followers may have seen Jesus' humility reflected in his claim to be "greater than Solomon," this affirmation would be scandalous to priests. Recall that Mark 14 portrays the high priest claiming that Jesus was guilty of blasphemy (Mark 14:61-65; cf. b*San* 43a).

Jesus' parables were often confrontational. He sometimes veiled his speech so the Romans would not grasp that he envisioned freedom for his nation. Often he couched his words pictorially so that the Pharisees and scribes would not be able to entrap him, but they sometimes knew he spoke against them: "And they tried to arrest him, but feared the crowd (or mob), for they perceived that he had told the parable against them" (Mark 12:12). The parables sometimes can be forms of offense (see McCracken).

A prophet sent to Jerusalem at the time of pilgrimage. There is evidence that Jesus imagined himself to be a prophet and that his mission was to go to Jerusalem. Probably authentic to Jesus' mind is the concept that he was about to be stoned; no one after 30, and the crucifixion of Jesus, would have created the following saying of Jesus: "O Jerusalem, Jerusalem, killing the prophets and stoning those who are sent to you" (Matt. 23:37; Luke 13:34 [Q]). Jesus perceived himself in line with the prophets; he claimed to be sent to Jerusalem. He thus imagined he might be stoned, as had Honi, the Galilean miracle worker, some years before.

Jesus went up to Jerusalem to fulfill the requirements of the Torah; three pilgrimages to Jerusalem were required of faithful Jews for the feasts of Booths, Weeks, and Passover (Exod. 23:14-17; 34:22-23; Deut. 16:16). The pilgrimage was a time of joy (Isa. 9:2, cf. 16:9-10). Jesus went up to Jerusalem to worship in God's House and to celebrate Passover. In light of the escalating tensions with the leading priests, he most likely thought he could be stoned. The fear of his disciples, on the way up to Jerusalem and in Gethsemane, indicate that many in Jesus' group felt the hour of confrontation was present: "And they were on the way, going up to Jerusalem. Jesus was walking ahead of them; and they were amazed, and those who followed were afraid" (cf. Mark 10:32).

The cleansing of the Temple. When Jesus was in Jerusalem, he exploded with rage over some excesses in the cult, and allegedly overturned the table of the money-changers. While it is clear that Jesus loved the Temple, worshiped in the cult, and respected most priests, it is also obvious that he was offended by corruption in some aspects of the Temple cult. We shall never know for sure what was in Jesus' mind when he was angry. Maybe he did want to symbolize the destruction of the Temple and the restoration of a new Israel (as E. P. Sanders imagines). It is conceivable that, near the end of his ministry, some priests found proof that Jesus might be illegitimate, or a *mamzer,* and thus may not enter the Temple, as prescribed by *More Works of the Torah* (cf. Charlesworth in *Archaeology,* pp. 60-63). Being shut out of the Temple would have angered Jesus and his followers.

All devoted to Jesus Research should avoid positivism and claims to know what cannot be known according to our sources. However, scholars can clarify the questions now before us: Why did Jesus knock over the tables of the money-changers? Was it deliberate, and if it was, what did Jesus intend by this action? Did the *hanuth* (the place for the large animals to be sacrificed) move into the outer Temple with Herod's expansion of the Temple Mount in 30 C.E.? If so, then Jesus' explosive anger makes more sense, since large animals leave evidence of their presence, and Jesus' weaving of a whip, from tethers, as mentioned in the Fourth Gospel makes much better sense. Whatever may be the answers to these intriguing questions, his action in the Temple sealed his fate for some of the leading priests.

Jesus' last evening. The Gospels and Paul stress that Jesus' last supper was the time when he did something special that is remembered as the Last Supper or Eucharist. Unique moments were remembered about that evening. The reliability of Jesus' actions are indicated by multiple attestation (1 Cor. 11:23-25; Mark 14:22-25; Matt. 26:26-29; Luke 22:15-20; contrast John 6:51-58). Perhaps at a Passover meal and clearly during Passover, Jesus and his disciples celebrated the old Jewish rite of how God delivered his nation from bondage; they knew an early form of the Passover *Haggadah.* As Jews, they broke and ate unleavened bread, drank wine, and relived the Exodus (Exod. 12:14). Was it then that Jesus spoke of "the New Covenant" (1 Cor. 11:25; Luke 22:20)? Many scholars concur that Jesus did something special at his last supper. A shared memory, preserved in 1 Corinthians and the Gospels, helps authenticate the basic importance of Jesus' last meal.

Jesus' Crucifixion

Jesus is arrested in the Garden of Gethsemane—most likely by soldiers attached to the Temple. What rules or conditions caused Jesus to be crucified (Rivkin)? Who crucified Jesus?

It is certain that the Jews are not Christ-killers, despite two thousand years of infamy cast upon them. Jesus died by Roman execution, decreed by the Roman prefect. Anti-Semitism in the telling of Jesus' story must cease; he was a Jew, and his early followers were all Jews.

Yet some Roman quislings among the priesthood, including Caiaphas and Annas, were probably behind his arrest. Did they wish for him to be crucified? It is conceivable that they knew Jesus was in danger and wanted him removed from the public scene for a week or so. We shall never know what was in the minds of Caiaphas and Annas.

It is certain that no official meeting of the Sanhedrin (an official court of seventy-one Jews [m*Sanhedrin* 1:6]) condemned Jesus to death. Some scholars think the Sanhedrin had the right of corporal punishment (Smallwood); others disagree (Brown in *Death* 1:365-66; and Bryan). The ancient sources concur that the Sanhedrin did not have the power to declare a death sentence (esp. John 18:31;

jSan 18a, 24b). Even if the Sanhedrin had the power to condemn Jesus to death, it could not have met officially. It did not meet at night, as Mark implies (Mark 14:53–15:1). We should discard into the dustbin of misconceptions the possibility that the Sanhedrin sentenced Jesus to death; it never met at night, as the earliest accounts report.

As we perceived in chapter 7, many names or episodes in Jesus' Passion are now easier to imagine, and most likely historical, in light of archeological research. The following nine discoveries were reviewed:

1) the steps Jesus walked on as he ascended up into the Temple,
2) the Temple walls built by Herod the Great,
3) an inscription preserving Pilate's name and title (*prefectus*),
4) an ossuary with the inscription "Joseph Caiaphas,"
5) the tomb of Annas,
6) the remains of a man who had been crucified about the time of Jesus' crucifixion,
7) the ossuary of Simon of Cyrene and his son "Alexander,"
8) Golgotha, and
9) pre-70 Jewish tombs with rolling stones.

Now, no one should perpetuate the hypothesis that the Jesus story is mere myth and legend. Recall that Josephus, a Jew, reported: "Pilate...condemned him to be crucified" (*Ant.* 18).

Jesus' ossuary: Has it been recovered? In March 1980, a first-century Jewish tomb was found in modern-day Jerusalem. The tomb was uncovered inadvertently by workmen driving bulldozers. They were preparing an area for the construction of apartment buildings on Dov Gruner Street in East Talpiyot, which is considerably south of the purported line of Jerusalem's first-century walls.

Recent sensational claims have focused on ossuaries (stone boxes for disarticulated human bones) found in Talpiyot. On the outside of one of these ossuaries are the words: "Jesus, son of Joseph." Some claim that this is the ossuary of Jesus from Nazareth. Is that likely?

No. Here are the main reasons: (1) The writing on the alleged Jesus ossuary is difficult to read. It may have the name of Jesus, but that is a guess, and the name is one of the poorest written in that tomb or any tomb. (2) "Jesus" and "Joseph" were as common in the first century C.E. as are "Bob" and "John" today. (3) The writing is not an inscription; it is graffiti. The writing is sloppy, yet some inscriptions in this tomb are neat and even elegant for ossuaries. (4) The ossuary is poor; it is one of the worst ossuaries I have examined. (5) Other ossuaries were found in the Talpiyot tomb; some of them had no names. Maybe they contained the bones of another man named Joseph who had a son called Jesus. (6) Another ossuary much earlier had been recovered from some unknown spot; it contained the remains of "Jesus, son of Joseph." When it was discovered, no one imagined the bones could be identified with any known person. (7) An ossuary sometimes contains the bones of many, sometimes more than five, individuals. (8) According to the Gospels and Acts, in 30 C.E. Jesus' family had no tomb in or near Jerusalem; Jesus had been buried in the tomb of Joseph of Arimathea. (9) It is bizarre to imagine that Jesus would have put his bones in an ossuary; his disciples would have done this for him. Jesus' disciples proclaimed him the Messiah, the Son of God; they would not have scribbled his name on an ossuary; they would not have placed his remains in an ordinary and unadorned ossuary.

Jesus' Resurrection

For more than a thousand years, Christian theologians have advised those who believe in Jesus that the resurrection is a mystery that they should accept and not try to understand. Often Christians are told "simply believe," you do not need to perceive. At other times Christians are instructed that Christianity is founded on mysteries that they do not need to comprehend.

That advice no longer suffices for millions of Christians and others. They live in a world culture that has led them to want to understand, to perceive, and to comprehend.

Those interested in the fruits of Jesus Research want to know if Jesus' resurrection is believable. If it is not, then another foundation for New Testament theology, and the Christian faith, should be found. In the process, the Christian is taken back to Jesus' life and thought. Central among the questions that now arise for many is this one: can a dead man rise from the dead?

Is the central question, Can a dead man rise from the dead? No; that is never an issue for the resurrection texts in the New Testament—and these are our only source for comprehending the Easter faith of eyewitnesses to the Jesus of history, including Jesus' resurrection appearances.

As has been stated by many, historians are the ones best trained to interpret the New Testament witnesses in their sociological contexts. The historian knows that belief in Jesus' resurrection by God appeared around 30 C.E. in both Galilee and Jerusalem. Why? And why is their creatively new claim important for Jesus Research?

Did such resurrection faith evolve merely out of a hope that collapsed and then revived because Jesus' closest followers had received from him a love that could not die? Is the wish simply the father of the thought? What is wrong with concluding that for Jesus' followers Jesus lived and died, but his presence was felt again? If so, for them, Jesus must be alive, and that may have meant he has risen from the dead.

Why is the resurrection impossible or possible; and what responses do the original witnesses provide? Reflections are organized into reasons against and for the historicity of Jesus' resurrection.

Seven Reasons against Resurrection

Those who doubt the historicity of Jesus' resurrection have offered many arguments, which can be summarized under seven claims.

1) *It is impossible given Newtonian physics.* Some critics, including Christians, point out that resurrection is an ancient idea based upon a belief in a trifurcated universe—heaven, earth, and hell—and that modern cosmology proves such faith mythological since there are only a heaven and an earth. People die; they do not

revive. No one has seen any proof that the dead continue alive somewhere. Ancient myths must be corrected so Christians may live in this scientific world. Some Christians reject belief in Jesus' resurrection as absurd; the most prominent among them is Bishop J. S. Spong, who stressed this position in his popular books *Easter Moment* (1980) and *This Hebrew Lord* (1974, 1993).

2) *He appeared only to those who already believed in Jesus.* One should not continue to believe in Jesus' resurrection. He appeared only to those who believed in him; thus, belief generated belief.

3) *The wish became the father of the thought.* When loved persons die, one often dreams about them. One remembers them present, often feels them close, and wishes they were still alive; hence, the wish fathers the thought. We are confronted with our own fantasies and absurd imagining.

4) *Jesus' tomb was empty because Jesus' followers stole the body.* Resurrection belief is based on an empty tomb. The tomb could be empty for numerous reasons. Jesus' disciples could have removed Jesus' corpse for secondary burial, and so his bones could eventually be placed in an ossuary. Some of Jesus' followers could also have stolen his body (cf. Matt. 28:13), and robbers could have stolen the corpse if it had been bound in linen with valuable spices (cf. John 19:39).

5) *Resurrection belief begins with Christianity.* Jesus' followers, who were traumatized by his horrific death, invented the concept of resurrection. The Messiah and the Son of God cannot end his life on a cross as a despised slave. There are no resurrection accounts in the earliest gospels: Mark and the *Gospel of Thomas*.

6) *Only fundamentalist Christians still believe in Jesus' resurrection.* Belief in Jesus' resurrection is an example of Christian apologetics that must be corrected. Only the misinformed or uneducated continue to believe in Jesus' resurrection. Easter is a time to celebrate the return of flowers and good weather, so it is wise to remember Jesus and his wonderful life without ancient myths.

7) *Jesus died; he did not raise himself from the dead.* A dead man cannot raise himself; either he is dead or he is alive. Jesus died. He could not have risen from the dead. Docetism, the worst of all the heresies, is shrouded in the claim that Jesus, a Jewish male, only seemed to die on the cross.

Summary. For those who doubt the resurrection, to focus on Jesus' resurrection can make his life and thought imperceptible—even meaningless. He was sent by God into this world; he taught us to pray for God's Rule on earth. He was the One who made God present in our mundane lives. We do injustice to his victory over violence by stressing an outmoded myth; we know that dead men do not rise up again. We render no credit to his inclusion of women and others cast into the interstices of society by emphasizing something he did not do. We honor his memory by calling on God the Father, as he taught us, and living a life that helps the needy and yearns for that far-off city of God in which there is room for all who love God and seek to do God's will.

Six Reasons for Resurrection

Those who are convinced that Jesus' resurrection is historical and not an example of ancient mythology have offered many arguments, which may be summarized under six perspectives.

1) *It is possible in an open universe.* The educated person cannot claim that resurrection is impossible; it is unperceptive to think resurrection is absurd simply because no one has seen a person resurrected. We see the earth flat, the sun moving around the earth, and a stationary land; but despite appearances, we perceive that the earth is an oblate spheroid, that the earth rotates around the sun, and that each of us is moving at incredible speeds in many directions at once. At the beginning of the nineteenth century, Heisenberg proved that one of the constants in examining reality is the principle of indeterminacy. Einstein theorized that time is not a constant, but that time is dependent on speed. Einstein's fourth dimension is not physical, but it is fundamental. We learn that of the four dimensions—length, height, width, and time—the most important is time; it is the invisible dimension and cannot be touched and seen as the other three.

Today, Newtonian physics has collapsed, and Euclidian geometry is too imprecise. The universe is no longer observed to be closed; the farther away a star is from the earth, the faster it is moving away from the earth. Black holes defy comprehension. The wave theory has been found wanting, and the string theory is used by almost all physicists, but few think it represents the complexities of reality. Physicians need autopsies to discern the precise means of death. Healing is usually considered miraculous and sometimes surprising. Birth is one of the wonders of the world.

To claim that resurrection belief depends on an archaic concept of a trifurcated universe (the heavens, the earth, and hell under the earth) misrepresents ancient cosmology. According to Genesis, God created a bifurcated universe: the heavens and the earth. That is precisely what astronomers observe today: many heavens and one earth. The concept of "under the earth" does not assume another region separate from the earth; it denotes what is under the surface of the earth: the realm of the dead. That is, the Hebrew word *ṭḥt* indicates "beneath" the earth's surface. It denotes the place where the dead are taken, the underground "houses." Before the sixth-century Babylonian Exile, Israelites and others buried their dead below the earth, in subterranean chambers that often mimic the rooms of a palace. Today, one can descend stairs to these subterranean realms and see bones of many who died before 600 B.C.E.

The early "Christian" belief that Christ descended into hell to save those who had not heard the means of full forgiveness (*descensus ad inferos*), which is recited in liturgies today, is found in the New Testament (1 Pet. 3:18-20; Matt. 27:52-53; Luke 23:43) and in documents contemporaneous with the later New Testament documents (esp. *Odes of Solomon* 42:10-20). This belief is not carried forward with the presupposition of a trifurcated universe.

The ancient cosmologers who developed the concept of resurrection, the Jews from 300 B.C.E. to 200 C.E., portrayed a bifurcated cosmology (see *1 En., 2 En., Apoc. Ab., 4 Ezra, 2 Bar.*). Damned sinners are not in hell beneath the globe called earth; they are in one of the heavens. There are not three regions—heaven, earth, and hell; there are only two: the heavens and the earth.

2) *He appeared not only to those who already believed in Jesus.* Did only those who believed in Jesus see a risen Jesus?

No. James, Jesus' brother, seems to have been embarrassed by Jesus' ministry (Mark 3:21; cf. Luke 8:19-20). James's frequent adversary in the Palestinian Jesus

Movement, Paul, reported that Jesus appeared to James (1 Cor. 15). Moreover, the archenemy of Jesus' movement, Paul, claims that unexpectedly, and without warning, he experienced the risen Jesus (Gal. 1; 1 Cor. 15; cf. Acts 9:3-4). It is false to claim that only those who believed in Jesus experienced a resurrection appearance.

3) *No wish or hope; the Palestinian Jesus Movement died Friday when Jesus expired.* According to the New Testament documents, there is no one who hopes or expects Jesus to be resurrected. There is no evidence of wishful thinking. Most important for our present focus, Cleopas and his companion dejectedly on the way to Emmaus admit: "We had hoped" (Luke 24:21).

Jesus' movement ends in failure. Jesus dies like a slave, embarrassed before all. Peter and the disciples go back to fish in the Sea of Galilee (John 21:1-3). The members of the Palestinian Jesus Movement never imagined or expected Jesus' resurrection. Mary Magdalene comes to the tomb and finds it empty. She thinks the gardener has removed Jesus' corpse (John 20:15).

4) *The open tomb was not a source of resurrection belief.* Those who claim the empty tomb is a basis for resurrection belief among the disciples either have not read the New Testament or have read it without understanding. The empty tomb is not evidence of resurrection belief. Four times, Mark, and only he among the New Testament authors, uses the word "to be amazed" (Mark 16:1-8; *ekthambeisthai*). He uses it to portray the amazement of the women when they see the empty tomb; they were "amazed" (Mark 16:5). They probably wondered why the tomb was empty.

When the Beloved Disciple bends down and looks into Jesus' empty tomb, the Fourth Evangelist reports he "believes." This verb either indicates the first inklings of resurrection belief (an inceptive aorist) or (more likely) denotes what "to believe" means in the Gospel of John: "These are written that you may believe that Jesus is the Christ, the Son of God" (20:31). Johannine belief is based on the incarnation (John 1:14); it does not begin with Jesus' resurrection.

5) *Jews developed resurrection belief centuries prior to Jesus.* Jesus and his followers did not create the concept of resurrection. This idea is too often confused with resuscitation. Resurrection should be defined as the belief that someone who had lived, has died, and is subsequently raised by God to a life that is eternal.

Jesus and his followers inherited resurrection belief from earlier Jews. During the time of Jesus, many Palestinian Jews, in Galilee and Judea, believed in the resurrection of the dead. The earliest evidence is in *1 Enoch* (ca. 300–250 B.C.E.). Later the concept appears in Daniel 12 (ca. 164 B.C.E.). Resurrection belief appears in pre-70 liturgies, including the *18 Benedictions* (earliest Rabbinics) and the *Psalms of Solomon*. Resurrection belief appears in many Apocrypha and Pseudepigrapha (see *Resurrection*).

The Dead Sea Scrolls introduce us to previously unknown texts that contain the concept of resurrection; the most notable are *On Resurrection* and *Pseudo-Ezekiel* (and neither was composed at Qumran). Prior to Jesus' time, resurrection belief appeared in different forms among Jews who believed in it. Some of these Jews refused to speculate who would be resurrected and how. Others claimed only the righteous would be raised. Some, as the author of Daniel, believed that all those "who sleep in the dust of the earth" will be raised. Some shall awake and receive "everlasting life"; others will awake "to shame and everlasting contempt" (Dan. 12:2).

Most likely, Paul believed in the resurrection as a pre-Christian Pharisee. Before Easter, some of Jesus' followers believed in the resurrection of the dead: "Martha said to him, 'I know that he [Lazarus] will arise (*anastēsetai*) in the resurrection (*anastasei*) at the last day'" (John 11:24). Some scholars have contended that the Evangelist Mark did not know about Jesus' resurrection; but it is presupposed in Mark: "After I am raised up (*to egerthēnai* [aor. infin. pass.]), I will go before you to Galilee" (16:7; cf. 14:28). The compiler of the *Gospel of Thomas* may have believed in the presence of the living, and resurrected, Jesus; see how that gospel opens: "These are the hidden words that the living Jesus spoke." Too often scholars have used their own interpretations of Mark and Thomas to claim that resurrection belief is not present in the earliest gospels (moreover, the *Gos. Thom.* is not one of the earliest gospels).

6) *Something revived the Palestinian Jesus Movement.* The historian perceives that Jesus' movement ends in failure. It was a failed mission. The treasurer betrays the prophet. The group's leader denies him three times. To the masses, an alleged pseudo-prophet is disgraced by public crucifixion, his followers express a lost hope, a woman seeks a corpse when a tomb is empty (John 20), and the disciples (including the Beloved Disciple) abandon the movement and go fishing (John 21). Historians note a feeling of failure within Jesus' group immediately after the crucifixion; for example, Cleopas states his former belief in Jesus: "We had hoped that he was the one to redeem Israel" (Luke 24:21).

The historian also observes evidence that unexpectedly a blazing zeal launches a massive missionary mission within Second Temple Judaism. It is headed by Peter and then Paul. Each of them is credited with a resurrection experience. Most historians imagine that without something happening, the Palestinian Jesus Movement would have drowned in lost hopes.

What revived the movement? Jesus' followers agree; they unexpectedly witness a resurrected Jesus. In *The Resurrection of Jesus: A Jewish Perspective* (1983), P. Lapide, a Jew, expresses his opinion why the disciples' resurrection belief is not impossible. He contends: "[A]ccording to my opinion, the resurrection belongs to the category of the truly real and effective occurrences, for without a fact of history there is no act of true faith" (p. 92). Historians have to explain what jump-started a dead movement. They have abundant evidence in the New Testament. It is multiply attested, coherent, and makes sense in pre-70 Palestinian Judaism.

Summary. The resurrection belief of Jesus' followers shows that Jesus Research should not end with the cross. Their belief might be perceived in light of Jesus' putative claim that he was the one sent by God, and accentuates the fact that his life and thought continued to be meaningful to them. He was the prophet who made God present in their mundane lives.

Authentic?

Is there any reliable history in the resurrection accounts? We may now apply to the resurrection texts the methodology defined at the beginning and used throughout this book.

1) *Multiple attestation.* Jesus' resurrection is multiply attested (Paul [viz., 1 Cor.

15], Matt., M [Matt. 28:11-20], Luke, L [Luke 24:13-35], John, Acts, and foreshadowed in Mark [plus Mark 16:9-20, which is apocryphal]). The accounts are markedly independent. Some resurrection appearances occur in Jerusalem (Matt. 28:9; Luke; John 20). Others are placed in Galilee (Matt. 28:17; John 21 = J²; cf. Mark).

2) *Embarrassment.* The origin of the earliest account seems to derive from women, not a reliable witness in Second Temple Judaism, and these reported to men who did not believe them. This is either a clever use of rhetoric or the stuff of history (see esp. Luke 24:8-11). The Evangelists seem to undermine the fact that the first appearance was to Mary Magdalene; they are embarrassed that a woman could be the first witness. They edited the story so that Peter is the first witness to Jesus' resurrection. Also, for anyone in ancient Palestine to claim that Jesus had been raised would have been embarrassing for two reasons. It could not be denied that Jesus publicly died as a slave or criminal. To state that anyone had been raised opened the speaker to ridicule.

3) *Coherence with Jesus' Judaism.* Resurrection belief had been evident in Second Temple Judaism for centuries before 30 C.E. The social-theological context in which the kerygma appeared was one in which many believed in the resurrection of the dead (*1 En.*, Dan. 12, *18 Benedictions, Pss. Sol., T12P, On Resurrection, Pseudo-Ezekiel*), but the basis for belief in Jesus' resurrection by God is the eyewitnesses who were surprised.

Conclusion

Five questions introduced this chapter. Let us now see how they are to be answered.

23) *What led to Jesus' confrontation with some of the leading priests?* Jesus was probably a revolutionary who sought to revive the old traditions of Israel, as represented by many, especially Jeremiah, Isaiah, and the authors of the Psalms. He offended the leading priests because he rejected their elevated definitions and demands for purity. His proclamations and a self-understanding would have upset the high priestly group. His miracles and the crowds who defined him would threaten those whose mandate was to keep peace in the East.

24) *Who crucified Jesus and why?* The Romans judged Jesus to be an insurrectionist. The Roman soldiers, following the command of the prefect, Pontius Pilate, crucified Jesus.

25) *Has Jesus' bone box (ossuary) been recovered?* No.

26) *If Jesus' bones have been discovered, is resurrection faith possible?* This theological question extends beyond the purview of historians. They can only point out that according to some of Jesus' followers, they saw him alive again, after the crucifixion, and that he was able to pass through doors and walls (cf. John 20).

27) *Did Jesus rise from the dead?* Historians cannot answer this theological question. They can only point to the witness of the earliest followers who claimed he did because they saw him alive again.

CHAPTER 10

Conclusion

The preceding chapters introduce the reader to most of the major questions involved in Jesus Research. Although many questions appeared during our search for a deeper and better understanding of Jesus' life and thought, twenty-seven questions focused our research. How have those questions been answered?

1) *Why is Jesus research necessary?* It is necessary because Christianity is a historical religion. Its theology is based on history. A particular person, Jesus, performed some particulars that are particularly important for my own self-understanding and salvation. The incarnation is fundamental to Christianity. Without a Jew named Jesus, there can be no faith in him. And a resurrection presupposes a person who has lived. It is imperative then to explore how much reliable information, and with what certainty, can be obtained concerning the life and thought of Jesus from Nazareth.

2) *How is Jesus Research possible?* Jesus Research is possible because there is reliable historical data in our Gospels, and because methods have been developed and polished for obtaining insights into Jesus' life and thought. In this endeavor, one needs to include all relevant data and employ all pertinent methods.

3) *When did the study of the historical Jesus begin, and what has been learned?* The study of Jesus began with some scientific rigor in the eighteenth century. In London and in 1738 Thomas Chubb published *The True Gospel of Jesus Christ Asserted*. Chubb was the first to discover historical reasons for concluding that Jesus' true message was the imminent coming of God's Rule (the Kingdom of God) and the true gospel was to be found in Jesus' preaching of good news to the poor.

4) *Is it important to distinguish between what Jesus said and what the Evangelists reported?* Yes; one should not confuse the mind of Jesus with the thoughts of his followers.

5) *What are the best methods for discerning traditions that originate with Jesus?* We defined and then applied numerous methods, each supporting the other. Among these the most significant were embarrassment, multiple attestation, coherence, plausibility within Second Temple Judaism, and dissimilarity from the kerygma and teaching in the Palestinian Jesus Movement.

6) *Do reports about Jesus exist outside the New Testament?* Yes; but these add nothing to Jesus' life, and only the *Gospel of Thomas* supplies important data to help in reconstructing Jesus' thought.

7) *Are the Gospels objective biographies?* It is wise to recognize the possibility that the Gospels are similar to Greek and Roman biographies, and that there are literary parallels among the Gospels and Jewish compositions (cf. esp. *Jos. Asen.*).

8) *Was Jesus not the first Christian?* No; Jesus was a devout Jew.

9) *Was Jesus an Essene, Pharisee, Zealot, or Sadducee?* Jesus was influenced by some Essene ideas and many Pharisaic thoughts, but he was not an Essene or

Pharisee—let alone a Zealot or Sadducee. He was unique and gave rise to a new Jewish sect.

10) *When and where was Jesus born?* Jesus was born about 7 or 6 B.C.E., somewhere in Palestine.

11) *Is there historicity in the virgin birth, and did some judge Jesus to be a* mamzer? The virgin birth is a Christological affirmation; it makes claims about Jesus' uniqueness. It is impossible to prove or disprove such a belief. Some Jews most likely judged Jesus to be a *mamzer.*

12) *Did Jesus travel to a foreign land to obtain wisdom and the powers of healing, or did he live with Essenes to obtain these powers?* No.

13) *Is there any reliable history in the noncanonical gospels that helps us understand Jesus' youth?* No; these are later legendary accounts.

14) *Was John the Baptizer Jesus' teacher?* Yes.

15) *Was Jesus married to Mary Magdalene?* No data enables us to obtain a clear answer. They were certainly intimate; but their relationship was primarily spiritual.

16) *Did Jesus perform miracles?* Yes; his opponents claimed he had miraculous powers.

17) *How and in what significant ways is archaeology important for Jesus Research?* Now, for the first time, thanks to excavations at various places—including Bethsaida, Capernaum, Migdal, Nazareth, Jericho, and Jerusalem—we can imagine Jesus' culture. We can even touch and hold objects his contemporaries held and touched. His parables take on new meaning in light of the images Jesus imagined.

18) *What are the most important archaeological discoveries for Jesus Research?* These are those that help us understand his thought, especially the Dead Sea Scrolls and the apocryphal works, and excavations that disclose streets he walked upon and houses he entered. Most important, we have archaeological evidence of Caiaphas, Annas, Pilate, Simon of Cyrene and his son Alexander, the remains of a man crucified about the time of Jesus, and Golgotha.

19) *Was Jesus a peasant?* No.

20) *What was Jesus' fundamental message?* He proclaimed the dawning of God's Rule and taught his followers to imagine God as Abba, Father.

21) *When did Jesus imagine God would inaugurate his Rule?* Sometimes, Jesus thought the end of time was very close in time; at other times, he imagined it would not dawn for some time. He was a man of his time; he was human.

22) *What term did Jesus use for God?* Abba, Father.

23) *What led to Jesus' confrontation with some of the leading priests?* We have discovered that the most important reasons are the following: those in authority, Romans and priests, would have been disturbed by his miracles, his proclamations and self-understanding, and the threatening crowds who were almost mobs. Priests would have been alarmed by his rejection of their concept of, and demands for, purity.

24) *Who crucified Jesus and why?* Roman soldiers crucified Jesus because Pilate judged him to be a threat to the peace in the East.

25) *Has Jesus' bone box (ossuary) been recovered?* No.

26) *If Jesus' bones have been discovered, is resurrection faith possible?* Historians cannot answer such questions; they can only point to the claims of Jesus' followers.

Some of them claimed that the resurrected Jesus had a body, but he could pass through doors and walls (cf. John 20).

27) *Did Jesus rise from the dead?* Again, this question extends beyond the methodology and focus of historians. They can claim, however, that Jews soon after Jesus' crucifixion claimed that they experienced him alive again. New Testament theologians would add that the New Testament has a coherent witness to Jesus' resurrection.

What has been learned? If we ask a question, we should not presuppose a desired answer or manipulate data to acquire a pleasing answer. We need to develop the maturity to be honest in asking questions, and be prepared for a possibly unattractive answer. In asking questions, we need to include all pertinent data and employ all relevant methods. We should also be able to defend to ourselves (and perhaps to others) why we have privileged certain data.

If we find a text that answers our question with pellucid clarity, we should ask *why*; then we should ask what motivated the statement or answer. Was it a need to defend a position or claim that prophecy demanded that particular aspect of Jesus' life? Have we been myopic and blind, looking only at texts? Have we forgotten the paradigmatic importance supplied by *realia* from Jesus' time, culture, and Judaism? If the concept is symbolic, have we studied the symbols in pre-70 marble and on coins? Have we studied *realia* that represent that symbol? Have topography and archaeology served us? Finally, is an answer improbable, possible, probable, or relatively certain?

Using these caveats, methods, and criteria, we have obtained a vast amount of information about that Jew who ventured out from the hills of Nazareth, centered his ministry in Capernaum, went up to Jerusalem and the Temple to worship, and eventually died on a wooden cross outside the western walls of Jerusalem. He urged all who heard him to be prepared for God's Rule, which at times seemed incredibly close to those standing near him. He taught his followers habitually to pray:

> Father,
> Hallowed be Thy name.
> May Thy Kingdom come!
> Give us each day our daily bread.
> And forgive us our sins,
> For we forgive all who are indebted to us.
> And do not allow us to enter into temptation.
> (Luke 11:2-4)

Suggested Readings

Introduction

One of the best books for studying the proper method for ascertaining Jesus' own words and reliable facts about his own life is G. Theissen and D. Winter's *Quest for the Plausible Jesus* (2002). This book helps the reader distinguish the fruits of historical research from thoughtless faith pronouncements. Theissen and Winter also demonstrate how confessionalism and anti-Semitism have created a Jesus who never lived and had virtually nothing to do with Judaism.

Reliable scholars devoted to Jesus Research clarify why Jesus Research is necessary in *Jesus Two Thousand Years Later*, edited by J. H. Charlesworth and W. P. Weaver (2000). The proper way to appreciate Judaism and to see Jesus within his Jewish environment is provided by E. P. Sanders's *Jesus and Judaism* (1985) and A.-J. Levine's *The Misunderstood Jew* (2006). The Jewishness of Jesus is illustrated in many books, especially *Jesus' Jewishness* (1991), edited by Charlesworth. The attempt to show that Jesus was a Jew and should be understood within his own Jewish world is illustrated in Charlesworth's *Jesus Within Judaism* (1988). For a brilliant demonstration of Jesus' genius, by a Jew, see D. Flusser, with R. S. Notley, *The Sage from Galilee* (2007). Impressive and insightful guides to Jesus Research are presented in Theissen and Merz's *The Historical Jesus: A Comprehensive Guide* (1998) and in Stegemann's *The Jesus Movement* (1999). In-depth, authoritative, and thoughtful probes into many aspects of Jesus' life and teaching can be found in J. P. Meier's multivolume *Jesus: A Marginal Jew*. For a perception of the Palestinian Jesus Movement as a family movement, see J. D. Tabor's *The Jesus Dynasty* (2006). For two very different attempts to explain Jesus' revolutionary teachings, see M. J. Borg's *Jesus* (2006) and O. M. Hendricks's *The Politics of Jesus* (2006). For the claim that the Gospels are corrupt records of Jesus' own traditions, see B. D. Ehrman's *Misquoting Jesus* (2005); and for an attempt to rebut him as well as those who sensationalize or claim conspiracies, see C. A. Evans's *Fabricating Jesus* (2006). For an argument that the Gospels are based on eyewitness testimony, see R. Bauckham's *Jesus and the Eyewitnesses: The Gospels as Eyewitness Testimony* (2006). For a stunning demonstration that the Gospels are indeed biographical, see R. A. Burridge, *What Are the Gospels?* (2004). For a lucid discussion of the significance of the historical Jesus, see R. A. Burridge and G. Gould's *Jesus Now and Then* (2004). For publications on authenticating Jesus' activities or words, see respectively B. Chilton and C. A. Evans, *Authenticating the Activities of Jesus* (1999) and Chilton and Evans, *Authenticating the Words of Jesus* (1999). For a study of the impact of Jesus' life on American culture, see R. W. Fox, *Jesus in America* (2005).

When comparing the Gospels, including the *Gospel of Thomas*, it is enlightening to work with a synopsis of the four Gospels; one of the best is K. Aland, *Synopsis Quattuor Evangeliorum* (= *Synopsis*).

For research up until 1996, one should consult C. A. Evans, *Life of Jesus Research: An Annotated Bibliography* (NTTS 24; Leiden, New York: Brill, 1996). For more recent research see "Abbreviations" at the beginning of the present book, the scholarly periodicals, and especially the *Journal for the Study of the Historical Jesus (JSHJ)*. Other works include the following:

Allison, D. C. "The Eschatology of Jesus." Pages 267-302 in *The Encyclopedia of Apocalypticism*. Ed. J. J. Collins. Vol. 1. New York: Continuum, 1999.

Allison, D., et al. *The Apocalyptic Jesus: A Debate*. Ed. R. J. Miller. Santa Rosa, Calif.: Polebridge Press, 2001.

Anchor Bible Dictionary. 6 vols. New York: Doubleday, 1992.

Anderson, H. *Jesus*. Englewood Cliffs, N.J.: Prentice-Hall, 1967.

Bammel, E., and C. F. D. Moule, eds. *Jesus and the Politics of His Day*. Cambridge: Cambridge University Press, 1984.

Batey, R. A. *Jesus & the Forgotten City*. Grand Rapids: Baker Book House, 1991.

Bauckham, R. *Jesus and the Eyewitnesses: The Gospels as Eyewitness Testimony*. Grand Rapids: Eerdmans, 2006.

Bellinger, W. H., Jr., and W. R. Farmer. *Jesus and the Suffering Servant: Isaiah 53 and Christian Origins*. Harrisburg: Trinity Press International, 1998.

Benoit, P. *The Passion and Resurrection of Jesus Christ*. New York: Herder & Herder, 1969.

Boers, H. *Who Was Jesus?* New York: Harper and Row, 1989.

Borg, M. *Conflict, Holiness, and Politics in the Teachings of Jesus*. New York: Mellen, 1984.

———. *Meeting Jesus Again for the First Time*. New York: HarperCollins, 1994.

———. *Jesus: Uncovering the Life, Teachings, and Relevance of a Religious Revolutionary*. New York: HarperSanFrancisco, 2006.

Bornkamm, G. *Jesus of Nazareth*. New York: Harper & Row, 1960.

Burridge, R. A. *What Are the Gospels?* Grand Rapids: Eerdmans, 2004.

Burridge, R. A., and G. Gould. *Jesus Now and Then*. Grand Rapids: Eerdmans, 2004.

Carmignac, J. *Recherches sur le "Notre Père."* Paris: Letouzey & Ané, 1969.

Charlesworth, J. H., ed. *Jesus and the Dead Sea Scrolls*. New York: Doubleday, 1992, 1995.

———. "The Historical Jesus and Exegetical Theology." *Princeton Seminary Bulletin* 22.1 N.S. (2001): 45-63.

———. "Jesus Research and Near Eastern Archaeology: Reflections on Recent Developments." Pages 37-70 in *Neotestamentica et Philonica: Studies in Honor of Peder Borgen*. Ed. D. E. Aune et al. Leiden: Brill, 2003.

———, ed. *The Bible and the Dead Sea Scrolls*. 3 vols. Waco, Tex.: Baylor University Press, 2006.

Charlesworth, J. H., and W. P. Weaver, eds. *Images of Jesus Today*. Valley Forge, Pa.: Trinity Press International, 1994.

Charlesworth, J. H., et al., eds. *The Lord's Prayer and Other Prayer Texts from the Greco-Roman World*. Valley Forge, Pa.: Trinity Press International, 1994.

Chilton, B., and C. A. Evans. *Studying the Historical Jesus: Evaluations of the State of Current Research*. Leiden: Brill, 1994.

———. *Authenticating the Activities of Jesus*. Leiden: Brill, 1999.

———. *Authenticating the Words of Jesus*. Leiden: Brill, 1999.

Conzelmann, H. *Jesus*. Philadelphia: Fortress, 1973.

Crossan, J. D., and J. L. Reed. *Excavating Jesus: Beneath the Stones, Behind the Texts*. San Francisco: HarperSanFrancisco, 2001.

Dahl, N. *The Crucified Messiah and Other Essays*. Minneapolis: Augsburg, 1974.

Davies, S. L. *Jesus the Healer*. New York: Continuum, 1995.

Davies, W. D. "A Quest to Be Resumed in New Testament Studies." *USQR* 15 (1960): 83-98.

Dodd, C. H. *The Founder of Christianity.* New York, London: Macmillan, 1970.

Dunn, J. D. G. *Jesus Remembered.* Grand Rapids: Eerdmans, 2003.

Ehrman, B. D. *Misquoting Jesus.* New York: HarperSanFrancisco, 2005.

Evans, C. A. *Life of Jesus Research: An Annotated Bibliography.* Leiden: Brill, 1996.

————. *Fabricating Jesus: How Modern Scholars Distort the Gospels.* Downers Grove, Ill.: InterVarsity Press, 2006.

Flusser, D., with R. S. Notley. *Jesus.* Jerusalem: Magness, 1998.

————. *The Sage from Galilee: Rediscovering Jesus' Genius.* Grand Rapids: Eerdmans, 2007.

Franzmann, M. *Jesus in the Nag Hammadi Writings.* Edinburgh: T & T Clark, 1996.

Fredriksen, P. *Jesus of Nazareth: King of the Jews—A Jewish Life and the Emergence of Christianity.* New York: Knopf, 1999, 2000.

Green, J. B., et al., eds. *Dictionary of Jesus and the Gospels.* Downers Grove, Ill., and Leicester, England: InterVarsity Press, 1992.

Harvey, A. E. *Strenuous Commands: The Ethic of Jesus.* Philadelphia: Trinity Press International, 1990.

Hendricks, O. M., Jr. *The Politics of Jesus: Rediscovering the True Revolutionary Nature of Jesus' Teachings and How They Have Been Corrupted.* New York: Doubleday, 2006.

Horsley, R. A. *Archaeology, History, and Society in Galilee: The Social Context of Jesus and the Rabbis.* Harrisburg, Pa.: Trinity Press International, 1996, 2000.

————. "The Kingdom of God and the Renewal of Israel: Synoptic Gospels, Jesus Movements, and Apocalypticism." Pages 303-44 in *The Encyclopedia of Apocalypticism.* Ed. J. J. Collins. New York: Continuum, 1999.

Jeremias, J. *The Sermon on the Mount.* London: Athlone, 1961.

————. *The Parables of Jesus.* 3rd ed. London: SCM, 1963.

————. *The Eucharistic Words of Jesus.* Rev. ed. Oxford: Oxford University Press, 1966.

————. *The Prayers of Jesus.* London: SCM, 1967.

————. *New Testament Theology: The Proclamation of Jesus.* London: SCM, 1971.

Johnson, L. T. *The Real Jesus.* New York: HarperSanFrancisco, 1996.

Käsemann, E. *Essays on New Testament Themes.* London: SCM, 1964.

Kazen, T. *Jesus and Purity Halakhah.* Stockholm: Almqvist & Wiksell Int., 2002.

Levine, A.-J. *The Misunderstood Jew: The Church and the Scandal of the Jewish Jesus.* New York: HarperSanFrancisco, 2006.

Meyer, B. F. *The Aims of Jesus.* Introduction by N. T. Wright. Eugene, Ore.: Pickwick, 2002.

Navone, J. *Triumph Through Failure: A Theology of the Cross.* Homebush, Australia: St. Paul Publications, 1984.

————. *Seeking God in Story.* Collegeville, Minn.: Liturgical Press, 1990.

Parrinder, G. *Jesus in the Qur'ān.* Oxford: Oneworld, 1965, 1996.

Patterson, S. J. *The God of Jesus: The Historical Jesus and the Search for Meaning.* Harrisburg, Pa.: Trinity Press International, 1998.

Pixner, B. *With Jesus in Jerusalem: His First and Last Days in Judea.* Rosh Pina, Israel: Corazin Publishing, 1996.

————. *With Jesus through Galilee According to the Fifth Gospel.* Collegeville, Minn.: Liturgical Press, 1996.

Pokorný, P. *Jesus in the Eyes of His Followers.* North Richland Hills, Tex.: BIBAL Press, 1998.

Reed, J. L. *Archaeology and the Galilean Jesus.* Harrisburg, Pa.: Trinity Press International, 2000.

Rivkin, E. *What Crucified Jesus?* New York: UAHC Press, 1997.

Rousseau, J. J., and R. Arav. *Jesus and His World: An Archaeological and Cultural Dictionary.* Minneapolis: Fortress, 1995.

Sanders, E. P. *Jesus and Judaism.* Philadelphia: Fortress, 1985.

————. *The Historical Figure of Jesus.* New York, London: Penguin Press, 1993.

Schaberg, J. *The Illegitimacy of Jesus*. New York: Crossroad, 1990.

Stegemann, E., and W. Stegemann. *The Jesus Movement: A Social History of Its First Century*. Trans. O. C. Dean. Minneapolis: Fortress, 1999.

Tabor, J. D. *The Jesus Dynasty*. New York: Simon & Schuster, 2006.

Theissen, G. *The Shadow of the Galilean: The Quest of the Historical Jesus in Narrative Form*. Philadelphia: Fortress, 1987.

Theissen, G., and A. Merz. *The Historical Jesus: A Comprehensive Guide*. Trans. J. Bowden. Minneapolis: Fortress, 1998.

Vermes, G. *Jesus and the World of Judaism*. Philadelphia: Fortress, 1983.

———. *The Religion of Jesus the Jew*. London: SCM, 1993.

———. *The Passion*. London: Penguin, 2005, 2006.

Weaver, W. *The Historical Jesus in the Twentieth Century, 1900–1950*. Harrisburg, Pa.: Trinity Press International, 1999.

Weaver, W., and J. H. Charlesworth, eds. *Earthing Christologies: From Jesus' Parables to Jesus the Parable*. Valley Forge, Pa.: Trinity Press International, 1995.

Yoder, J. H. *The Politics of Jesus*. Grand Rapids: Eerdmans, 1994 [2d ed.], 1995.

Young, B. H. *The Parables: Jewish Tradition and Christian Interpretation*. Peabody, Mass.: Hendrickson, 1998.

1. No Quest, the Old Quest, the New Quest, and Jesus Research (Third Quest)

Benoit, P. *Jesus and the Gospel*. Trans. B. Weatherhead. New York, 1973.

Borg, M. J. *Conflict, Holiness, and Politics in the Teachings of Jesus*. Studies in the Bible and Early Christianity 5. New York, 1984.

———. *Meeting Jesus Again for the First Time: The Historical Jesus and the Heart of Contemporary Faith*. New York, 1994, 1995.

Bornkamm, G. *Jesus of Nazareth*. Trans. I. and F. McLuskey with J. M. Robinson. New York, London, 1960.

Bultmann, R. *Jesus and the Word*. Trans. L. Smith and E. H. Lantero. London, Glasgow, 1934.

———. *The Theology of the New Testament*. Trans. K. Grobel. New York, 1951.

———. *History of the Synoptic Tradition*. Trans. J. Marsh. Oxford, 1963.

Charlesworth, J. H. "The Historical Jesus in Light of Writings Contemporaneous with Him." *Aufstieg und Niedergang der römischen Welt* 2.25.1 (1982): 451-76.

———. *Jesus Within Judaism: New Light from Exciting Archaeological Discoveries*. Anchor Bible Reference Library. New York, London, 1988.

———, ed. *Jesus' Jewishness: Exploring the Place of Jesus in Early Judaism*. New York, 1991.

———, ed. *Jesus and the Dead Sea Scrolls*. Anchor Bible Reference Library. New York, London, 1992, 1995.

———, ed. *Jesus and Archaeology*. Grand Rapids, 2006.

Charlesworth, J. H., with M. Harding and M. Kiley, eds. *The Lord's Prayer and Other Prayer Texts from the Greco-Roman Era*. Valley Forge, 1994.

Charlesworth, J. H., and L. L. Johns, eds. *Hillel and Jesus*. Minneapolis, 1997.

Charlesworth, J. H., and W. P. Weaver, eds. *Images of Jesus Today*. Faith & Scholarship Colloquies 3. Valley Forge, 1994.

Chilton, B. *Pure Kingdom: Jesus' Vision of God*. Grand Rapids, 1996.

———. *Rabbi Jesus: An Intimate Biography*. New York, London, 2000.

Chilton, B., and C. A. Evans, eds. *Authenticating the Words of Jesus*. NTTS 28.1. Leiden, Boston, 1999.

Crossan, J. D. *The Historical Jesus: The Life of a Mediterranean Jewish Peasant*. New York, 1991.

Dahl, N. A. *Jesus the Christ: The Historical Origins of Christological Doctrine*. Ed. D. H. Juel. Minneapolis, 1991.

Davies, W. D. *The Setting of the Sermon on the Mount*. Cambridge, 1966.

Dodd, C. H. *Parables of the Kingdom.* Rev. ed. London, 1936.

————. *The Founder of Christianity.* New York, 1970.

Dunn, J. D. G. *Jesus Remembered.* Grand Rapids, 2003.

Evans, C. A. *Life of Jesus Research: An Annotated Bibliography.* Leiden, New York, 1996.

Flusser, D., with R. S. Notley. *Jesus.* 2d ed. Jerusalem, 1998.

————. *The Sage from Galilee: Rediscovering Jesus' Genius.* Grand Rapids, 2007.

Fredriksen, P. *From Jesus to Christ.* New Haven, London, 1988.

————. *Jesus of Nazareth: King of the Jews.* New York, 2000.

Harnack, A. *The Mission and Expansion of Christianity in the First Three Centuries.* 2 vols. Trans. J. Moffatt. New York, 1908.

Jeremias, J. *The Sermon on the Mount.* Trans. N. Perrin. London, 1961.

————. *The Parables of Jesus.* Trans. S. H. Hooke. 6th ed. London, 1963.

————. *Unknown Sayings of Jesus.* Trans. R. H. Fuller. 2d ed. London, 1964.

————. *The Eucharistic Words of Jesus.* Trans. N. Perrin. Rev. ed. London, 1966.

————. *Abba.* Göttingen, 1966.

————. *The Prayers of Jesus.* Trans. J. Bowden, Chr. Burchard, and J. Reumann. London, 1967.

————. *Jerusalem in the Time of Jesus: An Investigation into Economic and Social Conditions During the New Testament Period.* Trans. F. H. and C. H. Cave. Philadelphia, 1967.

————. *New Testament Theology: The Proclamation of Jesus.* Trans. J. Bowden. New York, 1971.

Johnson, L. T. *The Real Jesus.* New York, 1996.

Kähler, M. *The So-called Historical Jesus and the Historic, Biblical Christ.* Trans. C. E. Braaten. Philadelphia, 1964 [original in 1896].

Käsemann, E. "The Problem of the Historical Jesus." In *Essays on New Testament Themes.* Trans. W. J. Montague. SBT 41. Naperville, Ill., 1964.

Levine, A.-J. *The Misunderstood Jew.* San Francisco, 2006.

Meier, J. P. *A Marginal Jew: Rethinking the Historical Jesus.* 3 vols. New York, London, 1991–2001.

Perrin, N. *Rediscovering the Teaching of Jesus.* New York, 1967.

Renan, E. *The Life of Jesus.* New York, 1927.

Sanders, E. P. *Jesus and Judaism.* Philadelphia, 1985.

————. *The Historical Figure of Jesus.* London, New York, 1993.

Schweitzer, A. *The Quest of the Historical Jesus.* Trans. W. Montgomery. New York, 1910.

Stegemann, E. W., and W. Stegemann. *The Jesus Movement: A Social History of Its First Century.* Trans. O. C. Dean Jr. Minneapolis, 1999.

Theissen, G. *Sociology of Early Palestinian Christianity.* Trans. J. Bowden. Philadelphia, 1978.

————. *The Shadow of the Galilean.* Trans. J. Bowden. Philadelphia, 1987.

Theissen, G., with A. Merz. *The Historical Jesus: A Comprehensive Guide.* Trans. J. Bowden. Minneapolis, 1998.

Theissen, G., and D. Winter. *The Quest of the Plausible Jesus: The Question of Criteria.* Trans. M. E. Boring. Louisville, London, 2002.

Vermes, G. *Jesus the Jew: A Historian's Reading of the Gospels.* Philadelphia, 1973, 1981.

————. *Jesus and the World of Judaism.* Philadelphia, 1983, 1984.

————. *The Changing Faces of Jesus.* London, 2000.

————. *The Authentic Gospel of Jesus.* London, 2003.

————. *Jesus in His Jewish Context.* Minneapolis, 2003.

————. *The Passion.* New York, 2006.

————. *The Nativity.* London, 2006.

Weaver, W. P. *The Historical Jesus in the Twentieth Century: 1900–1950.* Harrisburg, Pa., 1999.

Wright, N. T. *Who Was Jesus?* London, Grand Rapids, 1992.

————. *Jesus and the Victory of God.* London, 1996.

————. *The Challenge of Jesus: Rediscovering Who Jesus Was and Is.* Downers Grove, Ill., 1999.

2. Jesus Research and How to Obtain Reliable Information

Aune, D. E. *The New Testament in Its Literary Environment*. Philadelphia, 1987.

Bauckham, R. *Jesus and the Eyewitness: The Gospels as Eyewitness Testimony*. Grand Rapids, 2006.

Bultmann, R. *Jesus and the Word*. Trans. L. P. Smith and E. H. Lantero. London, 1934.

———. *History of the Synoptic Tradition*. Trans. J. Marsh. Oxford, 1963.

Burridge, R. A. *What Are the Gospels?: A Comparison with Graeco-Roman Biography*. 2d ed. Dearborn, Mich., 2004.

Charlesworth, J. H. *The Beloved Disciple: Whose Witness Validates the Gospel of John?* Valley Forge, Pa., 1995.

———. "The Historical Jesus: Sources and a Sketch." Pages 84-128 in *Jesus Two Thousand Years Later*. Ed. J. H. Charlesworth and W. P. Weaver. Harrisburg, Pa., 2000.

Charlesworth, J. H., with M. Harding and M. Kiley, eds. *The Lord's Prayer and Other Prayer Texts from the Greco-Roman Era*. Valley Forge, 1994.

Charlesworth, J. H., and L. L. Johns, eds. *Hillel and Jesus*. Minneapolis, 1997.

Chilton, B., and C. A. Evans, eds. *Authenticating the Activities of Jesus*. NTTS 28.2. Leiden, Boston, 1999.

———. *Authenticating the Words of Jesus*. NTTS 28.1. Leiden, Boston, 1999.

Crossan, J. D. "Why Is Historical Jesus Research Necessary?" Pages 7-37 in *Jesus Two Thousand Years Later*. Ed. J. H. Charlesworth and W. P. Weaver. Harrisburg, Pa., 2000.

Meier, J. "How Do We Decide What Comes from Jesus?" Pages 167-95 in *A Marginal Jew: Rethinking the Historical Jesus*. Vol. 1. New York, London, 1991.

Perrin, N. *Rediscovering the Teaching of Jesus*. New York, 1967.

———. *What Is Redaction Criticism?* Philadelphia, 1969.

Sanders, E. P. *The Tendencies of the Synoptic Tradition*. London, 1969.

———. "How Do We Know What We Know About Jesus?" Pages 38-61 in *Jesus Two Thousand Years Later*. Ed. J. H. Charlesworth and W. P. Weaver. Harrisburg, Pa., 2000.

Theissen, G., and D. Winter. *The Quest for the Plausible Jesus: The Question of Criteria*. Trans. M. E. Boring. Louisville, Ky., 2002.

Young, B. H. *Jesus and His Jewish Parables*. New York, 1989.

———. *Jesus the Jewish Theologian*. Peabody, Mass., 1995.

3. Sources, Especially Josephus

Charlesworth, J. H. *The Beloved Disciple: Whose Witness Validates the Gospel of John?* Valley Forge, 1995.

———. "Jesus, the Nag Hammadi Codices, and Josephus." Pages 77-102 in *Jesus Within Judaism*.

Crossan, J. D. "Why Is Historical Jesus Research Necessary?" Pages 7-37 in *Jesus2000*.

Davids, P. H. *The Epistle of James*. Grand Rapids, 1982. Pages 1-61.

Dickson, J. D. *The Christ Files: How Historians Know What They Know About Jesus*. Sydney, 2006.

Hengel, M. *The Johannine Question*. Trans. J. Bowden. London and Philadelphia, 1989. [For more reflection and research, see Hengel, *Die johanneische Frage*. WUNT 67; Tübingen, 1993.]

Jackson, J., ed. *Tacitus*. 4 vols. LCL; Cambridge, Mass., London, 1937.

Koester, K. *Ancient Gospels: Their History and Development*. London, Philadelphia, 1990.

McDonald, L. M. *The Biblical Canon*. Peabody, Mass., 2007.

Meier, J. "How Do We Decide What Comes from Jesus?" Pages 167-95 in *MJ*. Vol. 1.

O'Donnell, J. *Karl Rahner: Life in the Spirit*. Rome, 2004.

Pines, S. *An Arabic Version of the Testimonium Flavianum and Its Implications*. Jerusalem, 1971.

Rolfe, J. C., ed. *Suetonius*. 2 vols. LCL; Cambridge, Mass., London, 1914.

Sanders, E. P. "How Do We Know What We Know About Jesus?" Pages 38-61 in *Jesus2000*.

Schäfer, P. *Jesus in the Talmud*. Princeton, Oxford, 2007.

Thackeray, H. St. J., ed. *Josephus*. 9 vols. LCL; Cambridge, Mass., London, 1926–65.

Theissen and Winter. *Plausible,* pp. 1-26.

4. The Judaism of Jesus

Charlesworth, J. H. "The Historical Jesus in Light of Writings Contemporaneous with Him." *ANRW* 2.25.2 (1982): 451-76.

———. *Jesus Within Judaism*. New York, 1988.

———, ed. *Jesus' Jewishness*. Philadelphia, New York, 1991.

———, ed. *The Messiah*. Minneapolis, 1992.

Charlesworth, J. H., and L. L. Johns, eds. *Hillel and Jesus*. Minneapolis, 1997.

de Silva, D. A. *Introducing the Apocrypha*. Grand Rapids, 2002.

Flusser, D., with R. S. Notley. *The Sage from Galilee: Rediscovering Jesus' Genius*. Grand Rapids, 2007.

Neusner, J. *The Mishnah*. New Haven, London, 1988.

Sanders, E. P. *Jesus and Judaism*. Philadelphia, 1985.

Theissen, G. *The Shadow of the Galilean*. Philadelphia, 1987.

Theissen, G., and D. Winter. *Quest for the Plausible Jesus*. Louisville, Ky., 2002.

Vermes, G. *Jesus and the World of Judaism*. Philadelphia, 1983.

5. Jesus' Birth and Youth

Brown, R. E. *The Birth of the Messiah*. New York, 1993, 1999.

Charlesworth, J. H. *Jesus Within Judaism*. Garden City, N. Y., 1988.

———. *Authentic Apocrypha*. North Richland Hills, Tex., 1998.

———. "Jesus, the *Mamzer,* and the Dead Sea Scrolls." Pages 60-63 in *Jesus and Archaeology*. Ed. J. H. Charlesworth. Grand Rapids, 2006.

Chilton, B. *Rabbi Jesus*. New York, 2000.

———. "Recovering Jesus' *Mamzerut*." Pages 84-110 in *Jesus and Archaeology*. Ed. Charlesworth. Grand Rapids, 2006.

Davies, W. D., and D. Allison. Pages 149-284 in *The Gospel According to Saint Matthew*. Vol. 1. Edinburgh, 1988.

Elliott, J. K., ed. *The Apocryphal Jesus*. Oxford, 1996.

Schaberg, J. *The Illegitimacy of Jesus*. Sheffield, 1995. [Originally published by Harper and Row in 1987.]

Vermes, G. *The Nativity*. London, 2006.

6. Jesus, John the Baptizer, and Jesus' Early Public Life

Charlesworth, J. H. "Hanina Ben-Dosa." *ABD* 3:50-51.

———. "Hilkiah the Hasid." *ABD* 3:201.

———. "Honi." *ABD* 3:282.

———. "John the Baptizer and the Dead Sea Scrolls." *BDSS* 3:1-35.

Eshel, E. "Jesus the Exorcist in Light of Epigraphic Sources." Pages 178-85 in *Archaeology*.

Evans, C. "Jesus and Apollonius of Tyana." Pages 245-50 in *Jesus & His Contemporaries*. Leiden, New York, 1995.

———. "Jesus and Jewish Miracle Stories." Pages 213-43 in *Jesus & His Contemporaries*. Leiden, New York, 1995.

Eve, E. *The Jewish Context of Jesus' Miracles*. London, New York, 2002.

Fiebig, P. *Jüdische Wundergeschichten des neutestamentlichen Zeitalters*. Tübingen, 1911.

Green, W. S. "Palestinian Holy Men: Charismatic Leadership and Rabbinic Tradition." *ANRW* 2.19.2; pp. 614-47.

Kazmierski, C. R. *John the Baptist: Prophet and Evangelist.* Collegeville, Minn., 1996.

Labahn, M. *Jesus als Lebensspender: Untersuchungen zu einer Geschichte der johanneischen Tradition anhand ihrer Wundergeschichten.* Berlin, New York, 1999.

Labahn, M., and B. J. L. Peerbolte. *Wonders Never Cease: The Purpose of Narrating Miracle Stories in the New Testament and Its Religious Environment.* London, New York, 2006.

Meier, J. P. "Jesus with and Without John." In *MJ* 2:100-233.

———. "John Without Jesus: The Baptist in His Own Rite." In *MJ* 2:19-99.

Murphy, C. M. *John the Baptist: Prophet of Purity for a New Age.* Collegeville, Minn., 2003.

Neusner, J. "The Sage, Miracle, and Magic." Pages 13-30 in *Why No Gospels in Talmudic Judaism?* Atlanta, 1988.

Phipps, W. E. *Was Jesus Married?* New York, 1970.

Piccirillo, M. "The Sanctuaries of the Baptism on the East Bank of the Jordan River." Pages 433-43 in *Jesus and Archaeology.* Ed. J. H. Charlesworth.

Riesner, R. "Bethany Beyond the Jordan (John 1:28): Topography, Theology and History in the Fourth Gospel." *Tyndale Bulletin* 38 (1987): 29-63.

———. "Bethany Beyond the Jordan." *ABD* 1:703-5 [with a good bibliography].

Tatum, W. B. *John the Baptist and Jesus: A Report of the Jesus Seminar.* Sonoma, Calif., 1994.

van der Loos, H. *The Miracles of Jesus.* Leiden, 1965.

Vermes, G. "Hanina ben Dosa." Pages 178-214 in *Post-biblical Jewish Studies.* Leiden, 1975.

7. Jesus and Archaeology

Batey, R. A. *Jesus & the Forgotten City: New Light on Sepphoris and the Urban World of Jesus.* Grand Rapids, 1991.

Brown, R. E. *The Death of the Messiah.* 2 vols. New York, 1994, 1998.

Charlesworth, J. H. *Jesus Within Judaism: New Light from Exciting Archaeological Discoveries.* Garden City, N. Y., 1988.

Charlesworth, J. H., ed. *Jesus and Archaeology.* Grand Rapids, 2006.

Charlesworth, J. H., and W. P. Weaver, eds. *What Has Archaeology to Do with Faith?* Philadelphia, 1992.

Freyne, S. *Galilee: From Alexander the Great to Hadrian.* Wilmington, Del., 1998.

Hanson, K. C., and D. E. Oakman. *Palestine in the Time of Jesus.* Minneapolis, 1998.

Horsley, R. *Archaeology, History, and Society in Galilee.* Valley Forge, Pa., 1996.

Reed, J. L. *Archaeology and the Galilean Jesus.* Harrisburg, Pa., 2000.

Reed, J. L., and J. D. Crossan. *Excavating Jesus: Beneath the Stones, Behind the Texts.* New York, 2001.

8. Jesus' Proclamation of God's Rule (the Kingdom of God) and His Parables

Allison, D. C. *Jesus of Nazareth: Millenarian Prophet.* Minneapolis, 1998.

———. "The Eschatology of Jesus." Pages 267-302 in *The Encyclopedia of Apocalypticism.* Ed. J. J. Collins. Vol. 1. New York, 1999.

Allison, D. C., et al. *The Apocalyptic Jesus: A Debate.* Ed. R. J. Miller. Santa Rosa, Calif., 2001.

Borg, M. J. *Jesus: A New Vision: Spirit, Culture, and the Life of Discipleship.* San Francisco, 1987.

———. "Jesus and Eschatology: A Reassessment." Pages 42-67 in *Images of Jesus Today.* Ed. J. H. Charlesworth and W. P. Weaver. Valley Forge, Pa., 1994.

Capps, D. *Jesus: A Psychological Biography.* St. Louis, 2000.

Charlesworth, J. H. "The Historical Jesus in Light of Writings Contemporaneous with Him." *ANRW* 2.25.1 (1982): 451-76.

Crossan, J. D. *In Parables: The Challenge of the Historical Jesus.* Cambridge, Hagerstown, N. Y., 1985.

Dodd, C. H. *The Parables of the Kingdom.* 2d ed. London, 1935.

Flusser, D. *Die rabbinischen Gleichnisse und der Gleichniserzähler Jesus.* Bern, 1981.

Funk, R. W. *Honest to Jesus: Jesus for a New Millennium.* New York, 1996.

Hays, R. "The Corrected Jesus." *First Things* (May 1994).

Hedrick, C. W. *Parables as Poetic Fictions: The Creative Voice of Jesus.* Peabody, Mass., 1994.

Hengel, M. *The Son of God.* Philadelphia, 1976.

Herzog, W. R., II. *Parables as Subversive Speech.* Louisville, Ky., 1994.

Jeremias, J. *The Parables of Jesus.* 3d ed. London, 1963.

McCracken, D. *The Scandal of the Gospels: Jesus, Story, and Offense.* New York, Oxford, 1994.

Schweitzer, A. *The Quest of the Historical Jesus.* Minneapolis, 2001 [German original is 1906].

Scott, B. B. *Hear Then the Parable: A Commentary on the Parables of Jesus.* Minneapolis, 1990.

Via, D. O. *The Parables: Their Literary and Existential Dimension.* Philadelphia, 1967.

Wenham, D. *The Parables of Jesus.* Downers Grove, Ill., 1989.

Westermann, C. *The Parables of Jesus in the Light of the Old Testament.* Minneapolis, 1990.

Young, B. H. *Jesus and His Jewish Parables: Rediscovering the Roots of Jesus' Teaching.* New York, 1989.

―――. *The Parables: Jewish Tradition and Christian Interpretation.* Peabody, Mass., 1998.

9. Jesus' Crucifixion and Resurrection

Bammel, E., ed. *The Trial of Jesus.* London, 1970.

Borg, M. J. *Jesus: Uncovering the Life, Teachings, and Relevance of a Religious Revolutionary.* New York, 2006.

Bryan, C. *Render to Caesar.* Oxford, 2005.

Charlesworth, J. H. *The Beloved Disciple.* Valley Forge, Pa., 1995.

Charlesworth, J. H., et al. *Resurrection: The Origin and Future of a Biblical Doctrine.* New York, London, 2006.

Crossan, J. D. *Who Killed Jesus? Exposing the Roots of Anti-Semitism in the Gospel Story of the Death of Jesus.* San Francisco, 1996.

Goodman, M. *Rome and Jerusalem: The Clash of Ancient Civilizations.* New York, 2007.

Hengel, M. *Victory over Violence: Jesus and the Revolutionists.* Philadelphia, 1973.

―――. *Crucifixion.* London, 1977.

Horsley, R. *Jesus and the Spiral of Violence: Popular Jewish Resistance in Roman Palestine.* Minneapolis, 1993.

―――. *Jesus and Empire.* Minneapolis, 2003.

Jeremias, J. *The Eucharistic Words of Jesus.* Rev. ed. Oxford, 1966.

Kazen, T. *Jesus and Purity Halakhah.* Stockholm, 2002.

Lapide, P. *The Resurrection of Jesus: A Jewish Perspective.* Minneapolis, 1971.

Levine, A.-J., D. C. Allison, and J. D. Crossan, eds. *The Historical Jesus in Context.* Princeton, Oxford, 2006.

McCracken, D. *The Scandal of the Gospels.* New York, Oxford, 1994.

Rivkin, E. *What Crucified Jesus?* New York, 1997.

Schmidt, F. *How the Temple Thinks.* Sheffield, 2001.

Smallwood, E. M. *Jews under Roman Rule.* Leiden, 1981.

Vermes, G. *The Passion.* New York, 2006.

Winter, P. *On the Trial of Jesus.* Berlin, 1974.

Wright, N. T. *The Resurrection of the Son of God.* Minneapolis, 2003.

Yoder, J. H. *The Politics of Jesus.* 2d ed. Grand Rapids, 1994.